Creating a
POWERFUL
BUSINESS

Social Star ☆
Publishing

Creating a

POWERFUL
BUSINESS

The 12-Step e-ttraction method
to escape corporate, build your
own business and wake up inspired

Andrew Ford

Social Star ☆
Publishing

Published by Social Star
103/25 Gipps Street, Collingwood, Victoria 3066, Australia
socialstar.com.au

Typeset in National by WorkingType Studios
Cover design by WorkingType Studios
Author photo by Adam Tambakau

Printed in Australia by IngramSpark, part of the Ingram Content Group.

Paperback ISBN 978-0-6450386-7-5
eBook ISBN 978-0-6450386-8-2
Audiobook ISBN 978-0-6450386-9-9

Catalogue records for this book are available
from the National Library of Australia.

NATIONAL
LIBRARY
OF AUSTRALIA

A catalogue record for this book is available from the National Library of Australia

Dedicated to my mum
who always believed in me.

"Working with Andrew is truly a life-changing experience. He was exactly what I needed to help me believe not only in my business and ideas, but also in myself and my own abilities in harnessing my inner entrepreneur."

— Penny Grant (LLB, BA), Founder and CEO of Drool Experiences

"Andrew is a pleasure to work with, incredibly knowledgeable about personal branding and social media marketing as a whole, professional, easy-going and a great communicator."

— Daniele Tanner (BA), Co-CEO and Founder of Social Media College

"I have engaged Andrew and his company Social Star to work with me on incorporating this approach into my own personal and company branding, and am delighted with the results so far."

— Carol Benton (BA), Author and Business Communication Expert at Words2Win

"Andrew is the branding guru whom you want to engage for your personal and business branding needs."

— Evelyn Looi (PhD, CFA), Investment Consultant at Ascalon Capital

"Working recently with Andrew and the team at Social Star was a very positive experience. Their guidance and perspective were very important for the launch of SUMParts. Andrew made the process of personal branding so strategic and simple – every call we had was highly motivating. I sincerely recommend Andrew and team for Branding, Upgrading Personal Profiles, Strategic Communication, and Marketing your Business."

— Mitchell Batcha (BA), Former CEO of Valentino and CELINE, founder of SUMParts Consulting

"Andrew really knows his stuff. I engaged Andrew to advise me in running my freelance consulting business."

— David T Kearns (PhD), Principal of Carbon Capture Technologies at the Global CCS Institute`

Permissions

The publisher and author thank the following companies for permission to use their copyright material. The Association for Project Management (UK) for their chart that compares their IT Agile methodology with traditional methods.

Trademarks

Trademark information has been omitted from the main text to assist readability.

Contents

Preface

"The two most important days in your life are the day you are born and the day you find out why."

— Mark Twain.

I agree with the sentiment of this statement wholeheartedly, but something is missing, one more step in the process to ensure a full life. The day you are born is your opportunity for life, the day you realise your *why* gives you meaning, but the day you do something about it is the real day you start to live the life you really desire.

Being born is out of our control. It just happens and we are thrust into the world in whatever situation we find ourselves in. Our parents' circumstances and the local environment impact many of our decisions in life. Who we are today, our careers, religious beliefs, political affiliations, family situations, economic conditions and many other building blocks of life are set before we reach maturity. Most of this is beyond our choice yet it shapes a lot of who we are and what we believe. Once we reach maturity it's now over to us to make our own choices and shape our lives, but within the context of where we have come from.

I share my personal journey and life experience with you as an example to help reveal the unconscious beliefs, restrictions and motivations that help and hinder our entrepreneurship journey. It's difficult to shine a light on the past to reveal the future, but I think it's a necessary part of the process. My aim is to help you figure out your *why* and provide some tools to assist you in taking action to make it a reality.

My Story

Certain things happen in your life that are so profound they impact everything in your life. For me, this was my dad leaving me when I was only one week old.

Now that my mum has passed, I feel it's time to tell the background story of what happened to give some context and understanding to the situation, hopefully without blame and with some empathy for all the people involved.

Living in the 70's

Living in the 70's always reminds me of the classic Skyhooks song and album that was on high repeat in our household when I was a kid. It was black vinyl back then – classic. If you don't know it, do yourself a favour, as Molly Meldrum would often say.

At the start of the 1970s, Australia's prime minister was William McMahon, just before Gough Whitlam came into power. The Apollo 13 lunar mission launched and had its in-space emergency, The Beatles broke up, cell phones, digital cameras and post-it notes were being invented and Michael Jackson was a little kid in the Jackson Five cranking out the number one hits. Elvis was alive and doing Vegas while the Vietnam war was in full flight.

It was a very different time when my mum was having kids. Women's rights were progressing after the turbulent 1960s protests, but it was light years from the real empowerment of women to be themselves. There was no gender choice or "me too" movements and, without social media or the internet, free speech was limited. Women were mostly confined to getting married, having kids and being the primary carers.

Most families were very traditional with a stay-at-home mum, a dad who was the breadwinner, and a few kids living in the suburbs. My mum was different. She was a rebel and played in a variety of bands in her younger days and, by the time I came along, she had two kids from different fathers. She was also a yoga teacher, vegetarian, hippy, spiritual and personal development junkie. One of my earliest memories was sleeping behind an amp stack at a concert as she sang with her then-partner Peter, who played the keyboard, at the Swagman Hotel in the outer suburb of Ferntree Gully in Melbourne. It's strange how kids can sleep anywhere and what you remember looking back as an adult. Unfortunately, that establishment burnt down in a fire in 1991.

On weekends I remember being whisked off to an ashram in the countryside to see the latest Indian guru who would announce that I had great spiritual abilities, subsequently giving me a special name to guide me through life. I remember tagging along to various shared houses in Brunswick with strange smells and many half-naked people wandering around smoking joints whilst I was trying to find something to do to avert my eyes from the half-naked lady trying to entertain me. This was all before the age of six when I didn't understand the world or what was happening. It was the 1970s and there was a large division between the 1950s baby-boomer parents and their kids who grew up in the 1960s freedom movements.

Tom Wolfe called the 1970s the "Me Decade". Across the land, people seemed determined to escape from the wars and social movements of the previous decade. Disillusionment with national and global action led many to look inward and find solace in discovering more about themselves.

With this context, you might understand that when my one-year-old sister Peta fell ill, my mum decided not to take her to the doctor, but to a health guru in Sydney for "treatment". Peta was down to her birth weight and was failing to thrive. Mum travelled up there for three months to heal Peta with a juice and alternative milk diet whilst her husband Bill looked after Jon, my older brother. This all happened before I was born because in Sydney my mum met the man who would become my biological father, Geoff. How they met is a mystery, but I do know that Geoff was over from England. I'm not sure why he was in Australia or much about his background but, regardless, they obviously hit it off and he promised her the world. He was going to take care of her, and her two kids and life would be grand.

Geoff and my mother wrote a letter to Bill announcing their marriage was over and to send Jon up to Sydney. Bill was heartbroken and at 25 had lost his wife and children to another man. After some troubled times, he recovered and played an important part in my life. One of the positive male role models I was fortunate to have. Not only did he remain present to be a great dad to Peta and Jon, but he took care of me too. All throughout my childhood he gave me pocket money, showed me how to fix things and took me and my friends out for my birthdays. He was a good man and a big lesson I have learnt is that when there is a void in life, someone valuable will fill the space. More on that later.

A year after my mum met Geoff, I was born in Melbourne on 5 February 1971, healthy and happy. When my mum took me home to our rented house in Warrandyte, Geoff didn't seem to be able to cope with the responsibility of being the key provider. He now had three kids to support and the mother of his latest child. The responsibility was too much to bear, so a week later he left and broke my mum's heart. As I later learnt, he also tried to defraud some people on his way out of the country by writing fake cheques with their names to pay for things. He even tried to defraud Bill, which was a shitty thing to do considering how Bill had stood by our family – showing Geoff's weak character and the strength of Bill. In a way, it's like the book *Rich Dad, Poor Dad*, but instead of teaching me about money, this book, potentially called *Good Dad, Shit Dad*, taught me about being a father.

Of course, I was a baby at the time and didn't know any of these things were happening. Luckily for me and my siblings, my maternal grandparents, Ron and Gladys, stepped in and bought my mum a house near theirs in Ivanhoe in Melbourne to take control of the situation. We finally had a stable place to live, and life became somewhat normal. Apart from the new boyfriends who would move in and out periodically as my mother tried to form new relationships to fill the void. This pattern created new father figures for us kids.

The changing of the guard every few years meant that I learnt to not form attachments to any new father figure, and I became very used to change and drama. Perhaps even addicted to it. I have since read that adversity in childhood could be a precursor to making great entrepreneurs.[1] If you consider the similarities of starting a new business every few years – with the inevitable change, conflict and drama – it's synonymous with my home life back when I was a kid.

---

1   https://medium.com/@JasonShuman/why-childhood-adversity-creates-great-entrepreneurs-9b1ce015f06a

Meeting Dad #1

I first met my biological father, Geoff, at the age of six when he came back to Australia for a visit. He was in limited contact before we met and my only memory of him was that he used to send me a birthday card with a five-dollar bill inside. It was a nice thought, but a token effort as he never paid any child support. To this day the song from Everclear *Father of Mine,* still gives me goosebumps. Have a listen and you will know why. My surname didn't come from Geoff, it came from Bill, my responsible dad.

Being so young I don't recall how Geoff and my mum related when he returned, but I do remember our one outing when Geoff took my mate Cameron and me to the movies. We went to the now defunct Greater Union in Russell Street in central Melbourne to see *Star Wars.* Yes, the original one was on the big screen before they made the new ones and ruined the legacy for everyone. I had a great day. It didn't feel strange meeting him for the first time, in fact, I remember feeling so proud to finally have a father like the other kids. I was young and was having fun at the movies with my mate, plus Cameron didn't have a dad either as he had died a few years earlier. It's strange how kids from similar backgrounds form groups without really knowing why. My other friends, Bjorn and Kelly, didn't have dads either, so it wasn't unusual in our group to be in that situation. In fact, it normalised the situation for me. I heard later that my mum asked Geoff not to write to me anymore and not to come back to visit as she thought it was harmful to me. I don't know why or what happened, but I didn't see him for another two decades after that day at the movies.

Overall, we were happy kids. My siblings and I had a lot of friends in the local neighbourhood and did what most kids did in those days. Riding our bikes everywhere to explore the world, staying out late until the streetlights came on, kicking the footy over the powerlines and trying to break the streetlights. Making our own bows and arrows with our eight-inch Bowie knives (another gift from Bill for scouts) and shooting them over the houses, trying to hit each other. Most of these activities were with my best mate, Michael, who lived only a few doors down and had a birthday close to mine. We spent all our spare time together in primary school and are still close. He taught me a lot about loyalty and being there for your friends. He was solid, reliable and honest. A better friend you wouldn't be able to find. I was lucky we happened to buy houses near each other. Plus, his dad was a doctor, which was convenient as I was very accident-prone and needed stitches frequently.

Teenage Rebel

Then teenagerhood arrived and the focus moved from building cubby houses and riding bikes to trying to meet girls and testing our limits with drugs and alcohol. Most of our group had unusual family situations – no dads, divorced parents, adopted and so forth – so we had limited supervision. We got into trouble with the police and other groups but nothing that got on our permanent records. Not having rules suited me, perhaps creating an anti-establishment attitude that I brought into my corporate jobs in the future.

My grandparents were quite well off because they started an office products business after my grandfather came back from World War 2. RH Grierson & Co was a big part of my life growing up and so were my maternal grandparents. They supported my mother and us kids because she was on welfare, and we didn't have any father paying child support. They paid to send me, my brother and my sister to a private school and I was lucky enough to go to Ivanhoe Grammar, even though I didn't take advantage of the opportunity fully.

My friend Michael went to a different high school, so I started playing pool at Bjorn's every night with our gang of guys. We all went to primary school together, but Bjorn went to Ivanhoe Grammar with me, so we spent more time together. There were ten of us in our little gang, all from different schools, and we were tight. They were my family when mine wasn't there and gave me the foundation of security and reliability I needed when home life was nothing like that. We did everything together and they were good times. Not very productive, but fun as hell and I don't regret it one bit. I'd rather live a life of adventure than one of boring stability and we certainly have a lot of stories to tell now.

A pivotal moment came when I was in the middle of my teenage angst stage. I graduated from high school in 1988, with moderate results and wasn't sure about my next steps, so I got a job in the family business working in the warehouse. My goal was to work in business, and I thought being in the family business was going to be a good option considering my limited academic achievements – but I soon realised that working in the warehouse wasn't for me. This was a destructive phase because my weeks revolved around partying with my friends from Thursday to Sunday. I was drinking too much, more to escape than to have fun, and was blacking out regularly. Not good. Finally, I got fed up working full-time in the warehouse, so I quit and started doing odd jobs labouring on building sites and delivering pizzas at night, not exactly a smart career move but I wasn't sure what the next step was and I had already decided I wasn't cut out for uni since studying and I didn't get along. I almost failed high school as my English mark was borderline 50% and, if you fail English, then you don't pass Year 12. I think they gave me a pity pass, to be honest, to protect the school's reputation. I lacked career and life direction, so that pivotal moment came when my mum stepped in and arranged for me to spend a day with a psychologist she knew. At the time I was rebelling from life, blaming her and my dad for my situation, and escaping with alcohol and girls. It was fun some of the time, but mostly it wasn't, and it was damaging my health and hindering any real progress for my future. So off to the psychologist I went, thinking I was going to be diagnosed with something like ADHD, not that these conditions were around way back then.

I arrived at my psychologist appointment on a Saturday morning in my sky-blue VB Holden Commodore and was impressed with his fancy house in the green hills of Eltham. I was 30 minutes late and hungover from Friday night's drinking activities at the Gasometer Hotel, our favourite drinking spot. I wasn't my best self and was underprepared for what turned out to be a full day of work.

This psychologist was very professional. He was American and spent most of the day conducting a battery of tests on me. Word association, inkblot interpretations, stories with hidden meanings I had to uncover, written general-knowledge questions, multiple-choice questions, spatial-construction puzzles and more. Strangely, I enjoyed these tests, and he mentioned it was to measure my intellectual quotient (IQ), emotional quotient (EQ) and career prospects to help me find my true path. If you know my current business, you will see a lot of what this man did is what I do now for my clients, but with a business emphasis rather than a psychological one.

Who would have known back then that this would be a future career path for me? Certainly not me!

The Turnaround

I returned two weeks later for the results and they floored me. To my shock, I was quite intelligent – who knew?! Certainly not me. Apparently, my IQ was 127 based on his particular scale which positioned me in the top 5% of all people. He made a special mention that my EQ was equally high, which was rare, normally you have one or the other. My career options were all high-level roles like a lawyer, judge, doctor, CEO or professional. Strangely, these are my target market clients now. Up until that point, I thought I was below average when it came to my potential intelligence and abilities. That was how I was made to feel as a kid, that I wasn't quite as smart as the rest of my cousins or siblings. I was much younger and slow to develop, which didn't help much either.

But now I knew I had potential! It let me know that the path I was on wasn't where I should be, and I had the power to change it if I wanted to. I now had choices and a responsibility to live up to my potential. To not do that would be a waste. Unfortunately, knowing this and doing something about it are two different things. I still had the same routine and bad habits, which meant nothing changed in my life for a year or so. I continued partying and doing odd jobs. But slowly I started believing that I could do more and sought out more meaningful work and created positive changes in my life. Thanks, Mum!

It's interesting that in my current coaching work, I open people's minds to the potential for their careers. That working for someone else isn't the only option and that a portfolio career could be more profitable and fulfilling. Once they know this, they can't unknow it. Just like when I found out I had the potential to do more. It changes you and means you can't use excuses to justify doing less. I often wonder if this experience set me on a course to help others in the same way as this man helped me so long ago.

I returned to the family business with my newfound work ethic. I asked and received a promotion to work in the office. I sucked so bad at the start, but I quickly became useful and productive. I realised I could pick up things quickly and, if I focused, I could master areas as well as anyone. Sales became my passion as I loved building relationships with clients. It was the perfect blend of IQ and EQ for my situation and I loved it. My uncle Neil ended up allowing me to become a sales representative, which was cool because I got a car and new-fangled mobile phone. I remember that half-brick phone well, we only had one in the whole company, as everyone else used pagers, but I liked technology. I remember the first day I got to play with it and was amazed that it stored a whole six phone numbers. Crazy!

Learning to Love Learning

My other development plan was to return to further education, which my Nana, Gladys, encouraged me to do once she could see that I had potential as a businessperson who could take over the family business one day. I wasn't confident in my educational abilities, so I started with a short 12-week course in sales at the Council of Adult Education. That got me into a rhythm of weekly learning. Surprisingly, I loved it! I was studying something useful with other interesting people. Being an extrovert, the course fulfilled me and I felt good about myself for doing some self-improvement. With my confidence boosted, next came a TAFE (Technical and Further Education) course in marketing, circa 1995, which I excelled at. I still remember one of my marketing teachers, Mark Vincent, giving me a lot of kudos for getting 98% on my assignment. I never thought that would be me and it spurred me on to think bigger in my education. If I could do that well in TAFE, I might just be able to do a university degree. Something I never thought would be possible for me. I also realised how impactful an encouraging teacher could be for a student, a realisation that affected my choice to become a university tutor in later life.

After two years of TAFE, I transferred to the second year of a Bachelor of Business at RMIT University, majoring in marketing. I loved this course and found a passion for understanding people, once more utilising my IQ and EQ equally. I was a committed student and graduated with distinction after my six years of part-time studies. But wait there's more!

Not content with an undergraduate degree, my new company Hewlett-Packard offered me the opportunity to do an Executive MBA at the AGSM (Australian Graduate School of Management), which was a joint venture between the University of NSW and the University of Sydney. Interestingly, my boss at the time, Bill Dimopoulos, who approved the funding for this program, later became a client of mine to help him raise funding for his medical tech start-up. Strange how life turns out. I wasn't cut out for the structure of the EMBA program, so I switched to the newly formed Master of Entrepreneurship from Swinburne University. It was a fabulous program and I loved it from day one. I won lots of competitions and awards, but one of the best outcomes of the degree was meeting so many good friends that I still see to this day.

To finish off my elevation from an almost-failed high-school student to someone with three postgraduate qualifications, I wrote and self-published my first book in 2013 titled *Creating a Powerful Brand*. Not bad for someone who barely passed English in high school and was told he was dumb compared to my older cousin and brother by some of my teachers.

I still recall my Year 12 English teacher looking at one of my essays and making some very derogative comments about my level of intelligence. He wasn't wrong, mind you, as my writing was very poor in those days. But it wasn't because I wasn't capable, it was just that I didn't have a stable home life and studying was difficult, so I had missed most of my primary school education. I craved family support and that came in the form of my mates, so hanging with them was more important than learning, plus there was no supervision at home, so I did pretty much whatever I wanted. But that teacher couldn't have comprehended this. I'm sure he thought I was a privileged kid growing up in a nice traditional home, rather than living with the daily stress and disruption of not knowing who or what was going to be happening in my house that day. It wasn't his fault, he was likely trying to motivate me to do better. It had the opposite effect and made me give up trying. We all have different motivational triggers.

Luckily, my mum intervened years later and sent me to that psychologist who opened my eyes to the possibility of my future potential, otherwise my life could have been significantly different. I was fortunate that my grandmother pushed me to try further education and that my workplaces supported my studies. Many things continued my evolution from a lost teenager to a successful adult and I have tremendous gratitude for all those who played a part in it.

Meeting Dad #2

The second and last time I saw my biological dad was when I was 28 years old. I had flown to Canada to do my level 1 ski-instructor course and spend a season in the Whistler Blackcomb resort. By then I was over my teenage angst and just had some questions for him about what happened in the past, as well as picking up any useful tips about my genetics for potential future health conditions. He was married to a nice lady and had a three-year-old daughter Cerensa-Lee, who was so cute and delightful to hang out with.

We met in the afternoon at the Vancouver foreshore on a chilly but sunny Saturday. He brought the whole family, and it was all a bit surreal but pleasant, if not unremarkable. After all those years of wondering what happened, questioning why he left and feeling so many mixed emotions about him, it was a bit of a letdown. He was just an average older guy whom I didn't know. There wasn't any emotion left to resolve. We had a walk and talk, then went back to their place for dinner and I stayed the night at their place in North Vancouver. When I woke up the next day, he was gone. Apparently, he had a business trip, which wasn't mentioned earlier, so he was gone before I woke and I didn't even get to say goodbye. I tried to contact him after that trip, but he had moved house and changed his name as he liked to do regularly. Par for the course, it would seem!

I only know where he is now because Cerensa-Lee, now 27 and about to get married, found me on social media and reached out to me. He now has serious dementia and is living in a home, so it's likely he wouldn't recognise me even if I made the effort to visit him, which pretty much ends the chapter on my dad.

The reason I tell this personal story is that throughout my life the impact of my dad leaving when I was young, and the implications for my mum and family, has altered every part of who I am and what I do. The struggles and challenges I had, mostly related to not feeling loved and appreciated or being worthy to receive these even if offered, have left deep scars on me. The character I have developed of persistence, resilience, independence and resourcefulness can also be attributed to my childhood. We are all forged in the fires of our upbringing and reflect the way our parents raised us, then beaten to form our character on the anvil of life.

Reflection: Good Dad

The outcome of my background gave me some gifts worth realising. Firstly, it galvanised my desire to be the best father that I could be. I don't profess to be a perfect role model in this area, far from it, but I am committed to never leaving my kids. Always being there for them when they need me and having a strong presence in their lives. This is one reason I left the corporate world to start my own business. I could have got another job in an IT company as I was at the top of my game and respected in the industry. But the travel, work hours and culture weren't conducive to being a good dad.

When I reflect with a balanced viewpoint, I can see that instead of having a deadbeat dad, I had a range of father figures who positively influenced my life. A neighbour who was our scoutmaster taught me about building and construction. My best mate Michael's dad, the doctor, looked after all my scrapes and injuries with kindness and compassion. My good mates were like brothers to me and made me feel connected, appreciated and safe. On reflection, I realised that I only felt bad about my dad because others made me feel bad about it. Growing up, I didn't have any real feelings on the matter as it was just my daily reality. I didn't know any different.

But when I got older and out in the world, away from my core social group, others thought I should feel bad. I adopted that belief strongly and every Father's Day became my worst nightmare. The TV ads on high repeat would show the love between a father and son and stab me in the heart. Teachers would innocently ask about my dad and new friends ask about my family situation and I would feel embarrassed as I wouldn't know how to explain the complexity of our family tree.

We often don't know why things happen to us at that moment, but later in life, you can see the reasons clearly. When it was my turn to have kids, and I had two boys, everything turned around. Suddenly, Father's Day became the best day of the year! The TV ads would make me cry happy tears for my blessings and I would talk about my new family with pride. The void of not having a father created a strong value of wanting to be the best dad I could. I credit my mother not only for sending me to the psychologist but for helping me out a lot. Along with the hippy mumbo-jumbo were some quality personal development courses that had a significant impact on my knowledge. Courses like Love and Relationships Training (LRT), Discovery's accelerated learning camps, yoga practices, meditation, Reiki, and discussions on metaphysics and religion all positively influenced me.

My half-brother in the UK wasn't so lucky. He wrote a letter to me when I was 26, a few years before my trip to Canada to see our dad for the second time. He had heard about me and somehow found my address. He was 14 and struggling with his identity, angry at our shared dad for leaving him and his mum. She was on welfare and not doing well. He was depressed and seeking some solace in shared understanding from me. I wrote back but the letter was returned unopened as they had moved and didn't leave a forwarding address. Many years later he found me on social media and told me he was just out of prison, drug-affected, had a few kids with different partners, none of whom he was in a relationship with, and couldn't get a job. Life wasn't going well, and he blamed his dad for all of it. His messages were so poorly written and garbled that I could barely make out what he was saying most of the time, but I tried to offer some advice and support. But then he went dark, deleted his account and I never heard from him again.

I often think about this half-brother of mine. Lost and angry at the world for his circumstances. Without the supportive people around him and the tools of emotional resilience to get over his angst and do something more productive with his life. He felt compelled to repeat the mistakes of his lineage rather than using them as motivation to change the family story to something more rewarding for his kids. He didn't have that push from a psychologist right at the critical time in his life. This motivates me to mentor dozens of young people. To try to be a catalyst for positive change in their lives and assist where I can give them confidence and direction for the future. We all like to solve the problems for others that we have experienced ourselves.

I stood on the precipice of that life. I know I could have gone down that road, rather than the one I find myself on now. Without the support of an extended family with resources to buy my mum a house and send me to good schools, what would have happened to me? Would I have seethed and turned to violent crime to damage the world and get back at everyone for my situation? Soothing myself with drugs to forget and push people away who try to help? Perhaps it's luck or good fortune or something else I don't understand.

Lucky for me my dad had another family in England, so I have another half-brother there whom I am in contact with and he is doing well. I hope to meet him one day soon.

Reflection: Helping Others

Having some trauma in my history and my mother providing a myriad of personal development opportunities enabled me to understand what was driving my behaviour and decisions. It motivated me to help others do the same and shaped the *e-ttraction methodology* to delve deep into the background of my clients' lives to discover their true drivers and natures. This unique model supports the business that funds my lifestyle and supports my children. My story could be construed by some to be a little sad, but it's not as shocking as many. There were so many lessons that have helped me succeed in business and life. The key is to understand that it's not what happens to you that matters, what is important is how you choose to react to the situation. I had as much joy as sadness in my youth, great times with my friends and the challenges turned into benefits.

During my travels, I have met many people with far more challenging and shocking stories than mine. Clients of mine have shared horrendous stories of abuse that pale mine into insignificance. Others were not as fortunate as I was to have people to look up to like my siblings, grandparents and my friend's parents. By reframing our past and appreciating the good and bad situations we can have a different perception of what happened. I believe we can change our own story for the better. For me, I had a lot of angst that my dad didn't want to stick around and be with my mum because I was born. She suffered greatly and gave up her marriage to Bill for him and I blamed myself for ruining it. But when I reframe this thought, perhaps that was the best situation as he was a petty criminal and couldn't hold down a job to support his new adopted family. He made way for my mum to get re-married to a much more stable guy, Charles. That didn't last either, but that's another story.

But it left me with a lifelong curiosity about what makes people click; what drives them to do what they do, how they relate to others and what motivates them. I'm fascinated with this topic and that's why I started working in personal branding, helping others to figure out what drives them and building careers and businesses around their core values. By helping them see why the story of their lives drives their passion for certain things and how fulfilment can only be found by doing certain activities, like helping others overcome similar challenges to themselves.

This is why the first stage of my e-ttraction Method is called Understand, as it seeks to unveil some of your past to help you design your best future. It will only scratch the surface of your motivations, but I hope it sparks a curiosity to seek out ways to delve deep into yourself, to find the core reasons for who you are and what you are meant to do with the rest of your life.

Having got to know me personally, it's time to review your history and see how it can be used as fuel to find your why and create a personal business around this motivation. If you have blockers or negative patterns these can be highlighted and worked on too. I will not have all the answers, but I hope this process will enable you to see how your history predicts, in some ways, your future. But before we start the Understand process, it's useful to discuss who this book is most suitable for and provide some guidance around when to make a shift towards your own business. It can be a challenging journey so best to be prepared!

Introduction

"Be sure you put your feet in the right place,
then stand firm."

— Abraham Lincoln

have written this book specifically to help corporate escapees start and scale their own knowledge-based business utilising their personal brand. We will examine each element of this process and what this statement means in the coming chapters.

My first book *Creating a Powerful Brand* helped my clients build their personal brand by utilising the three-step approach I used in my coaching: Understand, Build And Leverage. It's been more than 10 years since I published that book and the methodology has grown considerably and now has the name *e-ttraction*, which means digital attraction. The theory is that if you Understand your personal brand, Build your digital assets, and Leverage them with authentic content to connect with the right people, then you don't have to sell your products; your perfect customers will come to you and ask to buy them. Another way of describing this process is *inbound marketing* or *inside-out marketing*. This is quite a different approach from most marketing theories. The vast majority of marketing agencies I come across use *push marketing*. The difference is both philosophical and practical.

Inside-Out Marketing

Inside-out marketing professes that if you create a business around a super niche target market and produce products specifically for them, all you need to do is communicate the benefits and then customers will buy them in enough quantity to meet your goals. Of course, this theory requires you to nail the niche, product mix and communication strategy to ensure this works.

However, the alternative is that you use push marketing. Most companies use this strategy and one of the most popular strategies is to attract as many customers as possible into the funnel. To do this, broader scale marketing is used, usually paid digital ads and traditional advertising to reach as many potential customers as possible. Once in the funnel, they use proactive sales tactics like cold calls, direct email messages and targeting on social media, to convert potential leads to customers. I'm sure most people reading this would have experienced cold calls from people who have no idea who you are, but try to sell you products because you once clicked on a link or visited a related website. Another annoying situation is when you just mention a particular brand and then you see ads for similar brands on social media for the next few weeks. Yes, our phones are listening to us. Most big companies use this approach as they have the funds to spend enough to dominate a particular industry. But how many people do they annoy to get the few that might purchase their product?

Push marketing of this scale is difficult to execute for start-up businesses and professional services businesses. The first barrier is that it costs too much money to reach any sort of market scale. Secondly, it can be seen as unprofessional to do paid advertising and use sales techniques that would be okay for other industries to convert leads to clients. Professionals such as doctors hold an esteemed place in our society and advertising their services for commercial gain appears to be at odds with their altruistic intent of helping patients. In 2006, the Australian Medical Association adopted the World Medical Association's (WMA) *Declaration of Geneva* as a contemporary companion to the 2,500-year-old Hippocratic Oath for doctors to declare their commitment to their profession, their patients and humanity. The first line of this commitment is: "I solemnly pledge to consecrate my life to the service of humanity."[2]

Furthermore, some professional services bodies, such as The Australian Health Practitioner Regulation Agency (AHPRA), regulate medical businesses' code of conduct and prohibit certain activities such as the use of client testimonials and cold email marketing. For instance, each professional industry has an association and code of conduct. Dentists, for instance, are prohibited from using before-and-after photos, overstating outcomes and getting testimonials from patients.[3] This isn't an unusual set of guidelines for professionals in their industry and it used to be far stricter in the past. One of my dental clients, who struggled with doing any form of marketing, said that when he was studying the profession the only marketing that you were allowed to do was a brass plaque on the front of your practice. The association regulated how large it could be and what it could say. That was it for marketing!

The other professional industries have similar bodies and rules. Working with the medical, legal, and financial industries over the last decade, we have seen a similar resistance to push marketing and a preference for more authentic marketing techniques. Similarly, architects, engineers, veterinarians, academics, consultants and so forth all have a professional status to uphold

---

2   https://www.ama.com.au/media/ama-adopts-wma-declaration-geneva
3   https://ada.org.au/policy-statement-6-9-advertising-in-dentistry

and prefer to gain clients by communicating their value rather than any pushy marketing processes.

This is why we specialise in helping corporate escapees start a knowledge-based business as it suits our inside-out marketing philosophy. The *e-ttraction 12-Step system* has been tested hundreds of times across dozens of industry sectors and found to work wherever the person's knowledge is an important part of the product. This fact inextricably links their personal brand to the marketing for their business and suits our system perfectly.

Therefore, I wrote my first book for businesspeople to build their personal brands to gain a promotion, new job or start a business. This second book extends the same three-step philosophy, now called e-ttraction, into how to be a corporate escapee who starts and scales your own knowledge-based business.

Knowledge Businesses

The types of businesses that best suit the processes in this book are based on your particular personality, knowledge, experience, education and network. That means there isn't a physical product that your client can touch and feel, it's intangible. Because the product is intangible, you become the product, even if you are not a traditional consultant you are a key part of providing the service to your client. Therefore, clients can't make a judgment about the product quality from touching or seeing it, they can only decide to use your service from what is presented online, reviews from past clients, and meeting up with you directly. Personal branding is of paramount importance to this type of business, and this is the type of business we specialise in. Because I have had so much experience in this sector, most of my processes built into the e-ttraction model fit these businesses best.

Knowledge professionals come in all shapes and sizes. However, there are three main styles we tend to see in our consulting business, and we have categorised them as Young Entrepreneurs, Fed-Up Middle Managers and Top-Shelf Corporate Escapees. It's useful to see whether you fit into these categories and examine a few examples to bring the theory to life.

Three Types of Knowledge Professionals

There are a variety of business models that can be set up when you leave your regular job: Young Entrepreneurs, Fed-Up Middle Managers and Top-Shelf Corporate Escapees.

Young Entrepreneurs

The first is a start-up that is represented by usually being based on a technology innovation and requiring start-up funding. If you are a Young Entrepreneur, then this book can help you position yourself in the market for fundraising and attracting staff. It can be difficult to start the process of investment here as you need to introduce yourself to many different prospective investors to gain the meetings to communicate your pitch. How can this be done? It can be via a referral from a colleague, in this way, the investor will want to see who you are before agreeing to a meeting. If you are cold prospecting, you will need a brand for them to see before they will even communicate with you. The same theory applies when trying to attract talent. Good people have many employment options and, as a start-up founder, you need to position yourself and the business well to attract people to work with you. Often start-up founders are younger (or young at heart), have experience in technology and desire a fast-growing business. They want an exit of some description within a few years of starting the business and are aggressive when it comes to their personal branding.

The young entrepreneurs are usually in their twenties and are smart and dynamic. They want to rapidly advance their careers, but the normal work system slows them down and doesn't have the opportunities they crave. They look for an entrepreneurial project to do themselves, but they lack the experience, knowledge and network to get things started themselves. The smart ones partner with more mature people for these projects and set off on their own paths. For a select few, I am that conduit between their passion and a process to get ideas into the market in a commercial way. But there are many mentors and great people out there who love to assist young people in creating start-ups.

I was recently at a careers day for RMIT University helping the next generation of marketing graduates with some career advice. One lady, Samantha, in the audience came to talk to me after and was dressed very professionally. She didn't look or act like a student and we had a great conversation about entrepreneurship. I misheard her and thought she said she was 28 and working in her own business and studying full-time. A mature-age student perhaps? In subsequent meetings, I realised that she was 22 and an undergraduate student who had been running her own businesses since she was 16 years old! She tried working at various companies, but they just held back her creativity and energy, so she wanted to have her own marketing agency, but customers didn't trust someone so young. So, we started working together.

Another example of this is a young professional named Sunayna or Sunny, as is her brand name. We had some mutual friends and so she approached me online to have a chat about her career. I arranged a coffee with her to see if I could help her and she told me her story. She was a 30-year-old speech pathologist who had completed her formal training and after a few years of good experience realised that she could never earn enough money to live the life she wanted to as a speech pathologist. She dreamt of starting her own business but didn't know where to start as it all seemed far too overwhelming. Having studied in the medical field, she had never had any exposure to business and felt there was too much to learn to leap into her own company. Imagine being great at what you do but not understanding marketing, sales, technology, finance, law, human resources, accounting, business structures and all the things that go into running a business.

I agreed to mentor her and guide her on her path to a business start-up. We are working on building her brand currently and plan to transition to her own company in 12 months, once she has established her following and core offerings. She has big plans for children's books, a YouTube channel and more!

Fed-Up Middle Managers

Another model is starting your own practice in the same industry. This is for the Fed-Up Middle Managers. This suits a range of professional service people in the medical, legal, finance or consulting industries. We have worked with a variety of medical practitioners building their own medical practices, such as physiotherapists, speech pathologists, chiropractors, pain specialists, general surgeons, dietitians and more. They have similar needs for their personal brands, such as working within the Australian Prudential Regulation Authority (APRA) guidelines, abiding by their particular industry's codes of professional practice, and similarities in their company structures and technology. These clients usually have very little time to devote to their personal branding as they are paid per time spent with patients. Therefore, we need to ensure our work is very time-efficient. We have developed specific content-creation processes for these clients that we will document when we get into these sections of the book.

The Fed-Up Middle Managers are doing the corporate grind. They ended up in a career by following what others thought best for them or just took the next best job on offer at each stage of their career, without a plan for their future. They know they are not happy and want more out of life. Given their life stage, they usually have significant financial commitments so feel that they can't afford to make sudden and unplanned changes in their career. They need stable income and if they were to change professions, they want to gradually ease into something else that's likely to be related to their current profession. With a few major differences around the style of work they do, the choice of clients they take, and the amount of time they dedicate to work compared to other priorities.

I was at this stage when I left my corporate job and became an entrepreneur. I had some success running Social Star as a side business (a branding agency that works with business professionals to build their personal and business brands) and knew that there was a demand for my services and that people would pay money for it. However, having a side business was one thing, relying on it to pay all my expenses was another thing, especially when I left my well-paying corporate job suddenly and didn't plan for this transition. I didn't have a large amount of savings to pay for set-up expenses or to support me while I grew the business. I just did it. I didn't even have a plan! It's the opposite of what I tell my clients to do! But I learnt a lot and I hope my experience provides a good lesson on what *not* to do.

I remember before I made this jump, a friend of mine who I studied with at Swinburne University during my Master of Entrepreneurship and Innovation degree, decided not to jump and for good reasons. Josh was in some of my classes, and we also did a business-planning competition called the BCG Strategy Cup competition. Each team of six people had three hours to review a case study and present to a panel of judges with a pitch to solve the business problem. We were representing Swinburne against all the MBA courses in Victoria and were lucky enough to win our division and progress to the Australian finals. Josh and I were key members of the team, and it was a great bonding time for us.

After university we stayed friends and I recall many dinners and conversations discussing the pros and cons of leaving the corporate world and starting our own businesses. I went down the path of starting Social Star and Josh stayed with employment, mainly due to his kids being so young and feeling it was too risky to go out on his own at that time. To be honest, he was right! As I said previously, it was a terrible time for me to start my own venture with the pressures of delivering regular income. Josh was more sensible than I and has done very well in his career and I'm sure he will branch out into his own side businesses at the right time when it's his time to be a Top-Shelf Corporate Escapee.

Top-Shelf Corporate Escapees

A final category of clients is those closer to retirement who want to run a portfolio business. These are Top-Shelf Corporate Escapees. These people are usually over 50 years old, but not always. The younger clients we have that sell their businesses want to build a new one, rather than create a portfolio of services they then provide themselves. This model is more suited to people who crave a better work-life balance, and they tend to be people who have worked for decades and want to enjoy some downtime. They want to deliver a range of services such as consulting, coaching, sitting on boards, investing, mentoring, speaking, writing and so forth. This style of personal branding requires clients to self-brand rather than use a company entity. That means the website would use your name specifically, instead of a business name. Andrew Ford Consulting, for example, rather than a business name such as Social Star. It's very flexible so you can take on any project that takes your interest and work as much or as little as you please. A portfolio business creates an entity that contains all your interests under one banner in a way clients can easily understand what you're offering without the complication of listing out all the individual services to explain your work. This entity is something you can build your brand around and have a personal website and a listing on LinkedIn functioning as your current career or experience in one legal entity.

The Top-Shelf Corporate Escapees are an interesting bunch. You would think that anyone who had started and exited a multi-million-dollar business or was the CEO of a billion-dollar organisation wouldn't need any business advice. Indeed, they are at the top of their game when it comes to their specific industry and their role within it. They are high-performance workers yet have large support teams around them to keep them focused on what they do best. They don't have to do things like setting up websites, marketing, bookkeeping and accounting, setting meetings, writing social content, sales, creating PowerPoint decks, writing plans and more. These things get them out of flow and that's why they have specialists to do them.

When they sell their businesses or want to retire from the CEO spotlight, they suddenly don't have these various teams to support them. Plus, their own brand identity has been protected by a company identity. They haven't had to put themselves "out there", so to speak. I have seen powerful people become very vulnerable once they must put themselves on the line and ask for an order or feel needy when they require people for assistance. They struggle to know how to position themselves separately from their businesses, let alone do all the work required to run a portfolio business, so some give up. Others call us or other experts in the industry to provide guidance and take over some of these elements. We provide confidence in the next best steps forward and outsource some of the tasks they dislike the most. They might have a family office for their finances, and we are the marketing office for their business endeavours.

Working with several people who have run billion-dollar businesses is very humbling. The first of which was one of the co-founders of SEEK, which was very early in my Social Star career. More surprisingly, he called me after being referred by two different people in his network. Another more recent example was the COO of a huge tech company that was recently let go in a whole top-level management reshuffle. He wasn't sure what to do next and was referred to me to go through our branding process. We built him a brand and website for his portfolio business, which was going well until he decided he wanted to start his own technology business. He very quickly assembled his contacts and started his own tech business. The man has so much energy and passion that he couldn't help but jump back into the game. That's the nature of successful people, they are hard-working and unstoppable.

From the three groups described above, you can see that there is no perfect time in your life to start your own business, each phase has different challenges and opportunities. That said, from my experience, the second persona, the Fed-Up Middle Manager, is the one that finds it the most difficult to make the transition to their own business. This was my transition time and it was tough. Having a full-time job, kids and responsibilities meant money and time were in short supply to apply towards building a new business whilst working. It also didn't help that I was recently divorced, which complicated matters too.

But you can't help it when your mid-life crisis hits. That was my catalyst to move from my high-profile corporate marketing executive role in the IT industry to running my own business,

Social Star. I have always been entrepreneurial, had a lot of business ideas and wanted to do my own thing. Having big dreams as a kid without the means to execute them was frustrating. Working in various corporations taught me a lot about business and my formal education added to that mix. But it wasn't until I started my own business, and a few other ventures along the way, that I learnt what it takes to run a successful start-up. Having worked for others was essential in my development, so choose your time of transition carefully. Once you are out it's hard to go back! One of my clients recently said they were unemployable now they have been working for themselves for several years. The benefits of working in a large business, such as parental leave and travel, should not be underestimated, so consider the long-term ramifications of your choice before making the jump. There is much safety in a regular income, and it certainly helps when buying your first house!

That is why many entrepreneurs are very young as they are yet to have serious commitments of a house or family, so they can take a risk and if it doesn't work out they can start again or get a job for some time. Similarly, at the end of your career, creating a portfolio business is very low risk. You already have a network of key people to help you find clients, skills in your area of expertise, and a strong personal brand and you can more easily afford to make the transition. I often work with the latter category, as these clients can afford to outsource their marketing and sales work to my team and are more coachable. They appreciate my advice and experience and pay for it willingly.

My goal for this book is that the e-ttraction process will help all three types of corporate escapees, regardless of their situation, to start planning for their transition so they are fully prepared for what's ahead. My journey wasn't quite as planned, and I will share more of how I ended up in my own business and how I ended up creating the e-ttraction model to ensure I was successful. It isn't just a model for others, it's what I use every day in my businesses.

My Corporate Escape

My career started at my family business, RH Grierson & Co, as I mentioned previously, where I worked for eight years and learnt the ropes of working in a company, sales and marketing.

Transitioning to Hewlett-Packard was quite an experience and culture shock! HP was Steve Jobs', the former CEO of Apple, favourite company. It was the first tech start-up in Silicon Valley in California and literally began in a garage in 1938 when Bill Hewlett and Dave Packard started it with $548 in capital after being encouraged to stay in the city and make it a tech hub by their Stanford professor Fredrick Terman.[4]

This site is now a museum. Jobs famously rang the founder of HP, Bill Hewlett, who conveniently lived around the corner and boldly asked for some spare parts to make a frequency counter. The HP founder was so impressed with this 12-year-old's boldness that he gave him a summer internship working in the factory. What a fortuitous meeting! As Jobs said in an interview, "I've always found something to be very true, which is most people don't get those experiences because they never ask. I've never found anybody that didn't want to help me if I asked them for help."[5]

At the time I started at HP, it was voted one of the best places to work in Australia and it was amazing. I took full advantage of the

---

4   https://en.wikipedia.org/wiki/HP_Garage
5   https://www.cnbc.com/2018/07/25/how-steve-jobs-cold-called-his-way-to-an-internship-at-hewlett-packard.html

opportunities and was captain of the ski team, member of the triathlon group, regular onsite gym attendee, on the social club committee and anything else I could get my hands on! I was a company man and loved working there. I travelled the world to awesome destinations such as France, Vienna, Chicago, Colorado, Japan, Korea, China, Thailand, Taiwan and many more. Over seven years I worked in five different roles, and I feel blessed for my time there. I learned a lot from the people and the work.

All great things come to an end and when HP merged with Compaq in 2021, it was the biggest tech merger in history at $25 billion. It was led by the new CEO, Carly Fiorina, who was brought in by the board to shake up the company. This was her way of growing the business and making a name for herself. She did make a name for herself, but likely not in the way she imagined. Her merger caused a lot of division in the business with a large and drawn-out dispute with the founders' children and the rest of the board, fighting to reject the merger. It ended up going ahead and cost all the shareholders a fortune. It reduced the value of the business by half and created a massive retrenchment process to reduce the cost of employees significantly.[6] More significantly, they destroyed the HP culture that was carefully crafted by Bill and Dave over 40 years. The company was never the same again. And it wasn't long before they retrenched the entire international division. It wasn't all bad for me as I got a generous exit package, and my biggest customer asked me to work for them, which was my first taste of consulting. They were based in New York, so I was a remote worker before the days of co-working spaces and the awesome tools to help people collaborate. It involved tough hours dealing with a boss in New York and after one year I wanted to head back into a more regular work style, especially as I had a growing family to support.

---

6   https://www.zdnet.com/article/
worst-tech-mergers-and-acquisitions-hp-and-compaq/

Hence, I ended up going to work for a local company, Sensis, the marketing division of Telstra. This was a great role as it was right on the cusp of the digital revolution. The internet was here, websites were common and social media was present, but it really hadn't caught on yet. My role was in the team transitioning the business from relying on the $1.2 billion of the Yellow Pages print-book revenue to a digital-based business. For those young people out there, this was pre-iPhone and the app store. I know it's hard to imagine a world without iPhones and social media applications like Instagram and TikTok, but there was life before these! As Apple led the way into the social media revolution, we did some crazy cool projects like the world's first mapping app on the iPhone. They were booming times in digital, and we had huge freedom to be creative and expand our products. We did Myspace marketing campaigns and influencer events well before everyone else caught on.

That positioned me as a digital expert and the recruiters started calling. After many offers of significantly more money and opportunities, I made the move to IBM to recharge their mainframe division. That was a fun year of making changes and breaking rules, as they had a very formal culture. The clash came when my global mainframe division wanted me to get out there training other countries in what I had achieved, whilst the local marketing hierarchy wanted me fired for not toeing the line. This is when my entrepreneurial spirit clashed with fixed-mindset corporate culture. I was flexing my creative ideas and pushing the boundaries and they didn't appreciate it.

The recruiter calls kept coming, so I ended up at my last corporate job for the highest salary I ever had. But also the worst job and company culture I had experienced. Bullying, misogyny, blatant sexism and inter-office affairs were all rife. You would think it was *The Wolf of Wall Street*, but this wasn't the 1980s and it wasn't conducive to stable decision-making. I clashed with the CEO over many of his tactics and, after one particularly offensive argument, I walked out. I remember the moment he called me into his office and was standing over me yelling about something and, in my mind, I was already deciding to leave and start my own business. It was so clear that the end of working for others had come and it was the start of working for myself. Corporate work had given me so much, but it was time for the next phase of my career.

Social Star became my full-time gig on the drive home. I called my ex-wife on the way to my rented flat. It was a terrible time for me, since I had recently separated from her and moved out of the family home. My finances were uncertain and emotionally I wasn't 100%. The company gave me two months' severance and I had to make a full-time income in that time to pay rent and child support. What a motivation to be successful! There is nothing like burning the boats to motivate you to hustle and make money. I got to work and followed my marketing process of e-ttraction, which at that time was unnamed, but I already knew what sort of process to follow. I networked, created content, helped people for free and built my reputation in the personal branding space. Having worked around Melbourne for many years, I had built strong networks and these people helped me so much to get started. Never underestimate the power of having a good reputation in your industry, it's a huge asset.

The first few years were challenging, but aided by the fact we had secured seed funding for our big idea to build an application for LinkedIn with automation and training to assist executives create strong personal brands. Unfortunately, that idea, whilst good, was ahead of its time and the technology, people and skills required to pull it off were not available. People said they could help but, when push came to shove, they couldn't. Consequently, we wasted a lot of time, money and energy on trying to get this new idea to market. My first developer said they could do it and ended up building a website. The second was similar, and the third stole all the funding and didn't produce anything at all. It was very frustrating and deflating. I remember one moment, whilst on holiday with my family in Fiji, writing an extremely detailed technical brief for my last developer. I thought if I spelt out in intimate detail what I wanted, that would solve all my issues. Unfortunately, it didn't and I called defeat on the project and almost gave up on the business entirely. It's a humbling moment when you must face your investors and tell them you have lost all their money, don't have a product to show them, and are completely spent. I was mentally and financially broken, but they still had confidence in me. They offered me a loan and told me to get back on my bike and come back with a new idea in a few weeks. People are wonderful sometimes and that confidence was a godsend during those difficult times.

This is when it's essential to have a strong belief that this is what you want to do and not go back to a job. If you dig into what you want in life and for your career and build the business to support your highest values, you will find a way to persist. You build resilience and keep moving forward. You learn the lessons and improve on them, time after time.

I regrouped and started consulting to earn a living and pay back my investors. It took me almost five years to chase down those who stole the money and retrieve it, pay back the loans and build the business to a size where we could reinvest into technology again. Since then, we have grown from strength to strength with many hard-earned lessons to support us. By not giving up, I built a strong business that provides me the opportunity to do what I love: helping and supporting people. It also allows me to work on other projects such as this book and my start-ups. Finding time and a level of financial freedom has been a ten-year quest and well worth the ups and downs of start-up life. But of course, I'm not done yet! There is much I want to do, such as growing Social Star into a multi-office business. I can envision every city having a Social Star to support students gain experience in marketing and helping individuals and local businesses to grow their brands.

I feel like the next chapter in our work is just beginning and it fills me with energy and excitement to share this journey with you, my readers and supporters. I hope you follow the advice in this book and join me on the other side of your career when you can create your own business around your lifestyle, rather than fit your life around your job. It's not easy, but it's definitely worth it.

How to Use This Book

As I mentioned in the introduction, I have written this book for people who want to escape corporate life and start their own businesses. Specifically, knowledge professionals who feel a "calling" to start their own business and are comfortable using their personal brands to build their businesses. They will be at one of the three stages of their career journey that I mentioned previously: Young Entrepreneurs, Fed-Up Middle Managers and Top-Shelf Corporate Escapees. But how do you know if starting your own business is the best option for you now? Before we progress to the main content, it's worth exploring the personal traits I believe are required to make starting your own business a better choice than working for others.

Of course, anyone can start a business anytime, the challenging part is to keep it going when things get difficult. Most businesses fail within the first three years, which is estimated to be at 60%, but I believe it is much higher, as many people don't register their small businesses officially.[7] From my experience helping people start businesses, there are two key reasons why they are not successful. Firstly, they don't have sufficient knowledge to start the business and make some critical errors in the set-up. Most of these issues are in product development, sales and marketing.

For example, we set up a coaching business for one of my clients using our 12-Step process and, at the end, handed over the brand assets to him to operate. He had a website, a great LinkedIn profile and blogs, and we had taught him how to continue the marketing process. But then he didn't do any! He just wanted to sell his services, so he ignored all the important branding processes and his business didn't work. Eventually, he was forced to go back to full-time work. Don't underestimate how much effort is required in sales and marketing to ensure you have a steady stream of clients. We estimate you should spend 30% of your time in this area, 50% of your time in delivery and 20% of your time in administration and company work.

The second, and more important reason businesses fail, is that the owners give up. If they make a mistake in the first iteration of the business, it can be changed and relaunched. But most people give up and don't persist through these market iterations.

Therefore, two of the most important considerations to review before you quit your job and start your business are: why do you want to start a business in the first place; what is your motivation to persist through challenging times? The most common reason to start a business is the desire for freedom.

7   https://www.investopedia.com/financial-edge/1010/top-6-reasons-
        new-businesses-fail.aspx#:~:text=According%20to%20the%20U.S.%20
        Bureau,to%2015%20years%20or%20more

Freedom

After working with literally hundreds of people who want to make the transition from working for others to working for themselves, I have discovered a commonality to their stories that I think is important to share and understand. They all have a passion for freedom, the freedom to choose who they work for, when they work and what they do each day. This value is so important that they will take significant risks and give up the security of income and employment to gain it. They know the path of entrepreneurship is more challenging, risky and time-consuming, but there is something in their DNA driving them to do it anyway.

The reasons are hidden in their past. Usually, it's a family trait like their parents are business owners, so they follow suit. Or it's the opposite: they have seen their parents work all their lives for other people and not get the rewards they deserve. Perhaps their parents didn't like their jobs, didn't get paid enough to live comfortably, or sustained an injury through work and their employers abandoned them. Whatever the cause of the drivers is, it's clear that the vast majority of people who successfully make the transition to self-employment have a deep internal motivation to do so. You need deep commitment to freedom to persist when it makes more sense to stop. I shared my story so you could see how my upbringing and circumstances impacted why I wanted to have my own business and what kept me going through significant challenges.

Growing up with no control over my home life and circumstances and feeling insecure created a strong desire for control in my life as an adult. Running my own business provides an ability to have more control over my circumstances. It's a strong desire, more than the safety and comfort of employment.

Persistence

We discussed how entrepreneurs often face large challenges in childhood. If you read the biographies of any of the most successful entrepreneurs of the last 20 years, you will read a similar tale of overcoming challenges and having to make decisions that were so risky that a "normal" person wouldn't have made them. For instance, Richard Branson famously went from a successful record company to running an airline. He didn't have the experience, funding or connections. Plus, British Airways, which was essentially running a monopoly, was determined to see him fail. Even his board of directors didn't understand why he would risk all his money, assets and reputation on a new venture when the current one was doing so well. Only entrepreneurs *get* why they did what they did. He couldn't help it, as he has a high-risk tolerance. Growing up with dyslexia, he solved his learning issues, absorbed the abuse and discrimination he faced, and used it to fuel his desire to see fairness in all industries. His quest wasn't about money, but his core values of overcoming challenges and helping others like him receive fair treatment in the market.

Jack Ma, of Alibaba fame, failed to get into university many times and had many other personal challenges. So, when he started an internet-based business ahead of the technology curve in China, he faced myriad challenges from battling the government, societal beliefs regarding web-based businesses, and ignorance of his business model, but it was par for the course. He was used to failing and people underestimating him, so he didn't fold, he persisted. My favourite quote from Jack is: "Never give up. Today is hard, tomorrow will be worse, but the day after tomorrow will be sunshine."[8]

8   https://www.ccamonash.com.au/articles/2018/1/2/
      jack-ma-a-story-of-success-through-failure

Steve Jobs of Apple was famously fired from his own company after making some disastrous decisions on the strategy for their personal computer line-up. He went on to start Pixar Animation Studios and revolutionised the animation industry with the launch of *Toy Story*, then came back to rebuild Apple after 11 years out of the company. He was an outcast from his youth, a brilliant hippy, he used to walk around his university with no shoes, unshowered and dropping into classes he was interested in but not enrolled in. He was very unusual and unconventional. He didn't conform to what others thought he should do, but he gave no fucks. Which is why he could create revolutionary products that challenged the status quo and changed industries. He didn't care what other executives or the nay-sayers thought. He just did what he wanted to do and what he felt was right. Few people have such personal belief in their ideas.

Finally, my favourite story is Elon Musk who failed so many times publicly. He was sent to the wall financially when the first three of his SpaceX rockets blew up at the same time as Tesla cars were not selling. But he persisted and overcame the doubters to become the richest man in the world.

You and I are not like these billionaire entrepreneurs, but our spirit is the same. We are built to persist no matter what. If this sounds like you, we will get along famously and I know this book will help you with your endeavour. I encourage you to examine your past, dig into your *why* and write it down so you can go back to it when things get tough.

One last thing I would like you to understand before we dig into the e-ttraction 12-Step model is some essential marketing theory to ensure we are speaking the same language.

Three Brands

A key marketing theory that is useful to highlight is that there are three different types of brands in the marketplace: personal, business and product. Understanding how people find, connect and perceive you in the market is critical to the set-up of your branding.

A personal brand is directly related to your name and persona. They are buying a service you deliver and expect you to show up, so when they ask for Andrew Ford to run a strategy-planning session, Andrew must run it.

A business brand is where the customer is buying the services and outcomes the business promises. When a client talks to Andrew and engages the services of Social Star, they might get one of our team delivering the workshop.

The product brand is the actual workshop and has its value in the market independently from Andrew and Social Star. There could be several services a client wants, such as a website, a new logo or a video, all of which have their unique value and conditions. We use creative credits to purchase these services which are independent from Andrew Ford or Social Star, albeit interrelated to each other.

All three of these brands are intertwined. They all have an impact on the final decision to work with someone, but there will be different levels of importance for each of the three depending on the style of business, how long the business has been in operation, and the services offered.

For instance, a new business that hasn't been in operation very long will rely on the personal brand of the founder the most. The business and products don't have any credibility yet, as they are new and haven't established their brands in the market. The trust is developed via the founder.

Once the business services many people, has staff and more reviews, it starts to develop its brand and trust independently of the founder. It can take several years to develop the business brand to this level, so the marketing focus when starting the new business is initially the founder's brand.

Generally, the last brand to be established is the products themselves. It takes the founder delivering the services hundreds of times to make it a routine and solidify exactly what the product range is and who it best suits. Only then, do we codify the service into a product and brand it independently, as it is less likely to change.

Final Thoughts

We are only on this planet for a limited time. You will never get yesterday back, it's gone, and tomorrow is the next chance to do what fills you up inside. Don't waste precious days, weeks or even years wondering what might have been. Be bold and do what is fulfilling to you. Many people I have met along my business journey tell me the same thing. They wish they had started sooner, but they were busy pleasing their parents, partners, bosses, friends and society. Doing what they thought they should, rather than what they felt in their guts they were meant to do. They played it safe and, in some cases, waited decades to be their true selves and live the life that they wanted.

When I was teaching at Monash University, many kids were just like this. I was teaching a capstone master's subject called Professional Development – Career Dynamics. It was an elective, but very popular with engineering, finance and business students as it didn't have an exam and they thought it would be an easy subject to take. The goal of our course was to prepare them for the real world after university with practical skills in networking, personal branding and essentially how to get a job and succeed in it.

It turned out not to be quite the soft subject they expected because many of them failed due to underestimating how difficult it is to delve into yourself and understand your values and drivers. How to represent this online so you can attract a potential employer, and then how to communicate effectively with other people so you can be successful in your role. It's not a 1 + 1 = 2 scenario. People are full of variables that are difficult to understand, predict and change. During the classes, we did a lot of activities and I recall one such day when we asked the students what their dream job was. There was a high percentage of international students in the class, mostly Asian and Indian, particularly from the engineering and accounting streams. When I asked them about their dream careers, most of them didn't even name their chosen course! I was dumbfounded. I asked, "Why study accounting, for example, if you want to be a race-car driver, chef, actor, game designer, etc?" The common answer was my father or mother were accountants, or this was the course my parents thought would be best for me. It's honourable to want the best careers for your children, particularly if you didn't have the same opportunities when you were young and want to give your kids a leg-up socio-economically. However, the problem with choosing for your kids and not letting them find their way is they end up in a profession that doesn't fulfil them.

They attend university to study, meet friends in the same course, which becomes their network, get an internship at a firm, start accumulating work experience, form connections with colleagues, and advance their careers. This is a very normal career journey, but the problem is the more they invest in that sector the harder it is to get out and do something else. They continue the same career trajectory as it's too hard to change. Some get married and start a family or buy a house, it's now too risky to start something new or change paths. Busy with life, they don't even think about what they want to do anymore, they just do. Then the mid-life crisis hits. Or the quarter-life crisis that is becoming more of the trend these days with Generation Z. They suddenly realise they don't like their profession or job they are in and want to do something else. But all their training, knowledge, contacts and experience are in that one field – how can they possibly change?

The good news is that it is possible. There has never been a better time to shift careers with the availability of knowledge, the change in work culture where it's accepted that you can do many different careers, and the ability to market your services far and wide easily with cheap technology. It's the right time to make a career change, if you feel like it's the best thing for you. Your happiness is more important than your income, and I am positive that doing what you love will bring more than enough rewards. Having helped well over a hundred people of all ages refocus their lives into more fulfilling careers, I have seen so many people pivot and know you can do it too.

There have been IT professionals who opened wine bars, recruitment consultants importing fine whisky from the UK, council officers importing tequila from Mexico (they are not all alcohol-related, I assure you!), middle managers becoming life coaches, doctors becoming authors, salespeople moving into AI and more. If you tell me a profession, I have likely had a client or two in that space. Some of the more unusual referrals I have received have been pole-dancing champions, professional skydivers, art curators, massive infrastructure developers, billionaire entrepreneurs, high-profile DJs, actors, politicians, high school students, AFL presidents, professional boxers and more. I love the eclectic nature of personal branding and meeting such a diverse range of people. That said, my regular clients fall into three distinct categories that I described at the start of this chapter: Young Entrepreneurs, Fed-Up Middle Managers and Top-Shelf Corporate Escapees.

As I've said previously throughout this book, I will introduce the e-ttraction Method. The e-ttraction Method has taken me 10 years to perfect after working with hundreds of clients in different industries and stages of business. There are three main sections to the e-ttraction Method: Understand, Build and Leverage. Each of these three sections has four Steps, making 12 Steps in total. Which you can see in the diagram below.

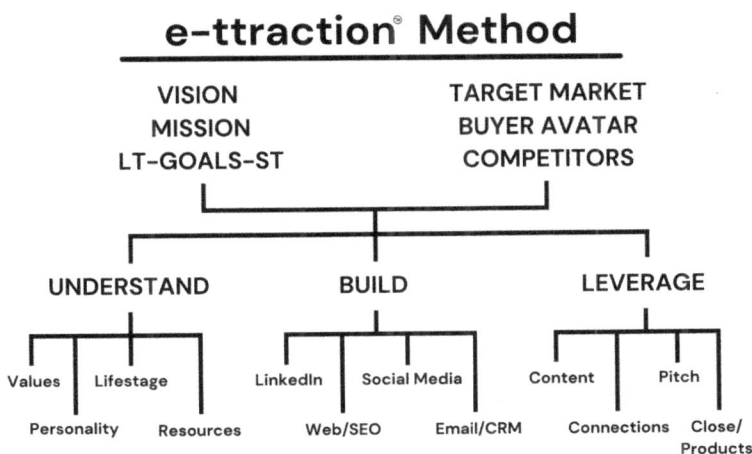

e-ttraction® Method

VISION	TARGET MARKET	
MISSION	BUYER AVATAR	
LT–GOALS–ST	COMPETITORS	

UNDERSTAND	BUILD	LEVERAGE
Values	LinkedIn	Content
Lifestage	Social Media	Pitch
Personality	Web/SEO	Connections
Resources	Email/CRM	Close/Products

Figure 1. The e-ttraction Method.

The method is structured around a university course, which has 12 weeks of content that makes up the course over one six-month semester. This structure has worked well for universities over many decades, so we leveraged this structure. The time it takes to go through this process will vary from person to person, but on average it takes my clients six months to fully change their branding approach, ready for their new business to launch. Keep that in mind when doing the timeline for your business.

Throughout this book, you can expect to learn new concepts in marketing and branding. Some might be logical and practical immediately. Others might be more foreign and require some more thinking to digest and fully appreciate. Everything in this book is here for a reason and will be helpful to you in the long-term. I pepper each Step with examples from my clients to assist with the practical implementation of the material and bring to life some of our work. These are real people in the same position you are in now and my aim is that they inspire you to see what's possible if you follow the process.

PART 1: **UNDERSTAND**

"When your values are clear to you,
making decisions becomes easier."

– Roy Disney

The first Step to creating your own business is to build your personal brand. As discussed in our three-brand methodology, when you initially launch your business your brand is the most influential way to gain trust in the market. Your business name isn't known or proven, and you haven't delivered your products yet, so there isn't another way to market your business other than your personal brand. To build a powerful personal brand we need to understand the person behind the brand. But before you jump right in and start making your website and posts on social media, it is important to sit back and reflect on what you really want, who you want to work with, how you are going to run your business effectively, and what you need to do to get started. The Understand section is designed to answer these questions and will challenge you to dig deep, to think about your situation in more detail, and to ensure the Build and Leverage sections are smooth sailing.

The Understand part is the most important to starting a business so don't underestimate its relevance. It sets the foundation for your goals, target market, business structure, and support required in the form of employees and software, plus what resources you need to get started. Let's begin.

Understand Yourself

"Know thyself" is the best-known of the three philosophical maxims that are inscribed at the entrance to the Temple of Apollo in the ancient Greek precinct of Delphi. It is an often-quoted rule to live by and, like most maxims that have stood the test of time, this one is a golden rule of success. The problem is that it is difficult to see yourself objectively because you are in your head 24/7, 365 days a year, without an opportunity to step outside yourself to critically analyse how you are made up. Therefore, it is vital to have a process to gain an objective perspective on your personality and traits.

In my first meeting with new clients, I spend the initial hour asking specific questions and listening to them to find out what they want from setting up a portfolio business. I ask questions like:

- What's most important to you?
- What do you want to achieve financially?
- What do you love to do most?
- What do you hate doing?
- If money were no concern, what would you do with your time?
- What do you daydream about?
- What are your lifestyle goals?

These questions get clients thinking about what they love to do, without worrying about how it relates to their current business. Sometimes clients don't see the relevance of this part of the conversation until I reveal the greater strategy, and then an "a-ha!" moment occurs, and the light bulb comes on. This is one of the reasons I love to help people with their brands and businesses:

to see the instant when they shift their thinking and can see the opportunities for themselves. When they can perceive themselves as the world does, they feel inspired to continue the process.

Understanding your brand is key to the success of setting up the business around your life, instead of setting up your life to revolve around your business. The clearer you are about what problems you solve, the more precise your target market will be attracted to you. The better you solve the problems that are right in your niche of experience, the greater the outcomes will be for your target market, and the more they will be prepared to pay you for your services.

There are four key Steps: Values, Personality, Lifestage and Resources. There are also a few extra sections that prepare us to do these Steps and a few we need to complete after the Understand section, which prepare us for the Build section.

To begin the Understand process, we must know why you are building a portfolio business in the first place. All good journeys start with a destination, so where do you want to go? Let's set some goals to get there.

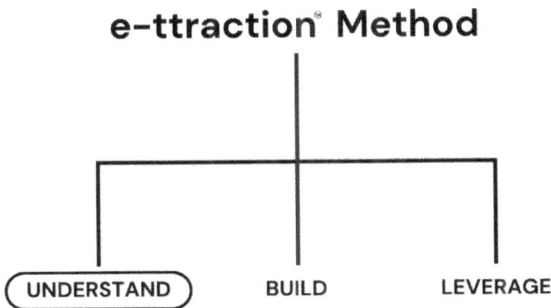

e-ttraction° Method

UNDERSTAND   BUILD   LEVERAGE

Figure 2. The first section of the e-ttraction Method is Understand.

The Future

Many of my clients have worked in large organisations and have often been a part of planning sessions to create goals. Often, they start with a vision that represents the overall purpose of the organisation. The vision leads to a mission, which is what we do in the marketplace to support the vision of the company. Then we create long-term goals, normally three-year goals, to bring the mission to life and short-term goals, usually 12 months, to create immediate actions to implement. This process leads to a cohesive organisation working together to achieve a common outcome.

For individuals looking to start their own business, this process is a bit different as we are not just looking at the organisation, we are examining our entire lives. We do this process based on what we want, and work and money are parts of this process but not the entirety of it. All our values matter when we set up our vision.

When you are running your own business, it's difficult to extract your personal life from the business. The point of these types of businesses is that you build your business around your life, not modify your life for your business. Therefore, let's start documenting your vision for your life and how your business works within it.

Vision

A vision is what you desire most for your life but are afraid to ask for it. It's a personal long-term (five-years-plus) wish list of a lifestyle that you don't know how you are going to get to. Some people don't like to aim for things they can't plan for, but in this case, put aside these doubts and just write how you would like your life to be in the future.

For example, my vision is to have the health, money and time to be able to spend it how I wish. Freedom to take my kids skiing overseas when they have holidays, and the snow is good. Freedom to enjoy a trip overseas with my mates or partner a few times a year without any stress or pressure of business commitments. Freedom to be fit and able to enjoy all of these activities to their fullest extent. Whilst still giving back to my staff, team and the wider community in a meaningful way.

Mission

Your mission is more of the specific plan that isn't personal, it's more about the business you want to start, which is useful to inspire the team and galvanise them together into action. For instance, at Social Star, our mission is to build a global branding agency that helps businesses in their local area to easily and effectively do marketing to gain their perfect clients, staff and partners. I don't know exactly when this will happen or how to do it, but that's not important at this Step. When we set goals, this mission will be converted into actions.

Goals – Long-Term

By long-term, I usually mean up to five years, depending on the business. This is long enough to project into the future and see actions take effect over time, but short enough that you can put some measures around it. For instance, the long-term goal at Social Star is to expand from a Melbourne-based agency to have a national footprint with six offices in Sydney, Brisbane, Adelaide, Canberra, Perth and Hobart within three years. Each agency will license the intellectual property of the Social Star head office and be led by a local business leader who has decades of experience in marketing but wants to establish a bigger business to improve their lifestyle. The businesses will all follow our blueprint to grow to a $1 million-plus business utilising the e-ttraction methodology. They will gain their clients from our central marketing and their network, following our personal branding plan. Employees will be easily hired from our sister company CampusLife which takes university students in marketing and trains them during their degree. Central creative services will be leveraged from our team at the head office.

Goals – Short-Term

Short-term goals are 12 months in duration and very specific. For this part, we utilise the SMART goals framework that we teach at university, which is utilised in many corporations. It is a great way to ensure we are planning in detail about what we want and where we want to go before we launch into creating the business.

To assist you in creating your own SMART goals we have some definitions from Monash University.[9]

SMART goals are:

→ **Specific:** it is clear enough that you know exactly what you have to do to achieve it.

→ **Measurable:** there are numbers, so you know when you have achieved it.

→ **Achievable:** you have the resources to be able to get there.

→ **Realistic:** there is a clear path to get there, which you can plan for.

→ **Time-oriented:** there are dates, so you know when it needs to be done.

They add two more attributes that I think are quite useful to make their goals SMARTER:

---

9   https://www.monash.edu/about/editorialstyle/planning/define-your-goals

→ **Evaluate:** regularly review and evaluate their effectiveness, and

→ **Record:** write down your evaluations and revised goals as part of your strategic plan.

Both are good additions in my opinion.

An example here might be useful to give context to the goal-setting process. I will use this example throughout the Understand process, as it will assist in explaining how the process refines your thinking and why it's so important to invest the time to get this right before moving on to the Build and Leverage sections.

Social Star SMART Goals for 2024:

1. Increase revenue to $1.4 million per annum via retainers by the end of 2024 with a profit margin of 20% and 10 staff members, which is the optimum level for the agency model.

2. To do this, build my personal brand during the 2024 calendar year.

   a. Appoint one of my marketing coordinators to manage my brand using our unique Expert Marketing System.

   b. Create four content pieces monthly: one podcast, one blog and two posts, which will be released weekly.

   c. Write, publish and launch my second book on e-ttraction by November of 2024.

   d. Relaunch my *Build Your Own Business* podcast by the end of June.

   e. Gain one speaking gig a month at $2.5K each and two external podcasts or interviews per month in the second half of the year.

3. Build the business brand to support sales to the company.

   a. Appoint one of my marketing coordinators to manage the company brand using our unique Expert Marketing System.

   b. Record a video series in February and July at the start of the 6-month sprints to drip into each month's content.

   c. Expand our social media reach into Instagram from 296 to 1,500 and launch our TikTok channel.

   d. Host one webinar a month to move audiences from Warm to Hot.

Let's use a few examples of these goals in our SMART sections to be sure they follow the process.

- Specific: *Create four content pieces monthly: one podcast, one blog and two posts, which will be released weekly.* Try not to be too generic such as posting more content; in this example, you know what type of content to post and when.

- Measurable: *Gain one speaking gig a month at $2.5K each and two external podcasts or interviews per month in the second half of the year.* I can tell if I gain this speaking gig at the value I wish to achieve. Remember it's a goal and gives you something to aim for, you might not get there, but at least you have a measure of your results to compare and can assess how to improve.

- Achievable: The numbers are all forecast, so they are my best guess on what I can achieve. However, the timeline is ambitious, for sure. With support from my staff helping me produce the content, my book coach Chris, and hiring a COO to assist in running the business to free up my time, I feel it is possible.

- Realistic: *Expand our social media reach into Instagram from 296 to 1,500 and launch our TikTok channel.* Getting reach is quite difficult and we have only just started expanding beyond LinkedIn, so we have set targets we can achieve with a moderate effort, because we don't want too much focus on these channels as they don't generate the business for us compared to what we use today.

- Time-oriented: *Write, publish and launch my second book on e-ttraction by November of 2024.* If I don't get it launched by this date, it's clear the goal hasn't been achieved.

Setting goals is a tricky balance between pushing yourself to be ambitious and making them comfortable and easy to achieve. There are two schools of thought with setting goals, make them achievable so you and the team don't get deflated, or set unrealistic stretch goals to push yourself and the team to achieve great things. The way I approach this is to have realistic goals that you and the team can achieve in most of the areas that are important for your success. But then have one stretch goal that is outlandishly large and a bit scary to push yourself forward. You want to be a little scared by the tasks ahead, so it motivates you to create space for it aside from the normal day-to-day operations of your business. This creates focus and good stress to work effectively. If you have already escaped corporate, setting ambitious goals will help you be focused on your daily structure and work ethic. It will be important to set up a space and time to work away from daily distractions.

An example of my stretch goal is to write this book between February and November. For context, our book-writing process is usually 18–24 months. So doing it in half the time is quite a stretch. Therefore, to get a large part of this book written in time for the November launch, I took two seven-day writing trips to focus on getting the book started and then to get the book finished. The point was to be away from daily work, household or family tasks. This meant I was free to just focus on writing. The first trip to Thailand yielded 30,000 words of content in five days and really helped me towards achieving my deadline. The second trip to the warmth of Port Douglas in Queensland during the freezing cold Melbourne winter was my editing time. It's a nice reward for the hard work, and since it's costly and time consuming, it greatly motivates me to ensure I get the work done.

The point of this story is to show you that you need a plan to achieve your stretch goals. When I set the goal initially, I knew I couldn't reach the target with my busy weekly schedule. So, it forced me to think differently about how to get it done. The weeklong writing trips and the addition of a book coach (thanks, Chris!) made all the difference. However, if this book wasn't that important to the business, then I wouldn't have made the time to do it. Furthermore, I don't have the mind space or time for another stretch goal this year, so I chose this one as the most important to me.

I used to be in the side of setting realistic goals. That if you aim a little bit higher, say 20% more, that would be a successful strategy as you can always work a bit harder, find a few more hours and be slightly more efficient. This is a good strategy for most goal-setting as you can progress without significant changes to your lifestyle. However, reading the book *10x Is Easier Than 2x: How World-Class Entrepreneurs Achieve More by Doing Less* by Dan Sullivan and Benjamin Hardy changed my thinking on this matter. In certain circumstances making goals that far outweigh your current perceived abilities to achieve them is important. It makes you think outside the box on how to achieve the result and promotes creativity and innovation, because the way you can reach a 20% growth target isn't the same as reaching a 200% growth target.

Writing my second book seemed too large a task when I thought of it last year but, upon reading *10x Is Easier Than 2x*, I put a plan together to see if it was achievable and decided that with the new team in place to assist me running the business, a book coach and dedicated time, it could be done. If you think about the natural cycle of things, you will find the principle of extreme versus moderate everywhere. Stockmarkets don't rise and fall in predicable increments. They have slight changes regularly, then sudden and violent swings up and down for a short time. Weather is usually pleasant most of the time, interrupted by extreme storms or other events occasionally. People are generally calm and orderly, except when they have a crisis or major life event and react differently in those circumstances. This cycle seems to follow the Pareto principle or 80/20 rule.[10] Applied to goal-setting, 80% of the time you would aim for incremental improvements that will promote stability in your personal, professional and financial life. But 20% of the time, you would make major changes in your business with a small number of large 10x goals, which will require an upheaval in all areas of your life as they create stress, consume time and change your daily routine.

Using our case study of my personal brand, when I first started Social Star, I had to do a significant amount of work to get the business set up and generate enough revenue to replace my corporate income. This was the 20% or 10x effort to set up my business for success. I wrote the first version of this book, created many videos, blogs and posts, and was very active on social media. My podcast and business networking group BYOB was formed and I did a lot of public speaking. After the business was well established, I was able to relax and have been coasting along for many years on the efforts of previous years' work. This was the 80% goal of gradual improvement or 2x. I would write a few blogs and do irregular posts on social media because it was enough to keep my business full of clients. Now I am back on the 20% or 10x

---

10   https://en.wikipedia.org/wiki/Pareto_principle

growth journey once again, completing a 10-year growth cycle for my business.

Learning from my example and from the other clients we have worked with, we see that these 10x moments of vastly higher levels of productivity are desirable only at critical junctures, say every five to seven years. It creates massive changes to your lifestyle and most people don't want to make this level of change too often in their lives, as it's too hectic.

The key to this work is the timing of the goal. In 2014, when I started my business and put the effort into creating these digital resources, I then leveraged them to spend more time with my kids and on servicing clients to generate revenue. A rest period, if you would like to think about it in that context.

In 2024, the environment is right for me to scale once more. We have developed a unique niche that delivers real value to our clients, and this can be directly transported to other cities. This requires a substantial change in my activity, with more hours worked, but also different work. Like writing this book. But I have the time because my kids are older and taking care of themselves. I have a management team in place to free up my time from the day-to-day running of the business and provide additional skills to our growth strategy, and I have a team to support me in my goals.

Step 1: Values

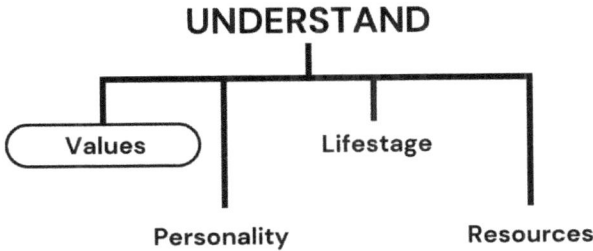

UNDERSTAND

Values　　　Lifestage

Personality　　　Resources

Figure 3. Values can be used as a basis for allocating time, money and resources when starting a portfolio business.

Values aren't what you think. It's not a list of what's right or wrong in the world and advice on how to act. The 10 Commandments spring to mind, likewise people usually associate company values with this section. Things like honesty, respect and tolerance are high on those lists.

The way we use values for our purpose of starting a portfolio business is to understand how we allocate time, money and resources. When you start a new business, your resources will be stretched by competing priorities and your values signal where you will naturally allocate them, so it's best to understand what they are.

According to Dr John Demartini, who first introduced me to his values methodology, every human lives to a set hierarchy of values that dictates how they live their lives. To discover someone's values, just examine where the person spends their time, money and energy. Look around their houses, examine their calendars, listen to what they talk about, see what they post on social media, and you will get a glimpse of their values.

I was fortunate to spend time with Dr Demartini through a mutual connection and I had lunch with him before hearing one of his inspiring presentations. He was a stranger to me before lunch, as I hadn't come across him before, but his speech blew my socks off and I was an advocate after that!

Like most methodologies, Dr Demartini didn't invent this material. It was popularised in the 1960s by Paul J Meyer[11] during the advent of life coaching as a framework to better understand our priorities and have a structured way to work on our goals.

There are now many versions of this method, including those by Dr Demartini, but they are all rooted in an ancient wheel-of-life philosophy Bhava Cakra[12] that has its roots in Tibetan Buddhism. This source code is a much more esoteric and complicated teaching that the practitioners from Meyer to Demartini have refined and personalised for the modern world and different circumstances.

We use the Demartini version as it's refined for businesspeople. His style isn't for everyone, as his theories are quite complex and deep but, if you explore his works in detail, I believe you will gain a great deal of understanding of how people work and relate to one another.

We ask clients to rank the top seven values on a scale from one to seven, from most important to them right now, to least important. These values are Money, Business, Family, Friends, Spirituality, Education and Health. I'll elaborate on what these values mean soon. But, as you can see, all these values are important and therein lies the challenge. How do you choose between things that are all important in your life?

---

11   https://positivepsychology.com/wheel-of-life-coaching/
12   https://en.wikipedia.org/wiki/Bhavacakra

Think about the order in which you put the values and the feelings that come up when you make your choices. Clients' reactions have been from: "How can I possibly choose?!" to "Can I add other values or change the list?" to "They are all equal." These reactions are understandable; however, I ask that you just follow the process because it's designed to create a discussion of where you are now with your values, any challenges you feel when making choices and why.

This is a daily challenge for all people. We have limited time, 24 hours a day, and we must make decisions about how we spend this time, our money and our attention to the different aspects of life. We make choices every day, but often we are not conscious of why we make them. At times we feel resentment for doing things we don't want to, but feel we ought to, should do or must do. These are signals of a clash of values.

Whenever you hear these words from someone, you know they are operating outside their values. They are adopting the values of others to please them, but giving up what they truly want to do. It is so common in our society that we hardly notice. I would go so far as to say that most people feel this is the way we should behave. That it is selfish to do otherwise. Putting others above ourselves is noble, surely? I would argue that having others happy with you and being unsatisfied with your own life doesn't help anyone in the long-term. A lot of people become givers. Feeling good about themselves by their martyrdom.

Others are takers. They don't comprehend that everyone is unique in their values and ideas. Takers desire others to operate in the same way as they do, believe the same things that they do, and operate in a way that is convenient for them. They believe the world revolves around them and it should bend to their wishes.

These people become frustrated when others don't operate as they do.

The truth is we are all givers and takers in different situations and times in our lives or with different people. Some common examples are useful to see how you feel about the situation, if you believe it's right or wrong.

A new parent may be a taker from their workplace because they suddenly place a high value on their family, since they believe their work "should" understand their family situation and provide time off to care for their children. But is this fair to the other workers who don't have children and can't get time off to spend time with their highest values?

A person may have high expectations for others to act in a certain way, say, giving back to the community with charitable contributions or improving the environment as part of their spiritual value. Yet they do not have similar expectations for themselves if it inconveniences them in any way.

An example that comes to mind of this was when Bono, the famous U2 singer, was advocating being carbon-responsible to the average citizen in order to reduce global warming. The issue was that he was flying his private jet around the globe for his band's tours, which left a huge carbon footprint, which was the opposite of what he was proposing others do – change their behaviours to reduce carbon emissions.[13]

Another example closer to our situation was a client who was a very successful business coach. He had been running his business for two decades and was branching out into a side business that he was truly

---

13   https://www.independent.co.uk/climate-change/news/u2-s-massive-carbon-footprint-called-into-question-1734827.html

passionate about. He lit up when discussing his new enterprise – it was great to see. However, he soon found that his coaching business started to reduce as he focused on his new business. He didn't spend any less time on his coaching clients, his methods were as strong as ever, but his energy changed, and people felt that.

We were discussing this change in business, and he was saying he wanted to grow his coaching business and I called him on it. I said that I didn't think that was true. He thought he should grow his coaching client base, he wanted the outcome of the revenue it brought in, but he didn't *really* want to do it. His ego was built into being successful in that area and it was hard to shift his thinking. But he realised the truth of my challenge and is now running both with the balance he desires, without the angst.

Life is more complex than all right or wrong, all black or white, and values will reflect this as they differ between different situations. So, the order in which we put these will need to be in context to the situation and nuance of the person and their circumstances. Trust your intuition when you do this first ranking and know that it's not set in stone, it's designed to make you aware of your preferences so you can understand the implications of your decisions on your life.

We want you to follow your passion. We want to avoid the situation where you say you want something, like a particular goal, but you only want that because you think it will increase your status in society, make you more attractive to a partner, or please your family. This only builds resentment and will not fuel your passion for your work, making it more difficult to build a powerful personal brand.

Now let's examine our seven values in the diagram below. Rank them on your first impression of what you feel to be most correct and then come back to this later to review.

UNDERSTAND

Value	Rank
1. Business	_____
2. Money	_____
3. Family	_____
4. Friends	_____
5. Spirituality	_____
6. Health	_____
7. Education	_____

Figure 4. Template for ranking your current values.

Money

Money is often a confusing and divisive one! It is interesting how different clients react to just the word. Some believe Money shouldn't be a value as it's not "right" to desire it. That is a perception and value projection of their beliefs onto the process. Money is neither good nor bad, it just is. Like all these values, there isn't a right or wrong answer or order. Everyone has their list and for different reasons.

The way I would like you to think about Money in this context isn't the desire for it. It's how much you appreciate it. Then find proof in your life to back up your choice. Do you read books about investing and finances? Do you enjoy researching and investing in the stockmarket, looking at your bank balance and learning how to make more money? If you voluntarily do this work because you find it intrinsically interesting, and you have friends who discuss this with you, then it's likely high on your list of values.

Subsequently, you are likely to have money because you value it. Furthermore, you are likely not to want to give up your money. You don't like to spend it on anything lower on your value list than where Money sits.

If Education was number six on your list and Money number two, you would likely avoid spending money on studying. You might prefer to do free seminars, read books, and listen to podcasts instead of paying a coach or large fees to universities. An exception to this would be where you could see that the investment would directly create more money for you.

A classic example of this is Warren Buffett, who is famously known as one of the best investors of our generation. He is worth billions yet lives in the same house he bought before he was rich. He drives an old car and doesn't seem to enjoy his money as others would expect him to. This is missing the point. He attracts money because it's high on his values and having the money is enough on its own. Not what the money can buy, that's a different value altogether.[14]

Another example that I like to use with my clients, because it's more relatable, is a friend of mine who has a high value on money as this is where he directs the conversation with my group when we catch up. He raises questions like, "How much money do you have in super?" and tells stories of the bargains he has negotiated, how he saved money or didn't pay for something, and it brings him great pride. I don't want to appear critical of my friend, but that's how he sounds to me and his friends. Happy to not do the right thing to save his money. His friends and I don't have Money as high up on the values list as he does, so we tend to judge him because his values are different from ours. Being aware of your

---

14   https://www.cnbc.com/2023/03/03/warren-buffett-lives-in-the-same-home-he-bought-in-1958.html

values, the fact that others have different priorities and that this is acceptable, can literally save relationships.

Imagine if two business partners were making decisions about paying a staff bonus. One has a high value on Money and the other has a higher value on Business. They would treat this decision differently as they are coming from different places. The businessperson could explain how the bonus would help the staff remain motivated and make more money. The money person could explain that keeping the money would be wise to ensure they could have reserves and wouldn't have to reduce staff in the case of an emergency. Both are right and the circumstances would decide the outcome. But if they thought each other was "wrong", rather than just having a difference in values, it could create a stalemate or one partner overpowering the other.

Business

Business is the work we do to earn a living. This often results in money, so people confuse these values, but I would argue that they are not the same.

For instance, your work of preference might be looking after your children or a family member. This is a productive capacity that doesn't directly earn an income, yet it is a perfectly reasonable choice for many people. If your highest value is Family, it makes sense to stay at home and look after your children. If your highest value is Business, you would likely work and outsource the care of your children or family to others like childcare or medical professionals. Many people judge these choices based on their values and feel they are "right" in their way of thinking. Others can be influenced by cultural, religious, societal or peer groups to adopt values against their own beliefs. This leads to people making choices based on what others want, rather than their true desires. This causes angst and unfulfilled lives. Which, of course, reflects poorly on your family. It can also have negative consequences on your other life choices, as you subconsciously try to get back to your true values.

I once had a client who was an expert in her industry. She was a wedding planner and loved helping couples experience their special day in amazing ways. This passion led to a slew of client referrals and her business grew. Soon she had a team of staff running weddings and she found herself disconnected from the creative process to become head of human resources, chief accountant, logistics manager and all the other managing director responsibilities. The only problem was she didn't love doing this role and started to hate it. This resentment of the change of role grew until she didn't want to work in the business anymore. She had lost her passion for it. She didn't care as much and let things slip. Her team didn't deliver to her standard and clients complained. Soon she was bankrupt, as her clients disappeared and she maintained her staff and overheads. It was then that she was referred to me and we explored what she wanted to do, not what her friends and family thought she should do. That was growing a big business. She wanted to keep it small, so we designed a lifestyle business for her that reflected her true values in the work, not the money that was the result of the work.

Another example is Mr Buffett, who some may criticise for focusing on making money above all other values. For example, when the United Steelworkers Union decided to strike at the Special Metals plant in Huntington, West Virginia, in 2022, many media commentators, such as Bernie Sanders, pointed out that at a time when Mr Buffett's company, Berkshire Hathaway, was doing financially well, why couldn't Mr Buffett be more generous to the working families of his companies?[15] Mr Buffett argued that his primary role was to provide

---

15   https://edition.cnn.com/2021/12/31/business/bernie-sanders-warren-buffett-steelworkers-strike/index.html

the highest return for his shareholders and not the workers. Plus, he has managers for these businesses who make the decisions, not him. However, I am sure that if the business wasn't performing financially, he would make some more direct recommendations. What this demonstrates is a difference in values between different parties. One values Money highest (Mr Buffett) and another values Community higher (Mr Sanders). However, it could also be argued that Mr Sanders is creating controversy to make himself more popular at the expense of Mr Buffett and isn't concerned about the workers.

What is interesting about this situation is that Mr Buffett is very clear about his values and, consequently, he has amassed a huge following of those who have similar values to him. Those who appreciate him also have a high value on Money and *get* him. Those who judge him for his wealth-focus will reject his brand and follow someone more like themselves. Therein lies one of the most important reasons for understanding your values. If you are clear about what you stand for and what you don't, your audience will be able to understand if they want to follow you or not. There is no use being vanilla about who you are and then opening later and having clients reject you based on having different values from you. It's a huge waste of time and resources for both you and the client. We suggest you tell them in advance and therefore attract the right clients, who match your values, become stickier with you, and refer more clients because, of course, they hang out with others like them, with similar values.

Family

Family is an interesting value as most people select it as their number one value. I can understand the reasons for this as it is a broad value, which could include your intimate partner, parents, children, close family or friends, even pets. It represents those most close to you, to the exclusion of your broader close friend group or other family members.

However, before you jump at the obvious and most politically correct choice of choosing Family as your number one value, let's apply some tests. Firstly, is this where you spend the most time, money and energy? Time is one of the key deciding factors here and let's not use the excuse that you work for money for your family. That might be true but, when push comes to shove, is it really for them or you? Do they get more benefits from you being at work compared to quality time and would they make that choice given the opportunity?

We often use these excuses when we justify values. For instance, you might argue that you must have a high-paying job because you want the best for your kids. But the house in the nice neighbourhood reflects on your desire for social status more than theirs, particularly when they are young. Your choice of expensive schools might be for their education, but how often is your desire to be in a particular social set, and feel good telling your friends how hard you work for your family, really not about you?

If we are honest with ourselves, we might put the Family value in a different order, and I have worked with many people who do.

One such situation comes to mind, which is my mother. Upon reading the first version of this book, she asked me what I thought her values were. I threw it back on her to offer her thoughts and she immediately gravitated to: "Of course Family is number one." I called bullshit on that, and we had a quality discussion that her highest values were Spirituality and Health. Not that there is anything wrong with that, of course.

During our childhood, Mum didn't play with us or spend much time taking care of us. She was free-spirited and we were taught to be independent, resourceful and resilient. We took care of ourselves, which had positive and negative implications. But the point is, she was always doing a new spiritual process, practising yoga, going to see the latest guru or meditating. Far too busy to spend time with us, hence the highest values being Spirituality and Health; Education would have also been right up there. Family was important to her, and she loved her kids, no doubt about that, but how she showed it was in her values.

This is important. We demonstrate our love and appreciation for others by bringing them into our most important values. Mum loved me, so she would take me to see spiritual gurus and educate me about personal development, sending me on courses costing thousands, as that was the way she showed me love. Not by playing games with me.

Parents with a high value on work will educate their kids about the value of hard work. Money people will give the kids savings and investment accounts, and so forth.

Another fun fact is that values change at major Lifestage changes. For me, Family became number one when my kids were born. How can I demonstrate that? I quit my high-pressure corporate job to start my own portfolio business so I could spend more time with them. Less money, more work but more time with them. Choices.

However, at the time of writing this book, my values have shifted again, and Business and Money have floated to the top. My kids are older, the oldest being 18 and they require less of me. I have more time now as they are less reliant on day-to-day support, so now is the right time to grow my business. Another factor in the shift is that I am over 50, which makes me look into the future at retirement and what that could look like in the next decade. It takes substantial time to prepare for a big change like this, so I am getting ready now.

Friends

Friends are your inner circle. The ones whom you see regularly, and you feel *get* you. They may be new or long-term friends, but you know who they are and how they are different from the other friends you have. You go out with them, share life experiences and ride the ups and downs of life together.

This value is a little misleading as this is related to your social life, which could be going out and doing activities or just talking. It depends on what you like to do, but if you do it with this group, then these are your Friends.

So, the question is how important are your Friends compared to your other values? Would you choose them over Family, Business or Money?

A client of mine represented this value highly and, because it's lower on my value hierarchy than hers, I will share her story. This client was a lovely soft person who worked in a corporate job, earning a good salary and living a quality lifestyle. She was married, chose not to have children, and had a close set of friends. She came to me to help her be more fulfilled with work, since the corporate life wasn't lighting her up like before. As she had become more mature, she desired more from her working hours than what she was getting from her corporate life.

We set up her portfolio business and she secured work in a new area that fuelled her passion. However, there were a few challenges throughout the process. She kept missing deadlines for the work. When I pressed her on why, it emerged that her friends were taking priority. Inevitably, each week she would recount stories of friends going through a rough patch who needed her support. So, she would drop everything and spend hours on the phone with them, bake them treats, take them out and generally be a quality best friend.

This clearly showed me that her Friendship value was far higher than her Business or Money value. She didn't *have* to drop everything, she *wanted* to because it was important to her. She could have calmed the person down enough until after she had completed her work for the week and then helped. But that isn't who she is. She has trained her friends that she will be there, it's her reputation and her love. It's high on her values and so we worked around that, rather than asking her to change. The alteration to the business model was to have fewer clients who were more long-term and understanding of her need for time off occasionally, rather than the additional workload of consulting short-term with higher pressure for deliverables.

Spirituality

Spirituality is the world not involving you or your loved ones. This could be represented by formalised religion, mindfulness or charitable activities. Some would call it the soul, as compared to the body and mind. It's non-material but it is represented by practices that yield no material satisfaction, such as money, status or ego success.

A client who comes to mind for this value is an African-American who recently moved to Australia from the US with his new bride. He was a devout Muslim and wanted to speak to groups, consult with schools, and write children's books to educate non-Muslims about the religion, to build awareness rather than fear regarding his spiritual practices. He had never written a book before and was new to this religion.

In his previous life, he was the tour manager for the famous rap singer Jay-Z and lived a crazy life of excess with all the trappings you could imagine. That was until he realised it was all very unfulfilling and he went in search of something more. A spiritual quest of sorts, just the sort of thing that people with a high value on Spirituality would do. Something my mother did do regularly.

This client explored various religions, including many forms of Christianity which were dominant where he lived. But something about the beauty of the Koran touched his soul and he became immersed in it. He converted and faced hostility and persecution in his native USA because of it. After all the international conflict with the Muslim world, it was a difficult choice to make. People seem to forget that Muhammad Ali also made that choice, changing his name from Cassius Clay and converting to Islam during the height of his popularity. But I digress.

My client's high value on Spirituality meant that many jobs or roles were not suitable for him. He would base his choices on his religious doctrine, and nothing could stand in the way of this. He did some consulting with me and went on his own journey. I am pleased to say that he has published several children's books and is a leading authority on his chosen niche.

Education

Education is the process of learning or teaching. Having a high value on Education comes in many forms, aside from structured education, such as what schools and universities offer. This can include self-learning, such as reading widely, listening to podcasts, attending lectures or just being curious enough about a topic to research it closely.

It is the joy in the process of learning something new that makes Education a high value. Similarly, teaching what you have learnt is also a trait of those with a high value on Education. I realised this once I had finished my 15 years of part-time business education. I felt I gained a similar satisfaction from teaching at university, mentoring younger marketers and giving back my knowledge as I did building it.

Education is lower on my values than Money, as I never wanted to pay for my studies, so I negotiated for work to pay for it. Once, when my company decided to not support my MBA program, I stopped studying as I didn't feel the learning was as valuable as the fees were compared to my mortgage. Others with different values would make a different choice. Lucky for me they resumed paying shortly after, so I finished my degree, although at a different institution.

Another reflection on this choice for me was that I prefer to do self-directed learning, such as reading and podcasts, which are free and valuable. Although I get paid when I teach, I prefer to spend countless hours mentoring for free. But that touches on my Family values as I feel like they are my alternative kids that I am helping. As I mentioned previously, values are not all clear-cut, they have nuances and grey areas that are worth exploring. The greater depth you understand what lights you up and what makes you resentful, the greater the chance of building a portfolio business that keeps you in flow and is truly fulfilling.

Health

The final value is Health. Everyone needs to be somewhat healthy to live and thrive. However, it comes in degrees of healthiness. The human body can withstand enormous abuse and still survive. This value also includes mental and physical Health, as they are inextricably linked.

A good way to know if you really have a high value on Health or if you just want to be fit, beautiful or hot, is the following. I am sure we all want rock-hard abs and slim legs, but does anyone need to remind you to do the healthy activities you desire? If you need external motivation to do something, then it's not a true value. High values are those you want to do and so you are intrinsically motivated to do them. This could be represented in many ways, such as needing a personal trainer to ensure you go to the gym and work hard, feeling like you must eat healthily but would rather eat something else, or your partner forcing you to meditate or keep a journal when you would rather be doing something else.

I once had a client who said Health was his highest value. I sat across from him in amazement after seeing him park directly at my office door because he was unable to walk more than 50 metres at a time due to his obesity. He also had several health consequences from that condition. I was curious as to why he said Health was number one on his list, and he said he desperately wanted to be healthy.

The problem with this statement is that if it was a true value, then he already would have been healthy. He would have made different choices with his eating behaviours and physical exercise so he wouldn't have ended up in the situation that he had. When something is truly a top value, you put it before other things – addictions can be mitigated – and excuses fall away.

This is one of the truths I have faced myself. I have loved exercise since I was 18 years old, after a particularly unhealthy patch. I ran regularly, swam and did fitness events. I ate what I wanted because of my training, but it was mostly healthy and nutritious with the allowance for alcohol to aid my social life and cheat meals.

That was until a combination of my mother passing away and COVID increased my drinking and cheat meals as an attempt to feel better, and this reduced my exercise potential. I gained more weight than ever in my life and, at an older age, found it very difficult to reduce. I gave up trying to manage it and just said, "Fuck it, I'm over 50 so it's okay to be fat." Discipline and diet just never overcame the role that drinking and eating played in my life. I needed the crutch and wouldn't give it up.

That was the case until I started wanting to 10x my business – then things changed. I joined a new business-coaching group and they helped rekindle my belief in myself and my business. I became acquainted with the passion I felt before those episodes and felt alive again. I realised that to work at the level I wanted in order to achieve the long- and short-term goals of the business, I would have to be sharp and fit. The brain can't work well in a low-energy body, so I stepped up my exercise and cut back on bad eating and drinking. The difference now was that I *wanted* to do it, rather than thinking I *should* do it to please others. Consequently, I have lost a lot of extra weight, but still enjoy my beer and burgers enough to not be back at my fighting weight quite yet.

This is the true nature of values. Your life can change when they change. But can you change your values yourself?

The answer is *Yes, you can.* To do this, we need to understand where values come from and what influences their hold on us.

Values and Voids

Values come from voids in our lives. That means where we perceive something lacking in our lives, we feel one-sided about that situation and want the opposite, which creates the value. The more significant the void, the higher up the hierarchy the value becomes. Sometimes these situations happen, but the change in values doesn't occur until the right circumstances occur or we enter the right Lifestage.

For example, my dad left me when I was born, right out of the hospital. It was a massive void for me when I was an angst-ridden teenager. I saw it as a wholly negative experience, but it didn't impact my values until I had kids. Having two boys really impacted the emotions from my dad leaving and caused a mini breakdown. I wanted so badly to make up for my dad's deficiency and be the best dad I could be, but I felt unworthy of that goal. I tried my best to be there for my kids but still felt inadequate at times, even though my friends said I was doing a remarkable job. It remains a void and high value for me to this day, but far less than when the kids were born.

I have worked on this emotional experience, however, and this leads us to how we change values with emotional dissipation and matching. When we experience one-sided events that we feel are traumatic, it stores emotions in our body. To release them we can take ourselves back to that situation in our minds and look for the balancing effect of others on that situation. This is difficult for most people, as we have fixed beliefs about our recollection of events and sometimes are unwilling to change them. But we must work to look for balance, as it's the key to releasing the emotion and reducing the void, which releases us from the obligation of the value. This doesn't mean that the values might change, but the feeling of why this value is so important does and that is a crucial difference.

In my situation, my dad leaving left a void of a father figure. I felt upset that he wasn't there and blamed him and my mother for what happened. But on doing this process, I realised that a bunch of father figures were there to support me during my life. People who were far better than my dad could have been with his issues and problems. A scout leader gave me practical advice on building and leadership, my grandfather showed me the importance of family and running a business, my best mate's dad showed me kindness and medical support when I got into a scrape, and so on. When

I did this process, I was grateful that my biological dad wasn't around as I wouldn't have had those wonderful experiences and mentors. It balanced my emotions to some degree and helped me understand that it wasn't so bad after all.

Consequently, I changed my high value on my kids from a feeling of fear of failure to one of empowerment to look after them because it brought me joy and fulfilment. The emotion associated with achieving the value was love and gratitude, rather than fear and obligation. It also provided me the space to change my values when I felt the kids were old enough and I could focus on building my business guilt-free.

Values are the cornerstone of our Understand process, hence the depth we have gone into in this book. As we progress in the process, we will revisit parts of this material to further reveal learnings. In the Resources section, we will review how our values help calculate our time available to build our portfolio business.

But for now, we will move on and explore how your personality impacts your role in the business you build.

Step 2: Personality

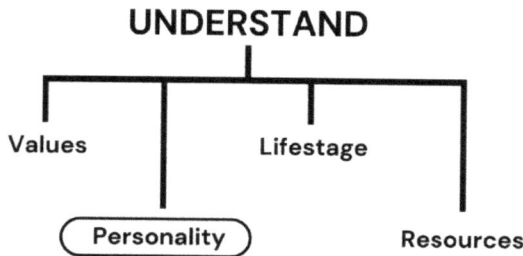

Figure 5. Understanding your personality helps decide the roles for you and others in your business.

Understanding your personality is an important part of the process because it helps decide what role you will have in your portfolio business, as well as the roles others play in ensuring you can build your business. There is a wide variety of ways to test personalities. Many are based on the tried-and-true Myers-Briggs test, which has a long history of helping people understand themselves better. The ones we use at Social Star are 16Personalities and the entrepreneurship test from Roger Hamilton called Wealth Dynamics.

However, many others can be useful if you want to delve into them. I am fortunate that my many corporate roles provided me with access to a variety of tests such as DISC, Big Five, CliftonStrengths and more. Most of these relate more to larger company structures, as they assess how you relate to each other in teams. Our focus is to understand yourself, potentially one or two employees, and your customers, most of whom will not do these tests so you can't attain the understanding they require to be useful. Therefore, we will not review these but feel free to explore at your leisure to gain an increased understanding of yourself.

Our chosen tests have been selected because they provide the insights we require to start your own portfolio business. Our tests are more related to you specifically and how you relate to business, plus they can be extended to a small number of team members if required.

The Myers-Briggs Type Indicator or MBTI was constructed by two Americans: Katharine Cook Briggs and her daughter Isabel Briggs Myers, who were inspired by the book *Psychological Types* by Swiss psychiatrist Carl Jung. Although they had no formal psychological training, this test became one of the most popular in businesses around the globe. The MBTI methodology has its critics, as most psychological tests do, but we find it very useful in our work.

However, it's worth understanding the pros and cons of the test so you can decide how much you want this to assist you with decision-making for your business.

Furthermore, being a test that has been around for a long time means a lot of people who may be potential team members may have done this test before you are interviewing them, which is useful. If not, they can easily do it before you decide whether you want to hire them, since they are easy and free.

It would be remiss not to review some of the critics' arguments against the Myers-Briggs test, so you are well aware of their potential challenges. Also, it's important to always assess who is criticising a test – are they trying to sell you an alternative test? Likely they are, which taints their advice. That said there are many reviews of the test online that are easy to find and digest. One I found was an online publication *Vox* that said: "The test is notoriously inconsistent. Research has found that as many as 50 per cent of people arrive at a different result the second time they take a test, even if it's just five weeks later."[16] Others say that the results of the test don't lead to accurate choices of career direction or employment positions and argue that it's not useful for businesses. One person I discussed this with said they didn't use it because it was old-fashioned. I don't feel any of these critics offer any comprehensive reasons not to try something that many people find useful.

My MBTI testing has been consistent over the last several decades and I find this test useful because it's quick to do, easy to interpret the results, and it's free. And it gives you some indication of your underlying personality, which I believe is beneficial in understanding how to position your brand and business. Finally,

---

16   https://www.vox.com/2014/7/15/5881947/
        myers-briggs-personality-test-meaningless

it has stood the test of time, with millions using it every year. Thus, I believe it's useful to do but with the understanding that it's not the only input into your brand, which is why we rely on the 16Personalities and Wealth Dynamics tests as well as the four different stages in this section that we combine to help assess how to position your brand and which type of business to set up.

There are four letters in the MBTI test worth exploring: Introvert/ Extrovert, Sensing/Intuition, Thinking/Feeling and Judging/ Perceiving. We call these opposites "preferences" because most people prefer one side more than the other, but can access and use both sides of a preference pair if a situation calls for it.

Each pair measures different parts of your personality and how you interact with the world. I call this your base personality, as it doesn't specifically relate to work or business, that is why we have other tests, but it is useful to better understand how you react to people around you. It also helps you understand how others operate, which is vital as you work through our process and start to produce content for clients, hire team members and choose partners.

There are many versions of the test you can take, which have similarities with the original research of MBTI. The one we use at Social Star is called 16Personalities. It's an online test, is free and has amazing reports that are generated instantly. Of course, there are many other options for personality tests but the results should all be the same, so choose the one that suits you best.

16Personalities

The 16Personalities test is the first one we ask clients to undertake. Here's the URL of the test so you can do it for yourself: www.16personalities.com. It is a very easy-to-use website with loads of great information and the basic reports are free and very useful. If you create an account you can share your test results with others in your team and compare profiles, which is useful too.

The test has similarities with the Myers-Briggs methodology, but it has been extended to include several other parameters that were not included in the original test. The Introvert/Extrovert pair is the same as Thinking/Feeling, but they have changed Judging/Perceiving to Judging/Prospecting and Sensing/Intuition to be Intuitive/Observant. But the biggest change is adding a new pair of measures Assertive/Turbulent. This likely sounds confusing, but it will become clear as we review each of the personality pairs and provide some examples.

I recommend reviewing their website to gain more clarity on how this test works and what the benefits are for your business. There are many other tests of this nature that you can find with a simple Google search. We have chosen this one due to the wonderful reporting and easy-to-use website. All of them have slight differences but are based upon the same Jungian theories and work completed in the MBTI original test. The 16Personalities test focuses more on the big five personality traits.[17] The five broad personality traits described by the theory are Extraversion, Agreeableness, Openness, Conscientiousness and Neuroticism. "The five basic personality traits is a theory developed in 1949 by D. W. Fiske (1949) and later expanded upon by other researchers including Norman (1967), Smith (1967), Goldberg (1981), and McCrae & Costa (1987).[18]"

Once you get your test results from 16Personalities or another site, you will end up with a four- or five-letter personality profile,

17   https://www.16personalities.com/articles/our-theory
18   https://www.thomas.co/resources/type/hr-guides/what-are-big-5-personality-traits#:~:text=The%20five%20broad%20personality%20traits,developed%20in%201949%20by%20D.%W.

also known as your "code". The first time I did this test was when I was 18 years old, and my mother sent me to a psychologist to review my intelligence, personality and capability. Back then, my code was ENTJ, a decade later I was ENFT, whilst my most recent test was ENFP, which would indicate that your base personality can change as you age. Similar to your values, which change at different periods of your Lifestage.

Your mood and frame of mind can impact how you answer the questions, so I advise my clients to think of their work situation when answering the questions. If you have this mental frame when you are doing the test, you are more likely to get the results that will be useful for this specific purpose.

Remember your code from the test, as it is quite common for people to ask you what it is. Some cultures and situations actually ask for it as a default way of understanding what you are like. I have seen it mentioned a lot in Korean social media as a shorthand for seeing what you are like. It also features on dating sites as a part of the About You area to see if you are compatible.

You will find the 16Personalities report is quite comprehensive as it reviews your strengths and weaknesses, romantic relationships, friendships, parenthood, career paths and workplace habits. Many of these would be extraneous to our uses, but are interesting for your overall life plan and useful for understanding your base personality.

I will reveal my personality type as a way of describing the value of the test and how to apply it. My results indicate I am an ENFP–T, which provides a broad guide of your personality, but the scale of each trait is very important to understanding the person. If you are curious about my full profile, you can review it here: https://www.16personalities.com/profiles/e749b125ef4d8

My style is a Campaigner, which is described as Free Spirit, Outgoing, Open Hearted and Open Minded. We like to be the life of the party, which is our extroverted nature, but are also deep thinkers and have a strong desire for emotional connection to others. This can be represented by the way we form teams around us in business and how we approach our clients as friends, rather than as customers.

This matches other tests I have done, including being an Aquarius in astrology, which is described by an article in *Cosmopolitan* as "Aquarians are clever, analytical, technical, truthful, assertive, confident, progressive and innovative. They like to solve problems, improve what's already working well, and push boundaries. They are activists, campaigners and progressors of the causes they think will make a difference to the world."[19] Some would baulk at the non-scientific planet-aligning star signs as a true form of personality assessment, however, it is similar to the other tests, so who knows?!

The true measure of any personality test is that the report resonates with the person taking the test. Mine sure does, the descriptions are dead accurate, which helps me understand what types of activities light me up and helps me identify the ways I best work. We take this into account when building your portfolio business.

Introvert v Extrovert

One of the most well-known parts of the MBTI test is the Introvert and Extrovert scale. This is represented by the E in my ENFP result, or I if you are an Introvert. As discussed, we have both traits within us, so what is relevant is the scale of preference, which oscillates differently depending on the environment and situation we are in, our mood and who we are with. I am 92% Extroverted, which means I get energy from being around people, I like to get things done and lead. It's a favourable trait if you are in sales because you genuinely

---

19   https://www.cosmopolitan.com/uk/horoscopes/a25735488/aquarius-traits/

enjoy networking and talking to people, which is why I made it part of my main job at Social Star.

I am highly Extroverted according to this test. But like many psychological tests, this result isn't as simple as it may seem. For instance, I am more Extroverted when doing activities and in groups that match my highest values, and less Extroverted when doing activities and in groups that match my lowest values. For example, I attend many networking events because I have a high value in Business. I like networking, meeting new people and hearing new ideas. Because I go to them often, I make friends there and start to develop a community. Therefore, the more entrepreneurial the event is, the more it fits one of my highest values. One example is Pitch Fest in Melbourne. I like to attend because my type of people go there and I have some friends who go regularly, which matches my Friendship value. This makes me feel comfortable, so I am more open to talking to new people and interacting with the presentations, such as asking questions, and feel at ease doing so, which matches my Business value. These behaviours would be considered being Extroverted, but if it wasn't hitting my highest values, then I would behave differently. Having multiple high values met at one event raises satisfaction and ensures you want to do more of them.

An example of the opposite situation was when I was raising capital for one of my ventures and ended up at the Australian Club for lunch with a potential investor. It's a prestigious club for the old money of Melbourne and they have specific rules, such as not talking about business during meals. Although I got along with the people there and made conversation with them, I felt like I didn't quite fit in. They were mostly lawyers, accountants and medical professionals, which are my target markets so they should have been a great fit for my personality. However, the style of these people was less entrepreneurial and more traditional, and not being allowed to talk business limited our conversation. Consequently, it took more effort to be outgoing and I would have been considered more Introverted in that situation. I'm the same person but exhibit different personality traits, depending on the values that were leveraged in the situation. A great learning for me was that even if someone was in my target market, it didn't mean they were compatible for our business. We deal with a lot of accountants but only the entrepreneurial ones fit our model and match with my style. We will discuss this more as we progress through the e-ttraction model.

A good test of your Extrovert and Introvert scale is if the situation and environment feed you energy, then you are more likely to be an Extrovert; whereas if you feel drained of energy after the situation, then you are more likely an Introvert. But also consider the values you are achieving in that same situation.

Sensing v Intuition

My current ENFP profile has a 78% leaning towards the N, which is Intuitive, compared to the opposite which is Sensing, or Observant (S) in the 16Personalities test. The second personality scale is a bit confusing because the first letters are not the ones in the profile.

Intuitive personality types rely on imagining the past and future potential of what they see. Those with the Observant style are more interested in observable facts and more straightforward outcomes. They prefer to avoid layering too much interpretation onto what they see. The compatible MBTI traits are Sensing (or Observant), which MBTI says: "pay more attention to information that is concrete and tangible".[20] They focus on "what is" and like to know facts and details. Whilst Intuitive people, like me, focus on the big picture and making connections between facts. We like to

---

20   https://www.myersbriggs.org/my-mbti-personality-type/
      the-mbti-preferences/

join the dots and trust our gut feelings and our sense of knowing, rather than any external data.

Steve Jobs made a famous speech to Stanford University graduates in 2005 that highlighted this personality trait well. He mentioned that you can't join the dots going forward in life, you have to trust your instincts. It's only when looking back at life, can you see how those dots were perfectly consistent to get you to where you should go. Easy to do for an Intuitive personality type and less easy for an Observant.[21]

It's quite a big difference in how one makes decisions, and you can see how this can be applied to a business. If your customer is high on Sensing/Observing, but you are a high Intuitive person, then you might present a wonderful strategy based on your beliefs of what the client should do, but they want to see the proof and data to back up your concepts. I have experienced this situation many times! Therefore, it's useful to have one of each personality type review your proposals before they reach the customers to ensure it has enough information for both personality types.

We are all born with each preference and can manage to stretch ourselves to do both roles in certain circumstances, but some traits won't seem natural and take more effort. So as your business grows, it's more efficient to have people naturally suited to each trait in the roles that suit their personality. So, if someone is more Observant, they might be better at reports with facts and figures, and if they are more Intuitive, they might be better at running workshops where you have to think on your feet and come up with fast solutions based on instincts. This is the benefit of personality testing, to ascertain people's natural styles and get them into the right roles for those styles.

---

21   https://www.youtube.com/watch?v=UF8uR6Z6KLc

Thinking v Feeling

The third pair of traits is Thinking v Feeling, which is self-explanatory. It's how we gather information and make decisions, and is an important trait to understand because it impacts our communication with team members, clients and partners.

MBTI refers to this pair as representing: "... the judging mental processes for coming to conclusions – opposite ways to decide. People who prefer Thinking put more weight on objective principles and impersonal facts when decision-making. They focus on logic and analysis. People who prefer Feeling put more weight on personal concerns and the people involved when decision-making. They focus on values and relationships."[22]

When I reflect on this as a business owner with a 78% leaning towards Feeling, I really resonate with the distinction. I make new employee decisions based on whether I like the person, new deals on whether I like the client and resonate with their business vision, and investment decisions based on gut instinct. Likely not the best way to make any of these decisions! However, since discovering my personality, I have put systems in place to ensure I have another point of view from others in my business. My COO is more on the Thinking side of the equation and helps with balanced scorecards and analytics for key decisions.

This might sound the same as the previous pair, Sensing v Intuition, and they are related, indeed all the traits are related, however, there is a subtle but important difference between these two. Sensing v Intuition has a greater emphasis on how we *gather* information from the outside world to make decisions, whereas Thinking v Feeling is how we *use* this information to make decisions. For instance, when deciding whether to hire a new team member,

22   https://www.myersbriggs.org/my-mbti-personality-type/
       myers-briggs-overview/

I will first need to evaluate if the business will grow based on market conditions to know if we will require new resources. As an Intuition personality, I will just know this or I will not. Data may influence this slightly, but I will likely just trust my gut. Then, when deciding on whom to employ, I will interview people and see who I resonate with the most, which is the Feeling personality trait.

This worked quite well when my business was small but, as you grow, you need more resource control and understanding of your team's productivity and client demand for services. Therefore, we now have many more processes (which I get my team to do) that aid in the effectiveness of these decisions. A blend of each of these decision-making processes is necessary to gain a full understanding of the situation, which is why your management should contain a blend of these personality traits.

Judging v Perceiving

The Judging v Perceiving is the fourth pair of the MBTI personality test, which is referred to as Judging (J) or Prospecting (P) in the 16Personalities test. They describe how people like to interpret the outside world, their outer life, and how the behaviours of others tend to be interpreted. People who prefer Judging like a more structured and organised lifestyle. They like to control their environment by making plans or at least knowing what the plans are when others make them. Interaction with the outside world is through their decision-making (Judging) mental process of Thinking or Feeling. Making decisions, coming to closure, and then moving on are important to people with a Judging preference. This is what the test prescribes here: "People who prefer Perceiving enjoy a more flexible and open-ended lifestyle. Rather than control their environment, they want to experience it through exploring options. Interaction with the outside world is through their information gathering (perceiving) mental process of Sensing or Intuition. Staying open to new information, last minute options, and being adaptable is important to people with a Perceiving preference."[23]

Perception involves all the ways of becoming aware of things, people, happenings, or ideas. People naturally perceive in opposite ways. Judgment involves all the ways of coming to conclusions about what has been perceived. These opposites are combined in ways that help individuals make decisions.

Both Perception and Judgment are mental processes. Differences in Perception (what people see in any given situation) and Judgment (what they decide to do about it) result in corresponding differences in personality characteristics, behaviours, interests, reactions, values, and motivations.[24]

People with high levels of Perception tend to be more structured in how they make decisions. They like to use checklists and formal criteria to assist in their decision-making and want time to analyse their thoughts. They gravitate towards roles such as Chief Operating Officers, financial managers and project leads. This personality type is suited for mature industries where change is limited, and types of businesses where there isn't a lot of new ideas required to be successful. Otherwise, it's useful to partner with someone who has more judgment to assist in the decision-making.

People with high levels of judgment tend to make more fluid decisions based on gut feelings and the immediate situation. They are good at connecting dots and seeing a natural order to decisions rather than a preconceived list of criteria. They make good CEOs (with a vision for the future), marketing managers and creatives.

---

23   https://www.myersbriggs.org/my-mbti-personality-type/
      myers-briggs-overview/

24   https://www.myersbriggs.org/my-mbti-personality-type/
      myers-briggs-overview/

An example of this complementary pairing is my business partner Adam and myself. I am the Chief Executive Officer (CEO), the "visionary" who makes quick decisions about the business. Adam is the Chief Creative Officer (CCO), who likes to take his time in decisions and consider all aspects before reaching conclusions. When we do client meetings, I immediately see the opportunities for a client and come up with ideas straight away. Adam likes to document his decisions and come back to the client later. Neither idea is wrong or less effective, they are just different and having this balance works well for us.

Assertive v Turbulent

The additional pair of traits that 16Personalities includes, which isn't part of the MBTI test, is Assertive (–A) v Turbulent (–T). This trait is made visually different with a dash between the main four traits because it impacts all the other ones. Essentially, it indicates how confident we are in our abilities and decisions. It can influence how we respond to success and failure, criticism or feedback from people and unexpected events.

As a 60% Turbulent trait, I tend to think longer about past decisions and worry about the future. My scale isn't as strong as the other traits, so I have 40% of the Assertive which pushes me to accept stress and use it positively. It helps me make decisions about the future, which I might be uncertain about, but I will ponder for quite a while before making those decisions. Unfortunately, this trait represents itself in waking me up at 3 am a lot of nights, worried about my business and the future. Even if things are going well, I worry it's going too well and disaster is just around the corner. I can't seem to help this, but if I was more Assertive, then I might sleep better, confident that it would all work out okay. This is an important trait to understand before you start a business because it's full of uncertainty, risk and challenges. If you are a very high Turbulent, it could significantly challenge your mental health.

Assertive types might be more bullish about their decisions and are likely high achievers, if they can make the right decisions often enough. But without a portion of Turbulent, they can burn bridges along the way, as they don't worry about the consequences of their decisions and push on regardless of the consequences. This isn't my personality, but I can relate to pushing ahead with ideas, even if others don't agree with my decision.

Turbulent people tend to be success-driven perfectionists who are eager to improve to offset their self-doubts by achieving more. They push themselves to be better and their companies to feel more successful because they worry about what others think. Even if they achieve great things, they often don't feel deserving of the success and listen to their inner critic, rather than their inner cheerleader. I relate to this because I struggle to celebrate success, as I worry that it will be short-lived.

Both traits can lead to running a successful business, but the fuel for the fire of motivation is different. Assertive types believe they deserve success, whereas Turbulent types don't believe they are owed success, so work hard to get it. Of course, if the person isn't driven for success, these traits can lead to the opposite reaction. Assertive people might believe the world owes them something and question why they should have to work for it, whereas Turbulent people might feel defeated and ask themselves, "Why even try?"

The MBTI style of personality testing is useful for self-awareness and understanding how we and others behave. It's useful for building a team and altering your communication for clients to best suit their styles. However, it doesn't fully address the role we should have in our business. That's why we utilise another test called Wealth Dynamics to drill down on how to be the best leader and get into flow more often when acting as the CEO.

Wealth Dynamics

The next test we use is more specifically focused on entrepreneurship and provides more clarity on what activities in your team are best for you to keep and which to outsource. Even in a solo business, you will have a team to support you. This could be your accountant, lawyer, virtual PA, marketing agency, software that does tasks for you, or a part- or full-time employee.

We are unable to run a business without any support because we can't possibly have every skill required, so we need to know what the best use of our time is and what we should seek a solution for.

Wealth Dynamics is from an entrepreneur named Roger Hamilton. I completed his training many years ago and liked his profile tests because they combined a few different information sources to form a test specifically designed for entrepreneurs. Its foundations are Myers-Briggs, so it uses that base personality testing but adds Chinese I Ching. As you can read on their website: "There are similar elements within Wealth Dynamics and popular psychometric tests, as they all have a common modern origin in Carl Jung's work on archetypes. But Wealth Dynamics is different in that it provides an intuitive structure, practical strategies, modern role models and a link back to how to run a new business."[25]

If you want to do the Wealth Dynamics test you can take it here https://wealthdynamics.geniusu.com/. We use it over more corporate-based tests because of the following five reasons.

Firstly, it's tailored to entrepreneurs. The reports have explicit recommendations for people wanting to start a business and examples of entrepreneurs who have similar profiles.

---

25   https://wealthdynamics.geniusu.com/

Secondly, one of the supposed criticisms of the MBTI test is that your profile changes over time. One of the benefits of Wealth Dynamics is that it shows how your strengths link to the cycle of time.

Thirdly, it's intuitive and easy to follow. The MBTI tests results, such as my code of ENFP, aren't easy to interpret if you haven't done the test. The names of the Wealth Dynamics results are a bit easier to follow. For instance, I am a Creator, which interprets logically that I like to create ideas. I am also a part Star and part Mechanic. You can almost guess what this means. We will explore all these terms shortly.

Fourthly, they link to your flow. I find this an important part of not just this particular assessment, but one of the main purposes of the whole Understand section because you align yourself with your business so you can be in flow more often. We will discuss flow states at the end of this section.

Finally, because Wealth Dynamics has also incorporated I Ching into the assessment mix, it will give you one of the five Chinese elements to ponder – it helps you better understand your purpose or *why*.

Figure 6. The Wealth Dynamics model.

The Wealth Dynamics test combines a range of different elements that are worth exploring.

As you can see in the above diagram, courtesy of the Wealth Dynamics instruction manual, which you can download from our website, there are four wealth frequencies and eight types of profiles. The frequencies are Dynamo, Blaze, Tempo and Steel. The frequencies summarise your personality and the profile types provide more details on how these represent you in your business.

Dynamo frequency is energetic and action-oriented, which relates to doing things or moving forward with projects. This profile makes for great entrepreneurs because they can energise a team and make things happen. Examples of people with this energy are Steve Jobs (Apple), Walt Disney (Disney) and Elon Musk (Tesla) – plus me! The range of profiles in this sector includes Mechanics who build things to perfection, Creators who like to come up with new ideas, and Stars who attract a spotlight.

If you lean more towards the Star profile, you are likely more Extroverted and gain energy from others; by contrast, Mechanics like to spend time alone tinkering. The Star and Creator profiles are great at starting projects but need support from more detail-oriented team members or systems. The more Introverted you are, the more you lean towards systems to solve the problems, and Extroverts choose people.

My primary profile is a Creator, which means the best use in my business is to come up with new and exciting ideas that the team will implement. The challenge is that I keep coming up with ideas and struggle to execute them all! So, often there are many half-completed ideas in my to-do list. That is why Creators need a team of people to implement. These don't need to be employees, as they could be freelancers, partners or software. But I am sure that you need someone to keep you on track. Having a personal assistant in my business changed my life and I highly recommend getting one as your first hire if you are this profile.

The Blaze frequency has some elements of the energetic approach but is more about the people rather than the projects. They are great at rousing a crowd and getting the best from them. Oprah Winfrey, Jack Welsh (GE) and Jacinda Ardern (former New Zealand prime minister) are all representatives of this energy and know how to engage and inspire people to action. Profiles with a Blaze frequency include Stars, Supporters who feel most fulfilled by their team's success, and Deal Makers who work with others to create maximum value.

As you can see, all the profiles have successful people who have achieved great things operating within their personality type. Choose your industry and team carefully so that it better matches your strengths and natural flow.

The following diagram shows my outcome from the full Wealth Dynamics test, which is available cn our website. It includes my personality profile results. As you can see, I have quite a strong Dynamo energy at 56%, with my dominant profile being a Creator.

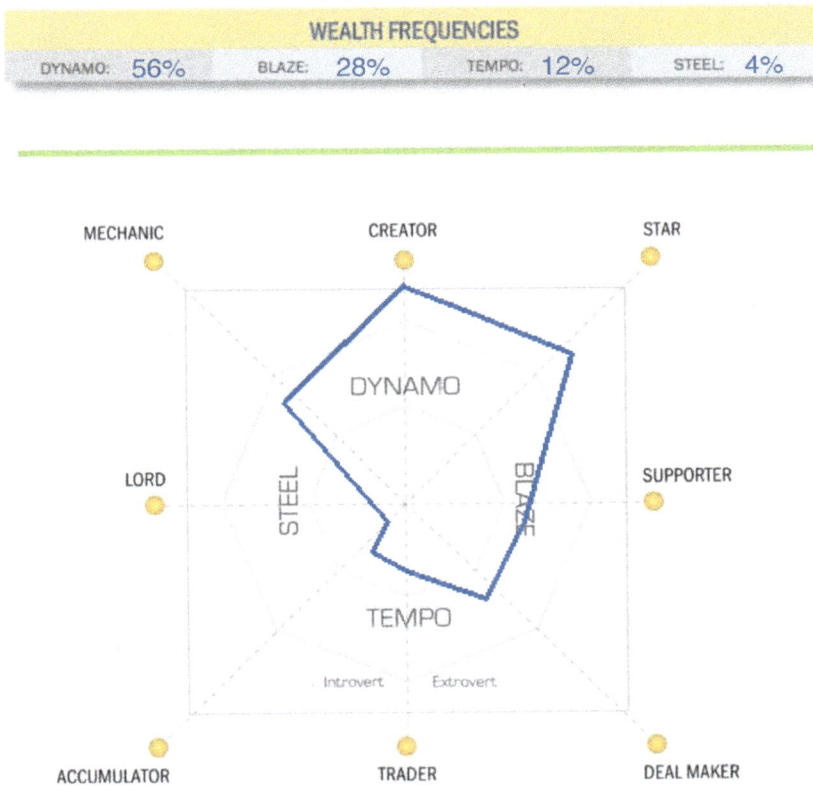

WEALTH FREQUENCIES

| DYNAMO: 56% | BLAZE: 28% | TEMPO: 12% | STEEL: 4% |

Figure 7. Outcome of the author's Wealth Dynamics test.

As the diagram demonstrates, I am a strong version of the Creator profile. The two profiles to either side of your main profile are your sub-profiles and have a strong influence on your personality too. As a Creator, I am also a part Mechanic and Star.

The areas I am not strong at are Lord, Accumulator and Trader, so these are the profiles I would be seeking when reviewing talent whom I want to hire to support me in my businesses.

Roger Hamilton describes the way his profile system works as follows. If you think of the eight profiles as eight games that are as different as basketball is to soccer or baseball, you can see that each one has different rules, different locations and different winning and losing formulas. In basketball, you're told to pick up the ball and not to kick it. In soccer, you're told to kick the ball, not pick it up.

In wealth creation, we constantly get contradictory advice, and neither is wrong, they are simply referring to different games.

To get the most out of your Wealth Dynamics profile, begin by committing to one game, and one game only, which is the one that gets you into your flow. Mastery comes from consistently playing that game until it is second nature.

Gain clarity on what that game is for you by recognising the times in your life when you tuned into your path and were in the flow, and the times when you were not, and life seemed like hard work.

Hamilton makes an important point here, in that to get the best out of your work performance, you follow your natural personality, rather than trying to follow other styles. Therefore, if you follow other entrepreneurs who have the same profile, then that will give you a role model for how to operate and succeed.

For instance, Elon Musk is a Creator, so he operates very differently from Warren Buffett who is an Accumulator. Elon loves his ideas and that is his main currency, his second profile of Star allows him to be in the spotlight and out front leading his team, and his Mechanic secondary profile enables him to start building projects. But he easily gets bored and wants to move on to the next project, as Creators love to create!

This is the opposite to Warren Buffet, who doesn't feel the need to create because he is more into accumulating assets, rather than building them. His Lord secondary profile is a master of detail and plays business like chess, always one step ahead. His other secondary profile is Trader, so he knows when to buy and sell as he has his ear to the ground for the latest changes in the market.

If these two master entrepreneurs changed roles, they would feel out of flow and quickly try to revert to their natural elements.

Furthermore, you can see how values relate to this personality test too. Warren would have a high value on Money, and being an Accumulator is his matching profile. Elon would have a high value on Business, which matches his Creator profile.

Once you understand yourself better with these three personality tests, you will be better able to structure your team and resources to fill in the gaps in your skills. This keeps you in the flow and working in your optimal style. Most importantly, it means you will love working in your business, rather than feel like it's a chore, which is vital to pushing through the challenging times.

Step 3: Lifestage

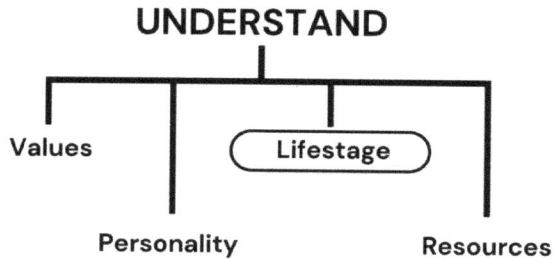

```
                    UNDERSTAND
                         |
        ┌────────────────┼────────────────┐
        |                |                |
     Values         ( Lifestage )
        |                                 |
                                          
     Personality                    Resources
```

Figure 8. Lifestage is the third Step in the Understand section.

Your Lifestage refers to where you are right now and where you want to be in the future. It's your long-term plan and can be anywhere from a 5- to 10- to 20-year vision of what you would like your life to look like. This is where your goal-setting process starts to take effect practically, and it helps us to structure your business for your needs.

We include this process for a few reasons. Firstly, the choice of what you do with your business when you stop your usual work needs some consideration. What's your exit plan? For most people moving from corporate to their own business, this new business stops when they stop working in it. For others, they can build enough assets to potentially sell their business when they want to exit, but this is a different approach and one that we will cover more fully in my next book. One is a cash business and the other is an asset business.

A cash business is one in which you spend only as much time and money on the business assets as required to operate it effectively. Your website, social media and content are designed to help you gain clients but not to be able to be operated by anyone other than yourself. So, if you choose to sell it, it's worth very little as the real value is *you*.

An asset business is one where you invest substantial time, money and energy in building intellectual-property assets for future staff and owners of the business. An example of this would be documenting processes, having a website that is more about your ideas and systems than your experience, writing ebooks or books that explain your methodology to potential clients, and having staff do the delivery work whilst you build the business and create your technology applications. Essentially, you are putting all you know into a tangible form so that others can use this to engage and deliver meaningful results for your clients.

Businesses can start as cash-oriented and transition to asset style once they are operating effectively, but they are difficult to reverse from asset to cash because of your original investment so, if in doubt, start a cash-style business. An example of the difference in these styles is Andrew Baxter who is a legend in the Australian advertising industry. I started working with Andrew on his personal brand five years before he was planning to transition to his own portfolio business. His goal was to sit on a few boards and do some consulting and speaking gigs to earn a moderate income with a great lifestyle for his family. He was a successful CEO of high-profile advertising agencies, so it was relatively easy to position himself as an expert in his industry and he set about to change his focus from an employee to an independent worker.

His transition was very successful as he prepared well by building his network, publishing a book, creating his personal website and publishing content regularly.

Then he noticed that he was invited to do a lot of strategic-planning sessions with clients related to marketing, so he created a framework that made it easier to run the sessions. His 24 Hour Business Plan business was born and soon scaled to have many practitioners and dozens of high-profile clients. Before creating this framework, Andrew ran a cash business that couldn't be sold. But by codifying his knowledge into a framework that others could deliver, he created an asset business that has value and can be sold when he doesn't want to work in it anymore.

The second reason that this part of the process is important is that we need to know when you want to exit the business and transition to retirement. I often ask my consulting clients the question, "When do you want to retire?" They often look at me confused and say something like, "I don't want to retire; I just want to work a bit less and choose when I work." This response is typical as I attract clients who have a high Business value and enjoy the work they do. They just want to have the time and freedom to work when it suits them and not be dictated to by others. Even as a CEO or owner of a business, you still have shareholders, staff, customers and suppliers who all need to be satisfied when running your business. Moving towards retirement in a specific timeframe means you need to plan financially and logistically to exit your business, which brings us to the third reason we need a Lifestage timeframe: exit readiness.

Being *exit ready* means you are preparing for the next phase of your business journey, but it doesn't necessarily mean selling your business. There are many forms of exits such as management buyout, transfer of ownership to children in a succession plan, selling to a competitor or supplier, listing on the stockmarket or just putting in a management team to run the business for you. Essentially, you are removing yourself from the business in the day-to-day operations. This is what most of my clients want to achieve eventually, and some of them still want to have the business remain so they can draw an income for the foreseeable future.

An example of a successful exit is one of my clients Mouaz, who runs a successful cyber-security business. He came to me from a referral and wanted help with marketing and sales as he was unable to grow his business beyond his single large client. I worked in a coaching capacity with him for a year or so and he adopted the e-ttraction formula with his team. His long-term goal was to put his partner in the CEO role, and he would move to a director role. It took a while for the methodology to sink in, but he had patience and, once it took hold, they rapidly expanded and he gained several new large clients. He completed his Master of Business Administration and trained with the Australian Institute of Company Directors, and now sits on the board setting strategy but letting his team do the work.

From this example, you can see a few of the e-ttraction elements at work. I haven't shared all his personal information, but he had a strong vision of what he wanted his lifestyle to be about – his family and community – then a mission for his business with his partner. His long-term and short-term goals were SMART, and he put in place actions, such as hiring me and completing his education, to ensure these came to fruition. He has a high value on Family, Business and Education, and a lower value on Money, which is demonstrated by his willingness to invest in learning so he can grow his business and spend time with his young family. He has a Supporter profile with Blaze energy, so he works very effectively with his team, but didn't have the ideas on how to grow his business, so he came to me, a Creator, for this knowledge. Once implemented, his Steel energy business partner could implement the plan on his behalf.

The exercise now is to plot your current age and your desired retirement age on the following graph.

Lifestage

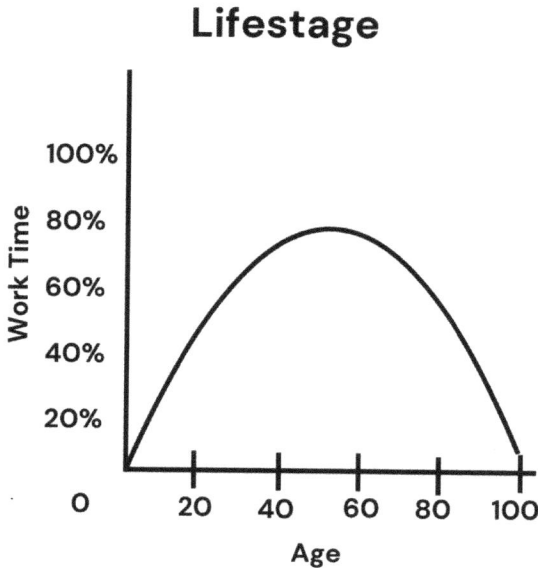

Figure 9. Graph to assist planning the balance of preferred time at work against age.

Once you have done this, you will see how long you must plan for whatever exit you choose and the format that best meets your life vision. Calculating the cash you will need to live a quality life each month and what you need to accumulate before you exit your business is useful at this stage, so work with your financial planner on these aspects.

Remember, when you do these calculations, that people are living longer and better than ever before. At the time of writing, the official retirement age of people in Australia is 56.9 years.[26]

However, the age when you can receive the aged pension is 67, so there is a gap that needs to be filled for some people.[27]

26   https://www.abs.gov.au/statistics/labour/employment-and-unemployment/
       retirement-and-retirement-intentions-australia/latest-release
27   https://www.dss.gov.au/seniors/benefits-payments/age-pension

However, given the average life expectancy is 83 years,[28] the average number of years living in retirement is 16 years; and longer for some people, especially women living into their nineties. Therefore, you could be faced with a few decades of funding your lifestyle. Not to mention the desire to have control of your life before 67 and the fact that, if you have children, they often require more financial support as the cost of living steadily increases.

This creates a strong need for a shoulder career that bridges the gap between when you don't want to work full-time and the point when you are unable or unwilling to work at all. This is where starting your own business and structuring an exit that retains an income for life is very attractive. For most of my clients, their long-term plan is to run their business for a minimum of 10 years, which will provide ample time to set up, run and exit a successful business. I stress to my clients that it will take a full year to gain e-ttraction and start earning income from this business. Add another year to test and refine your offering to achieve product-market fit before trying to scale it to an above-corporate income. So, there is a lot of preparation required before you consider leaving your job. It takes time to design what the business will be, set up the digital assets, and learn how to operate it with systems and a team.

Furthermore, you want to have done all the preparation to a high level *before* you are ready to inform your network of your new business so they can refer clients to you. Some people are in a hurry and want to start in a few months, but this is unwise as you can set a poor impression with your network if you position yourself in a certain way, and then change it once you start to refine your offering. I have witnessed some people in my network, not clients of mine, rushing the Understand and Build process. They test their new business

28   https://www.abs.gov.au/statistics/people/population/life-expectancy/latest-release#:~:text=Life%20expectancy%20decreased%20in%202020,and%20 1.0%20years%20for%20females

to everyone all at once and then realise it's not what they really want because it's not delivering enough value to the market, so they start changing their entire business focus. I have seen them change their models three or more times in a few years, which confuses your market and creates distrust in your network. How can they refer clients to you when they don't know when you will pivot your brand and business again? Investing two years to plan and set up a completely new business is time well spent, especially when you have 10 years to recoup your investment and create a lifetime of income.

Many of my clients engage me whilst they are still working in their corporate jobs, so they have the funds and time to set up their personal brand for the new business before they make the transition. This is especially important when you are lacking some of the key resources to start your business, which we will examine in the next Step.

Step 4: Resources

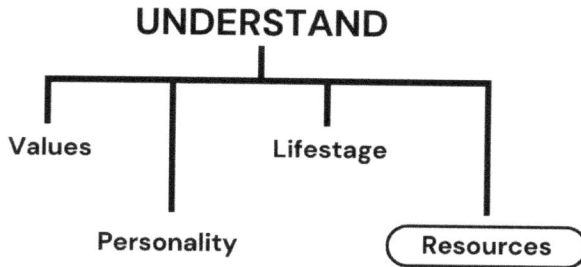

UNDERSTAND

Values

Lifestage

Personality

Resources

Figure 10. The fourth Step in the e-ttraction Method is Resources.

One of the biggest factors in any new portfolio business is managing the resources you must apply to it. We classify these resources as time, money, connections and knowledge. These factors relate strongly to the other areas of the Understand process because they are all interdependent areas that need consideration before you start to build your own business.

Time

Time is our one fixed resource. We all have the same 24 hours a day to apply however we wish. We can't get more time, although the quality of our time spent does vary and so does how we use this time effectively through leverage. We will discuss these concepts as we review the resource section. How time relates to the other Understand Steps is that our Values depict how we prioritise the time we have each day, our Personality shows us the most efficient way to spend our work time, and our Resources help decide who does the work.

It is useful to document how much time you want to apply to working on your new business and where these hours will come from. For instance, if you are working full-time and have a family but want to prepare for your new business in a few years, how many hours per week can you spend on this project? Where will you reduce your hours in other areas like exercise, family, time with friends or sleep? Perhaps you will reduce your job by one day a week to focus on building your brand, but can you afford to do this? Perhaps you are a young entrepreneur and have boundless time and energy, but no other resources like money. You could partner with someone who has money but not the time to start the business, either as an investor or by providing a loan.

If you are nearing retirement, what is the desired number of days per month that you want to work in the business? This amount normally changes from week to week, but try to estimate an average that considers your desired lifestyle. Most of my clients feel three or four days a week is a good range, but some end up working more than five days a week, as they really enjoy the business and don't consider it work. Having the flexibility to choose how many days you work is one of the outcomes a lot of people in this demographic seek.

If you have limited time, it's recommended that you employ others to assist you with this work, so that you don't feel the need to compromise your values to add this project to your activities. However, this costs money, which leads me to the second resource.

Money

Money refers to the amount of money you want to make and the amount you have to invest to get the business set up.

To decide how much you would like to earn, consider the following questions. And for those with a low value on Money, yes, this is an important section to do as it frames the entire marketing process. The questions are:

1) At what income level per year would you feel that it's not worthwhile setting up your new business? If I suggested that you would earn $50K per year, would your instant reaction be that it's not worth the effort, or would it be acceptable? There is no right answer; however, most of my clients place a certain value on their time and want to earn at least $100 to $150k to even bother going through the process, then substantially more once they are fully set up.

2) The second question is at what income level would you be absolutely delighted with your new business? Would $500K a year bring a huge smile to your face? If so, then set a high-water mark on your earnings to stimulate you to plan for something larger.

These two questions provide us with a range of floor and ceiling prices to work with. Be aware that if you are planning on having a cash business with limited staff, then it is difficult to earn more than $500K in revenue, as the time required to do the work is fixed and, without the leverage of people or assets to support the delivery of the service, it's difficult to scale past this point. In addition, the more income you desire, the more investment and effort is required to get the business set up and structured to deliver services at scale. You will likely require ongoing support, rather than an initial set-up and there will be higher levels of complexity, which means mistakes and missteps will be taken. Nothing comes for free, so be aware of all these circumstances when setting your floor and ceiling goals. You also might want to go back and revise your initial goals once you complete this section.

Another useful part of this section is to decide how much money you can invest in the set-up of your business. Some clients have no idea what the right figure is, and I can fully understand this because it depends on so many factors. What is the return on investment over the short- and long-term for the money invested? What assets do you have already to utilise in the business and what do you need to build? How much time do you have to spend doing the work compared to outsourcing it? All of these are relevant to the decision of what to invest.

The way we approach it is to work on a ratio of desired income to investment. If you budget 10% of your expected revenue over the first two to three years, this would be a good guide to what would be required. So, if you are nearing retirement and want a part-time portfolio business with $150K revenue, like a recent client of mine, then you would invest $15K a year in the set-up of the business in years one to three.

If you are setting up a cash business, you would only require the first year to set up, as you need limited assets to run the business. But for an asset business, you are more likely to need ongoing support, so the 10% would be ongoing. Of course, there are many variabilities in this estimation, such as your experience, network, skills and personality.

In the Build section, we will use these parameters to work out a system to ensure your income comes within this range. However, remember Newton's third law of physics: that every action has an equal and opposite reaction. So, any increase in income chosen will come with commensurate investment in the business as well as the required hours of work to produce this additional value. So, choose carefully!

Connections

Connections refer to the size and quality of your current network. How many people do you know and, more importantly, can you easily communicate with them right now? If you conducted a personal audit of your network, how many people would you know in total? Try to add this up now, because we will require this for the start of the Build process, which is coming up shortly.

A good way to calculate this is to add up the following areas:

- LinkedIn first-level connections and followers
- Facebook friends
- Instagram followers
- TikTok subscribers
- YouTube subscribers
- Email addresses in a database
- Contacts in your phone.

This will give us a volume metric that will be the first part of our calculation.

The next step is to assess the quality of these contacts. How many have you been in contact with over the last year? Would you be able to set up a coffee chat if you reached out? If you posted something online, would they like, comment or share it for you? Most importantly, if you launched a new business, would they refer their network to you? If you can estimate the total number of quality contacts as a percentage, that will give a starting point to know how far away you are from being able to start your new business, as you will be relying on your network to refer your initial clients. I understand it's difficult to do this estimation, but we don't need exact figures, more of a round number on which to base some calculations in the Leverage section for our marketing and sales efforts.

Take your overall number of connections and multiply it by the quality score to gain your total number of effective reaches. It will look something like this:

17,000 connections x 20% quality score = 3,400 effective reach

Of all the resources, I have come to believe that connections are the most important. We can gain more time through leverage and efficiency; we can get money with investment and borrowings, and both can be achieved relatively quickly. But a trusted network takes years, if not decades, to establish. In the old days, your reputation was your best asset and not much has changed today. It's just easier to ruin it with poor brand decisions. Just ask Will Smith, who after his Academy Awards slap of the host, has struggled to regain his beloved movie star status. He gained the respect and appreciation from audiences worldwide over decades of work, then lost a lot of it in one ill-thought-out action caught on global TV. Forever to remain accessible on the internet.

Knowledge

The final resource is Knowledge. Do you have the required credible and proven Knowledge to be considered an expert in your chosen area?

What would you put on your LinkedIn profile and website to support the assertions that you are good at what you do, and why someone should refer their contacts to you?

Some ideas of these assets that you can consider are:

- University qualifications, such as undergraduate degrees and postgraduate qualifications

- Short courses and certificates

- Associations from industry bodies

- Awards and honours from credible sources

- Published books, articles or papers

- Recommendations on LinkedIn, Google, Facebook or other sites

- Followers on social media and their engagement on your posts

- Guest appearances on media such as podcasts, interviews and other media.

If there is a lack of independently verifiable evidence of your credibility in an area, it is highly recommended that you spend the appropriate time to gain these, as it will take longer to start your own business if you don't.

This Resource takes time to establish. Just like Connections, it takes years to do a university degree, apply for well-regarded awards and get recommendations from clients and colleagues. If you haven't started collecting this information, we suggest you start now.

Some clients question this Resource and say that the proof they are good at what they do is in the results. I agree, but a new prospect will not go through the process of investigation and choose you if you don't have enough credibility online to assist them in their decision-making process. Even with a strong referral from a credible source, at some stage in the journey they will review your credibility online. We will review this trust metric in more detail when we look at the sales funnel in the Leverage section.

One factor of the Resources we have examined is that they all interrelate as complementary opposites. What I mean by this is that if you lack Time or Connections, you can use Money to hire someone to help you do the work to gain these. If you lack Knowledge, you can spend Time and possibly Money to gain these skills. If you need Money, you can use Connections to gain investment or initial clients for income.

A warning to those who lack all the Resources is that it will be difficult to spend the appropriate time and money investing in your own business, if you don't have a significant number of Connections and Knowledge. This creates a scarcity mindset and can lead you to try to skip over important sections in the Understand or Build section to rush sales. Unfortunately, if you do this, your offering will be less well-crafted and you might not be able to create e-ttraction and you could ruin your launch. It's far better to wait until you can do the process thoroughly.

Some examples of Resources can help show these principles at work. A client came to me who had recently migrated to Australia.

She was an expert in her industry in her homeland but had no connections here and, worse, her knowledge couldn't be applied due to local laws. She was keen to start her own business in a new but related area to her training, as it was difficult to find work. I stressed that without Connections we would need to spend a significant amount of time building her brand in this new market to offer something she hadn't done before. She would have to establish contact and trust with a core market before she launched, and this would take time. She agreed and started the process to fund her efforts and create more networks by working at a not-for-profit organisation to develop some cashflow and build her Knowledge and Connections list whilst we set about building her brand online.

Another client I worked with had a reasonable network of Connections, some Money to invest, and Time to work on his portfolio business. The barrier was Knowledge, as his experience of the area he wanted to work in was limited. We presented him with many opportunities to demonstrate his capability, but he failed to convince the Connections of his expert status and, after several tries, we advised him that he needed to work on his Knowledge. No number of Connections, Money and Time can make up for not being great at the core service of your business. As a postscript, years later I caught up with this client and he had managed to secure a few clients and was gradually establishing himself in his niche. Luckily, he had a trust fund to support him during the Knowledge process.

Finally, one client had very limited Money after a divorce but enough to start the e-ttraction building process. She had Time, Connections and Knowledge, which was why we took her on as a client. I am pleased to say that, post launching her brand, she has gone on to thrive in her chosen field and in record time too.

By setting some realistic goals and completing the four sections of the Understand process – Values, Personality, Lifestage and Resources – you will have a much better foundation to complete the Build process.

Case Study: Helen the Health Coach

Helen was referred to me by a mutual business connection many years ago, when she wanted to set up a new portfolio business after being a corporate CEO for many years. A typical Top-Shelf Corporate Escapee. It did not matter that the corporation was her own software business, she had the highly responsible role of CEO in a large company with the commensurate responsibilities and pressures that affected her lifestyle.

She didn't know the term *portfolio business,* but she didn't want her previous lifestyle and wanted something different. She just didn't know what that was yet. Hence, this was why she found herself sitting outside a café in Brunswick on a Thursday morning with me discussing her life vision.

She told me the story of how a few years back, she was a high-powered executive running her own software business turning over millions of dollars annually. She had a supportive husband and two young children and yet still worked 12-hour days to ensure her company thrived. *Super Mum* she was, until she realised that cancer doesn't care about your company's deadlines and budget. The first time she was diagnosed with this life-threatening disease, she adopted treatment like a work project and took on the chemo with gusto. She worked from her bed during therapy and took calls when she should have been resting. Pushing herself to keep going and growing.

At the time her Values were oriented towards Business, Money and providing for her Family. She didn't always enjoy it but was on a rollercoaster that was high speed, and she didn't know how to get off. Her whole life was geared to her business success. Her finances were predicated on a high income paying the mortgage, private school fees, prestige cars and overseas holidays. Her ego was based on being considered a *Super Mum*. Her friends were all similar high performers and peer pressure kept her from exploring other options. She felt she had no choice but to continue her life as she had always done.

She got better and redoubled her efforts to ensure her business was successful and it was. Then came the relapse. Helen thought she was bulletproof after successfully shrugging off cancer the first time, but this time the doctors told her it wasn't going to be that simple. This time she would need major, invasive surgery and there was a strong possibility she wouldn't make it.

When people face their mortality and realise that one day they will die, it has a profound impact on their choices and decisions. It's a major life event that restructures their Values and how they want to live their lives. Some have these feelings and then revert to their normal ways, as Helen did after her initial diagnosis. Others have an altered perception of life, and their Values change forever.

That was Helen after her second bout of cancer. She reflected on her life of success, yet at the cost of spending more quality time with her partner and children, plus the impact on her health. Her lack of attention to her health and wellbeing was offset by her lovely house in a nice leafy suburb of Melbourne. We all make decisions on how we want to live and what we prioritise; these choices come with benefits and costs. Helen now faced the ultimate cost.

She recounted an emotional story of the night before surgery. Facing potentially her last night on earth, prostrate on the floor, crying her eyes out, she prayed to God to help. Promising to change her ways if only she had another chance, acknowledging the chance she had already squandered, and regretting that opportunity lost to change her life.

In that moment of deep personal reflection, she told me she felt the presence of a higher power. She believed that she had a higher purpose and felt certain that it would all be okay. I am not a highly religious person, most of my clients are similar. However, as they say, faced with this sort of life-and-death situation, there are no atheists in foxholes.

I'm pleased to say that Helen's operation was a success, and she recovered not only physically, but mentally and spiritually. The experience broke her away from the lifestyle and habits she was used to and allowed her the time and space to reflect on what she wanted for her life. Not what society, her peer group, her company or anyone else expected from her. It's a powerful shift in thinking and one that often takes my clients until they are over the age of 50 to come to a point where they are ready to take ownership of their lives. Often, they have spent decades doing what everyone else wants, and it isn't until they peek over the edge of the end of their lives that they dare to demand something for themselves. They feel selfish for doing so. But what is the gift of your life if you give it to someone else to use?

What was fascinating about Helen's situation when I met her at that café, was she knew she wanted to change, yet hadn't fully changed her mindset.

When I asked about her goals, she said that she wanted to help women thrive after cancer and expected her new coaching business to turn over more than $1 million in revenue. This is about double what a normal portfolio business would make in the best-case scenario, but she was a high performer so I quickly outlined what would be required to build towards that sort of revenue. By doing some back-of-a-napkin maths, we worked out how many clients she needed at the industry average per-hour rate, plus the marketing, admin and business running time needed. It was a huge workload to even get close to half of this goal.

At the time, she didn't even know what her portfolio business would do yet, so there were no assets to leverage for making income that weren't related to personal effort. Nor did she have a strong reputation in her niche, so she wasn't about to command large speaking fees, consulting pay rates or board positions. So, in that situation, creating a $1 million portfolio business would have required a significant amount of work and investment over an extended period to make it happen.

Her Values had shifted but not her expectations. She wanted the large outcome, based on her previous mindset, but her Values said otherwise. The old Helen's highest Values were Business, with Money, Family and Friends close behind, and Health and Spirituality right at the end. But in our conversation in the café that day, that all changed. She said she couldn't possibly work the hours we outlined because she now starts the day with meditation and yoga, followed by a walk on the beach before dropping her kids at school. Work can only start at 10 am and then she wants to prepare a nutritious lunch before picking her kids up at 3:30 pm and spending quality time with them before dinner, and then time with her partner. Oh, she also only wanted to work three days a week and have lots of holiday time too!

This lifestyle represents Values of Health, Family, Friends, Spirituality and (dead last) is Business and Money. Pretty much the opposite of before, but her old mindset goals hadn't caught up with her new mindset's desired lifestyle.

After reflecting this back to her, we briefly discussed her Resources, and it was clear she didn't have any Money issues since she had sold her software business, and her husband worked. She then did a complete backflip on her short-term goals to support her ultimate vision and said it didn't matter what Money she made, she just wanted to help people in her situation. Supporting women who had been through a life-changing health scare was more important to her than her desire to make income.

Many business coaches would have received the brief from Helen and built a large digital marketing ecosystem to generate significant amounts of leads for her new business. She would have started off allowing this to happen because her goals were to generate a large income that she was used to. As her time was eaten away and she had to make choices between her new business and her Values of Health and Family, she would have been torn and started to resent the new business. It would have annoyed her to get what she asked for! Potential clients would feel this energy and probably stop coming, which would have created some angst. She would feel unfulfilled and eventually would have rejected the business completely.

Your lifestyle vision needs to match your Values closely. This is why it's important to create your Vision, Mission and initial Goals to start your brain thinking about the process, then complete the full Understand process and then, in the end, refine your Goals and hone them into something that is truly reflective of your true Mission and Values. Having realised this change of Values, Helen and I did the work to set up her portfolio business. She supported women through their health situations so they could thrive after cancer and her business is still going strong to this day. It's a smaller business, but it matches her lifestyle, health and family time. There were glimpses of the old mindset that came up from time to time. Frustration with the speed of business-building, pay rates and more, yet as she relaxed into her new portfolio business, she felt the fulfilment that only those who have a purpose in their work feel.

Conclusion

After working through the four parts of the Understand process – Values, Personality, Lifestage and Resources – plus reviewing several examples and a case study, I hope you feel more aligned in your Vision, Mission and Goals. Make sure they are up to date before we begin the Build process where we will take your desired business and make it a reality.

PART 2: **BUILD**

e-ttraction® Method

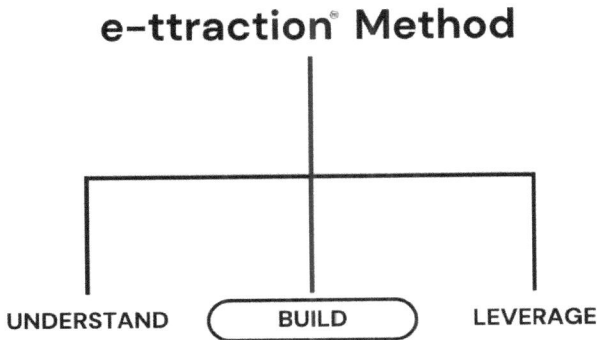

Figure 11. Part 2 of the e-ttraction Method is Build.

We appreciate that going through the Understand process is an introspective process, and those with Blaze or Dynamo energy can easily get frustrated at the lack of progress. However, as we enter the Build section, you will see it's very practical and easy to see the benefits.

We will now take all those ideas and give you step-by-step guides to implementing your brand. Resist the temptation to skip ahead or outsource this work, as it's essential you are involved in building your own brand. That said, you should get expert assistance with the areas you find difficult. For example, getting a website built will require many skills such as SEO, design, copywriting, photography and technical set-up of your domain and hosting. Your LinkedIn profile will require a headshot, biography and designed banner, so that could be outsourced. Even with the overall project management of the process, it could be useful to get assistance if you are a Creator profile like me, who struggles with the details and is easily distracted.

The Build process has four main steps: LinkedIn, Social Media, Websites/SEO and Email/CRM. But before we get into these areas, we need to review some results from the Understand section, such as your ideal target market, buyer persona and competitors.

Target Market

A target market is a group of your contacts who would best represent your ideal customers. This is based on the traditional marketing theory of market segmentation and it is important to define who this is, as not everyone is your perfect client. Only those who match your values and have the problem you solve will likely gravitate to your brand.

We start this process at a high level, using various mechanisms to hone the market down to the best group for you. Just like a sculptor taking a raw block of marble and chipping away at the surface piece by piece to reveal their vision. We will do the same to unveil who your perfect customer is.

Geographic Segmentation

Let's start with geographics. Where would you like to work? If you live in a big city, do you only want to operate there or would you travel to other destinations and how far? For those extroverts amongst us, we will likely want to conduct business face-to-face at times and so we will likely travel to see clients as it's in our nature. If travel is an option, then is it by car, bus or train, or would you fly to see a client?

The more introverted entrepreneurs will likely want to do more online types of work. Video calls, automated services and less direct interactions with clients. They will find it easier to have a larger geographic footprint business.

The process we did for Money in the Understand process is useful for this section too. Write down the preferred location of your ideal clients, then the limitations to where you would go. Where do you draw the line in terms of travel and how would that change the conditions of your deal?

Demographic Segmentation

Next, let's review demographics. Could you chip off some marble by choosing a certain age, nationality, income, gender or other circumstances for your ideal client? Some might find this challenging because they want to help everyone and wouldn't turn a client away due to something like gender. Please consider that you don't have to turn away those clients, if you don't want to. But you need to create an online brand that e-ttracts a certain person and, the more specific it is to your ideal client, the more it will be a direct hit for them.

Some of the demographic segmentation variables are as follows: age, gender, marital status, family size, education, occupation, nationality, religion, income and lifestyle. Any variable that separates your group from others in the market helps you to find your ideal client.

In this process, we are trying to find a group who is large enough to support our revenue goals, but small enough to form a niche we can access with marketing. The group should believe and understand why they are in the target market and why the others who are excluded are not there. This could sound elitist or exclusionary, but that's how humans have been thinking for thousands of years. Take Australia, for instance, we believe we are a group separate from the world. When you travel overseas and meet a fellow Aussie, you bond because you are from the same culture. Then each state has its own identity, as the rugby state of origin exemplifies between NSW and Queensland. Similarly, the battle for the best city between Melbourne and Sydney (obviously, Melbourne wins that one!). Then in each city, like Melbourne, you will have people in different areas loving their suburb or region. Like the bayside tribes who love living near the beach or the inner-city trendy folks who wouldn't dream of living away from the city. We divide into smaller groups of football teams, local clubs, and every smaller niche until we reach families and crews of friends.

The key here is to ensure you can access this target market somehow. Otherwise, this theoretical exercise doesn't translate to anything we can utilise in our business. A good way to test your target market is to do a search on social media for these groups. If there is an already-established group, then you are likely to have some way of reaching them with your marketing. For example, I had a client who was a mortgage-broker in Mornington, down the coast just outside of Melbourne. After we had completed the Understand section, we realised that she only needed a small number of clients monthly, as she was a new mum and didn't want to work full-time. She wanted a home-based business that was flexible around her baby, and she didn't want to travel too far, such as going to Melbourne to work. We decided her best target market was new mums, just like her, who live near or in Mornington. This is often the case that we service people who have the same problems we have, as we can clearly understand them.

We established her brand as being flexible appointments for mums around feeding and sleeping times. Lucky for her, there was a Facebook group called Mornington Mums that had over 10,000 members in it. The group swapped advice and gave each other support. There were only two mortgage-brokers in the group and because her website and branding were spot on for this market, she took the lion's share of business from that group. Her clients were incredibly loyal, and she ran her whole business based on these referrals. Marketing done! The key was to understand her perfect market and design her whole brand around how to help solve their problems, so when they went to her online assets – it was a perfect match.

A contrasting example of someone who didn't do target marketing well was a client who asked me to help her friend with some free advice on her brand as she couldn't afford to engage me directly. I like to take on some pro bono clients, so I provided some free consulting to her. Her business was helping children with autism thrive with schooling and her traditional client was from the lower socio-economic areas of Melbourne. She had a lot of similarities with her target market, as she had a son with autism, so helping them was in her highest Values. The only issue was she found it difficult to make a reasonable living from this work. She worked part-time because she was the primary carer for her kids, and this exacerbated the issue.

During our session, I asked her about her goals, which were far too modest in my opinion, and I suggested she aim higher and that it was no use providing a service that didn't fulfil you because it reduced your capacity to help people. Then we addressed the target market, which was mostly made up of families who were on welfare, as these had the highest propensity of autism in the population. She often helped them for free because they were unable to afford her assistance and the necessities of life.

My question to her was whether there were any children with autism with wealthy parents and if they would value her services. She seemed put off by this suggestion, but I continued by suggesting that if she worked with more families who could pay her more, then she could provide for herself and her family and help more families in need because it would take the pressure off her finances.

I would love to say she accepted my advice and chose the path that reduced her burden, but after several years I ran into her again and she was stuck in the same situation. Those who are unwilling to change or alter their circumstances will not change the outcome. As Einstein said, the definition of insanity is to do the same thing and expect a different result.[29] The issue, I believe, stems from past trauma related to self-worth and money specifically. However, I can only coach people who are open to coaching, which is one part of our target market definition that comes from psychographic segmentation.

Psychographic Segmentation

The next area to examine is psychographics. This is an important overlay to our geographic and demographic segmentations, as it highlights how our potential customers think.

As an example to explain psychographic segmentation, I will use a scenario from my own business Social Star. We have two main target markets: the over-50-year-old corporate escapee who wants to start a portfolio business in Australia; those who work with professional services firms in Australia who want to grow their businesses, as we defined in the previous section. The psychographic component of this second target market is that they are willing to be coached and are entrepreneurial. These clients are all experts in their fields: specialist surgeons, leading finance professionals, the highest-paid lawyers and consultants. They are used to giving advice, not taking it, so at times they believe they can do marketing better than others and are unable to treat other consultants as peers, not service providers. They are smart and know they don't have the knowledge and experience to do what we do, but are still unable to take direction and advice on

---

29   https://www.scientificamerican.com/article/
      einstein-s-parable-of-quantum-insanity/

things they don't understand. Particularly when it confronts their personality, as many of them are Lords in their Wealth Dynamics profile, so have a high attention to detail and have a desire to control and have certainty on outcomes for any action. Unfortunately, marketing isn't a science, it's an art, so outcomes are not verified with double-blind longitudinal studies and published in peer-reviewed journals, like in medicine. We operate in a very fast-moving industry where new techniques and technologies come out weekly. With the advent of Artificial Intelligence, this pace of change will accelerate. Therefore, it's essential that the client has the belief that the brand manager knows better than they do when it comes to their personal and business branding.

Therefore, the best clients for us have shown us that they can accept us as the experts in our industry, listen to our advice and adopt our strategies. It's soon clear that we know what we are doing, as the results speak for themselves.

The other critical psychographic element is an entrepreneurial spirit. This means they have an ambitious vision that they want to fulfil and need support to do so. Without a clear goal, it is difficult to support a client through the journey and know when you get there. This also necessitates an element of risk and operating out of their comfort zone, which again, requires them to seek support and reinforces the first point of trusting outside advisors.

If you have worked on these three segmentation variables, you would have a pretty good view of your best target market. If we continue the analogy of Social Star's target market, they would be Australian-based professional services businesses with revenue of over $5 million annually, an entrepreneurial leader who is coachable and looking to grow their business towards some type of exit, and who believes branding will help them achieve their goals.

The next step is to define your perfect buyer avatar, which is the absolute best customer you will aim for and use to create your marketing content.

Buyer Avatar

The buyer avatar or buyer persona is a representation of the best customer you can imagine for your new portfolio business. If you have already been working with clients in this capacity, you can choose your avatar from a real-life person. If you are not yet operating but have a strong idea of what your business will be, you can choose someone you know who you would like to work with. This is a good option because you can then research the person in detail and understand them before building the marketing assets.

Otherwise, we will use our imagination to come up with someone from our target market parameters who would be our desired choice. We must have a level of detail here, so we can immediately identify these types of clients from others when we come across them.

To start the process, write the segmentation information for them: their geographic location, demographic situation and psychographic tendencies. Find or create a name, get a photo and their biography. The more detail, the better. Try to predict their Values, Personality, Lifestage and Resources so we understand them more fully and, finally, outline their core problem that you would help them solve.

If you haven't started your portfolio business and are unaware of your avatar, you might find this exercise difficult. Please persist, as it's important to do the thinking now before we start crafting your website and social media to suit this person. It is more difficult to retrofit digital content than it is to spend time upfront carefully crafting this persona.

An example of a buyer avatar or persona might help illustrate this work. I will use one of our long-term clients as an example.

Michael Kenihan has been a long-term client of Social Star, and I would love more clients just like him. He lives in a leafy suburb of Melbourne, is over 60 years old and in fine health, and works in a variety of medical businesses. He is married with three kids and earns an above-average income from his variety of businesses. I first met Michael when he was a manager at a large physiotherapy business, and we were referred to do some marketing consulting work there. This was over 15 years ago, before Social Star was incorporated officially. I was doing work part-time whilst working in my job at Sensis.

Michael is 10 years older than me, but we got along immediately. He took my advice seriously and accepted that I was good at marketing and he was good at management and being a physiotherapist.

He is very entrepreneurial and started several new businesses, which he brought us in to work on. The work was meaningful and made a difference to the businesses, so he referred me to his colleagues, and I still have a variety of clients that he referred to me over a decade ago.

When he made the jump from corporate to his portfolio business, we helped him build his brand and then write his book a few years later.

We have the kind of working relationship that is very honest and has give and take. Due to our strong relationship, when he asked me to give his son an internship, I immediately agreed and even hired his son's best friend too.

Michael represents the essence of a good client: he appreciates our work and us as people. He treats my staff with respect and understands his role in the process. This translates to providing us the time to be briefed properly on work, paying invoices promptly and listening to our advice. We, in turn, appreciate his business and will go the extra mile to help and support him in his efforts. It's far more than a transactional relationship between a supplier and a customer – I consider him a friend. For our company, he is the avatar for our Corporate Escapee product.

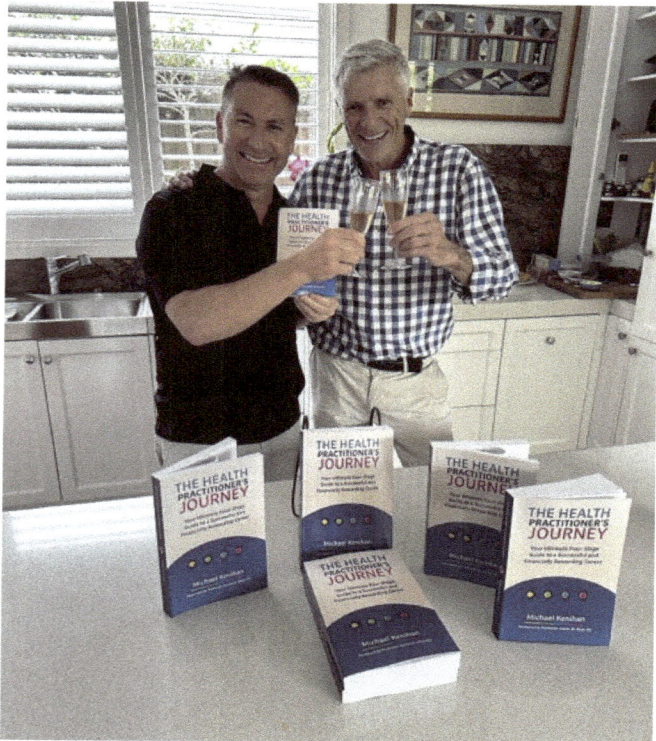

Figure 12. A photo of Michael and I when I dropped off his first box of books.

The other buyer avatar we have is for our professional services business. Sevan works for one of our great clients as the managing partner of a professional services firm, and he is a very dynamic leader. He believes in marketing and accepts advice from marketing experts. He is willing to invest in the brand of his organisation and has yielded the results of this investment.

Figure 13. A photo of Sevan and I at his new office opening.

When we do our marketing, we often remind ourselves that these are our ideal clients, so we can ensure that what we produce will e-ttract these individuals.

I suggest you create your own buyer avatars and share them with your team and marketing agencies.

Competitors

When we look at competitors for your business, it's important to realise that if you set up your personal and business brand correctly, there are no real competitors, only substitutes. Competitors are an exact replacement for your service from a similar organisation. A substitute is a different solution for the problem you have, but not like your organisation. For instance, if you were feeling tired and wanting to write a book on your holiday, you might go to a café and have a coffee. Caffeine is a stimulant and will help you be more productive. The different coffee shops are competitive with each other for your business. A substitute could be to go to a bar and have a Red Bull energy drink. This would have a similar effect of giving you a caffeine boost, but it's not coffee and you are not going to a café.

There are normally more substitutes for your offering than competitors. For instance, cafés outside of my local areas wouldn't be competitive, since I wouldn't bother to travel the extra distance to go there. In terms of substitutes, I could stay home and make tea or coffee there, or consume another energy-based product, do some exercise, or find any number of ways to increase my productivity. All would be substitutes for the coffee at the café.

In a business context, if you do your target market work well and create a super niche and create products that are a direct hit for those avatars, it's unlikely that anyone in your area, in your network, with similar values to you, would have that same solution.

You become unique and the only solution for those clients. All other perceived competitors are substitutes because their offering would be different from yours. This is particularly true for our clients who are knowledge professionals, as it's very difficult to compare services because they are directly connected to the person delivering them.

Product-based businesses can be copied more readily because they all come from the same source materials, so can be backwards-engineered to create something similar. For instance, Apple came out with the very first touchscreen smartphone and now every company has one that looks very similar. There are differences in the products, of course, as they try to make it not the same, but the overall design and approach are similar enough to look the same. If one of the companies invents a new feature, it's not long before the rest of the industry catches up with something similar too.

However, with people, it's not the same. One person can't just become like another. They can offer a similar solution to the same target market, but they are not the same. Each person has a unique background, work experience, value system, personality and approach which makes them 100% unique. You can't retrofit a person to be the same as others, and we shouldn't try either.

This is why going through the Understand process in detail is so important, because when we build a personal or business brand, and make it very compelling for the perfect customer, it's unlikely they will go anywhere else.

Like Apple phones, they sell in vast quantities and for a higher profit margin than any other phone brand. Not because they have access to some miracle resource that no other manufacturer can access. Or because they have better technology, since their competitors caught up long ago. It's because of their brand.

Your brand will mean that you can charge a higher rate too. Without a direct competitor, you can set your prices and, for the right client, they will not bargain with you. This doesn't mean you can charge whatever you want with no regard to the value you are delivering. It means a fair price for the work provided. After all, we want to be in our portfolio business for at least a decade, so we want to have long-term relationships with our clients and have them refer us to their colleagues. Creating enormous value for them is our goal.

Furthermore, there will be substitutes for your offering, which will reduce your opportunity to price too highly. A substitute is an alternative way to solve the same problem, not a direct competitor.

An example to illustrate this could be restaurants. If I feel like some Thai food, there are many Thai restaurants in my area. They are similar but not the same, yet are considered competitors because they offer similar meals for similar prices with similar décor in the same general location. Therefore, their prices are dictated by the market, and one can't charge substantially more than the other. A substitute for going to eat in their restaurant could be getting it home-delivered by Uber, cooking Thai food myself, or not even eating Thai food, but choosing Japanese or Chinese food instead. The problem of hunger is still solved but in a different way.

In the Leverage section, we will further explore how we go to market to make our brand unique and exclusive. But for now, we will delve into LinkedIn, the foundation for our credible brand.

Step 5: LinkedIn

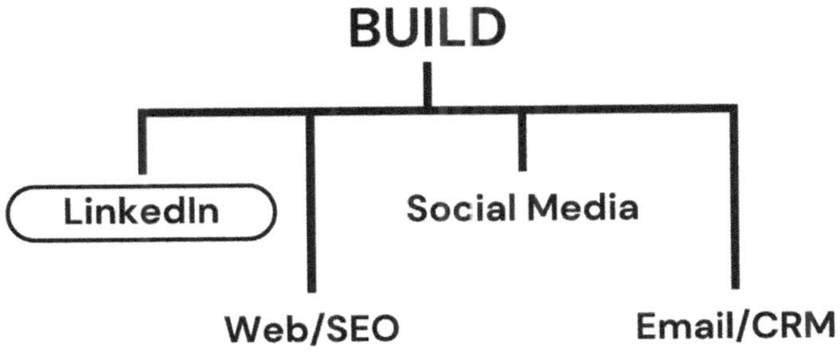

BUILD

| LinkedIn | Social Media |

Web/SEO   Email/CRM

Figure 14. LinkedIn is the foundation of a credible brand.

LinkedIn is the main professional network in the world. Since 2002 it has been the go-to social network for employment and business networking. Started by Reid Hoffman and Eric Ly, it was purchased by Microsoft for $180 billion in 2016 and has made some dramatic changes since its acquisition.[30]

Most of my clients are aware of LinkedIn and have a profile, but not many use it effectively. Therein lies the opportunity to build your personal brand on this platform.

Some key features make LinkedIn different from other social media, such as Facebook, Instagram or TikTok. The main compelling factor is that it has a very comprehensive area to list your work experience and education. Most social media are based on the newsfeed and not your details. They are built on an advertising model, so they prioritise the views of content first and the creator second.

LinkedIn is built on a subscription model. It does allow advertising, however, this is a relatively new offering and was added after the platform was structured on subscriptions. LinkedIn has a blogging

---

30   https://www.cnbc.com/2016/07/07/linkedin-co-founder-hoffman-why-we-sold-to-microsoft.html

platform that runs independently, although it's integrated into the interface. What this means is that your blogs or *articles*, as they call them, are crawled separately in Google and can help prospects find your brand.

Finally, and probably most importantly, LinkedIn is based on networking. The basis for how the algorithm works is that you can chat with your first-level connections and they see your content. Second-level connections, or mutual connections, you can reach out to connect with, but if you are less networked than a particular person, then you can't see these second-level connections at all.

LinkedIn is built to help you network for business, and the culture of the platform means it's appropriate to reach out to people you don't know to see if there is a mutually beneficial reason to network with each other. Of course, some people find this feature annoying as they get many unsolicited messages, however, you take the good with the bad on all these platforms.

I don't necessarily like pre-roll ads when watching my YouTube videos, but the platform is free, so I understand that this is the trade-off. Same with Facebook, which sells my information to the highest advertising bidder in exchange for using their services. This has been the way since newspapers, radio and TV were the main communication mediums and social media is just the latest in these mediums.

If you compare this to other social networks, you can reach out to connect, but it can seem inappropriate to try to make friends with people on Facebook or follow people on Instagram to form business relationships. They are more for personal matters, which is why LinkedIn doesn't call your network *friends*, but *connections*.

I have been on LinkedIn since very early in its development, 2005 to be exact, as I was working in digital marketing and using social media early on. I recall when the only image you could have on your profile was your photo and there wasn't a newsfeed at all. They have experimented with many different changes to the interface, so when you read this book some things might have changed – this is the nature of social media, it constantly changes.

At the time of writing, I have over 17,000 connections and followers, written over 150 blogs and have been invited to contribute to the intellectual property of LinkedIn with written advice for everyone on the network.

I tell my clients LinkedIn is a lot of 1% changes that add up to a great profile. Let's work our way through these now.

Building a Quality LinkedIn Profile

Figure 15. Profile photo of the author.

Humans are attracted to looking at each other's faces, hence the Facebook name. Most of the work we do on social media reflects this, as the posts we create with people in them generally outperform those that don't.

Therefore, the first thing that will attract someone's attention to your profile is your profile photo. More than that, your photo will stir feelings in the viewer that will either attract them to your profile or repel them. Let's give you the best chance of having your profile work for you by having an optimal photo.

From our experience, the photo should be very simple and straightforward. Avoid the desire to be tricky or have an overproduced image. It should look like you in real life. If you were meeting a prospect and they couldn't recognise you from your LinkedIn image, this is a problem. It creates distrust.

Filters, too much makeup, or using a photo from a decade ago isn't helpful. Also, avoid having anything else in the image apart from your face. If you look at the image on your phone, it's quite small, so use the space for someone to see you, not the fish you just caught or all your mates at the races or a wedding. It should go without saying that you shouldn't have alcohol in your images or anything that could easily offend people, but I still see this regularly.

For my target client this is sound advice, however, for some people reading this, the exception would be if your brand is very out there and based on something that would change this advice.

For example, I remember a colleague in the LinkedIn marketing space who created a point of difference for himself just to stand out. He was called the only CEO with a mohawk, referring to his haircut of choice, which was unusual at the time and for the circumstances. His name is Chris J Reed, and you can search for him on LinkedIn. He has turned that gimmick into a massive brand and business;

so it can work, but it is something you must go all in on, so ensure it's something you can maintain!

I understand the use of a "thing" to stand out, however, most of my clients would rather use their experience and network to gain clients, rather than something like a mohawk.

Have a look at your current photos and assess if you need a new one. If in doubt, get one. It can't hurt to have a portfolio of images anyhow.

Banner

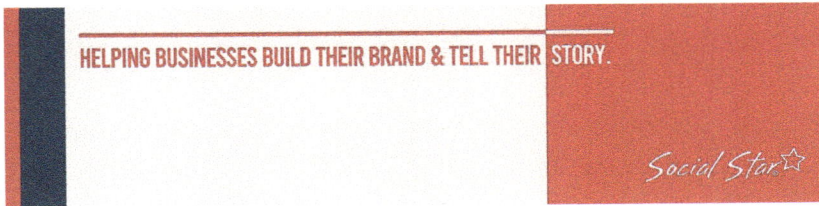

Figure 16. An example of a banner image.

The next most visual element of your profile is your banner or background image. This is a large area where you can put almost anything, although it is partially obscured by your profile image, so be careful not to put anything important in the bottom left-hand corner. Keep in mind that LinkedIn has a history of changing the placement of the photos. Only recently they moved it to the centre of the profile, which meant everyone was faced with redesigning their banners. LinkedIn quickly moved it back, after backlash from users.

What goes into the banner? That's a good question and the many answers depend on the stage of the journey you are on towards a portfolio business. If you are still deciding on what your business will be, you can put up a picture of a landscape of something meaningful to you. This is temporary until we get through the business set-up process, so don't stress too much about it. My clients usually use a picture they took of a holiday destination, the city skyline of their hometown, or even a quote that represents their brand. For some examples of this visit the Social Star website.

Once you establish your brand logo and guidelines, we will suggest a banner that more accurately represents you to your target market. As a rule, we don't like faces in the banner as it distracts people from your face. The exception would be if you were focusing on speaking and had a good image of yourself on stage. If you have written a book, you can focus your banner on that. But most of our clients have a banner that is more of an on-brand colour image with their logo. Plain and simple but ties their face to their business.

Banners are easily upgraded and changed, so don't think of it as a permanent brand item, more like something to be revised each year when you do a brand audit and make changes to your overall digital presence.

Headline

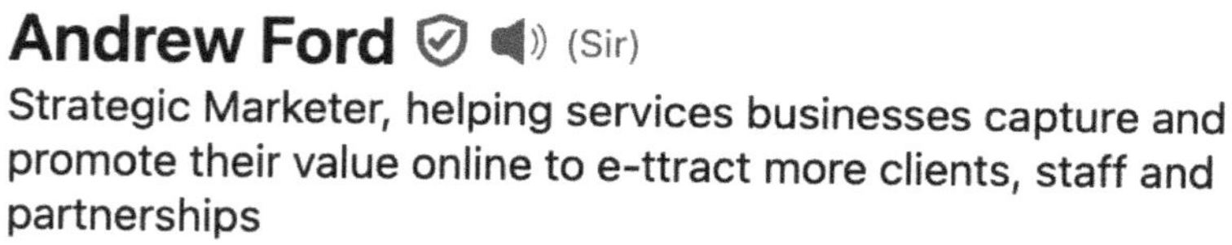

Andrew Ford ✓ ◀)) (Sir)
Strategic Marketer, helping services businesses capture and promote their value online to e-ttract more clients, staff and partnerships

Figure 17. An example of a headline.

The headline is one of the most important elements to consider after the visual elements of your photo and banner. The right-hand side of the brain will automatically activate and see the visual elements first. Then the left side of the brain will activate to review the words on your profile.

The headline, which we often call the *tagline*, spreads across all your social media profiles and into your website. It's an important positioning statement of what you do, for whom and the benefits of that work. This can involve quite a bit of work to get it honed to a suitable point and, like the banner, it can be adjusted over time as your brand matures.

The situation with the headline reminds me of an experience I had with my partner in crime when I was a little kid. My sister is only 18 months older than me and, when we were little, she found the recipe to make a chocolate cake. It was very simple with only a few ingredients and, if you put them together in the right quantity, it pretty much worked out. Then there was half a whole cake each! Once we made it a few times, I started to experiment with different measures of the ingredients. Could I make it even chocolatier? Perhaps add vanilla essence and see what happens. The point of the story is that once you have a base recipe that works, it's much easier to tweak it to suit your needs. But if you start with no recipe and just put a bunch of ingredients together with no plan, it's unlikely to work out. Let's develop the base recipe for your tagline.

There are four key parts to a tagline:

- What you do
- What you do specifically
- Who it's for
- What's the outcome?

For example, at the time of writing my tagline is:

"Strategic Marketer, helping services businesses capture and promote their value online to e-ttract more clients, staff and partnerships."

The four key parts of my tagline are:

- What you do: "Strategic Marketer". I work in marketing, have a degree from RMIT University and teach in the undergraduate program, I have run a marketing agency for a decade, therefore, I can claim this statement.

- What you do specifically: "capture and promote their value online", we use our unique methodology called the Expert Marketing System to capture the clients on video to make it super easy for us to create monthly videos, posts and blogs.

- Who it's for: "helping services businesses", we work specifically with our niche of services businesses like medical, financial, legal and consultants. We might take on other clients if we see them as a fit, but we are set up to work with these niche clients and hope to attract more of them.

- What's the outcome?: "to e-ttract more clients, staff and partnerships", this is what they will get from our service offering. I have used our trademarked word "e-ttraction" and specified we can help not only in *e-ttracting* clients but, importantly, staff and partners. This is different in the marketplace and helps us work with busy professionals who need more than client acquisition.

So, there is our simple system to create your tagline. Notice that I didn't mention your job title or company here. This is on purpose because running a portfolio business is vastly different from being the CEO or founder of a company. No one will have heard of your new business so it's irrelevant to them, plus it's right on the other side of the profile when they visit your page, so there is no need to duplicate it. When we work with CEOs and founders, we do include their job titles as it's relevant.

I recall working with the Social Media Manager for Telstra and advising her on what to call the CEO on LinkedIn. In Australia everyone knows our national phone company, so there is no need to position him any other way than the "CEO of Telstra", as it says all that it needs to. However, when David Thodey left Telstra, he changed his headline to "Board Director". This was likely enough for his target market, but he also didn't consult me on this decision, as I would have recommended more.

Contact Information

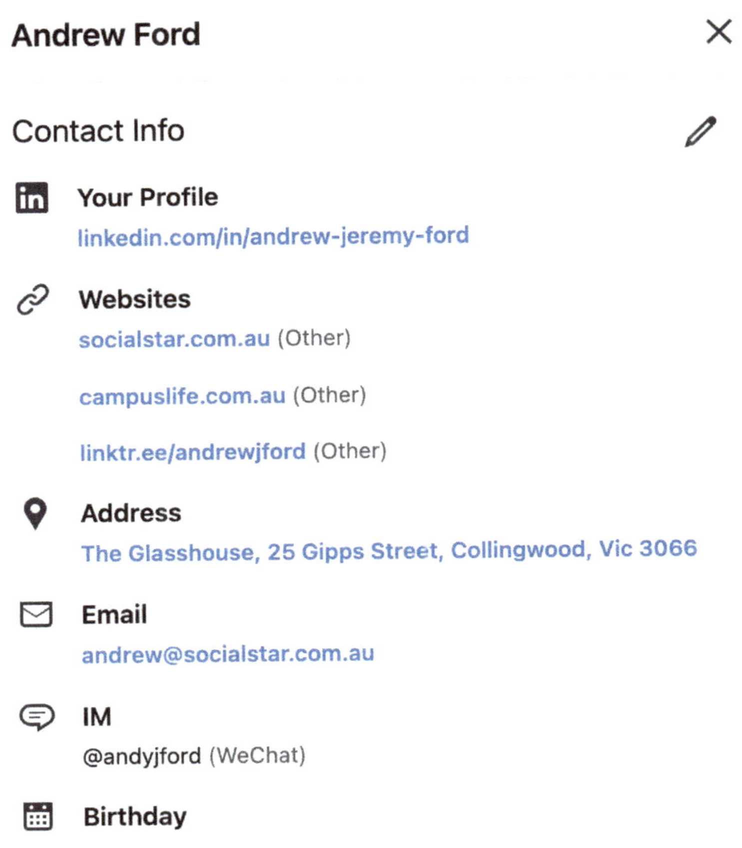

Andrew Ford   ✕

Contact Info   ✎

in **Your Profile**
linkedin.com/in/andrew-jeremy-ford

🔗 **Websites**
socialstar.com.au (Other)

campuslife.com.au (Other)

linktr.ee/andrewjford (Other)

📍 **Address**
The Glasshouse, 25 Gipps Street, Collingwood, Vic 3066

✉ **Email**
andrew@socialstar.com.au

💬 **IM**
@andyjford (WeChat)

📅 **Birthday**

Figure 18. An example of contact details.

Under your profile heading is a little button called "Contact info", and although a lot of people miss this, it's kind of a big deal. For those who use LinkedIn regularly, we use this to direct ourselves to your content and the next steps in your sales process.

There are several elements it is wise to address to ensure someone who wants to contact you, can.

There was a client I was working with recently and one of the salespersons had attended two of my LinkedIn training sessions and still hadn't updated his profile. I wanted to contact him to see what the issue was, but I couldn't find a way to message him. I didn't have his email or phone number because he was on a group call during the training. His profile photo was of him at the races, with his arm around a girl, drinking a beer, with sunglasses on. Cool shot for sure, but not necessarily the responsible businessperson who a potential client would trust to spend thousands of dollars with.

The issue was his private gmail was on LinkedIn and there was no other contact information, he hadn't accepted my connection request, so I resorted to calling his manager and asking for his details. But what if a potential client was interested in getting in touch, would they bother to research other ways to connect or just move on to the other – well-branded and proactive salesperson – in that competitive industry?

The key areas to update, and like I said, these are all 1% differences that add up to a lot, are as follows:

- Change your profile URL. You can make this anything you like, but your name is the best, if you can get it. If not, add an initial or something to do with your business. One client with a popular name used his name_CPA – very effective.

- Add an email address. Most people set up LinkedIn to find a job, so at least have a university email, gmail or something similar. As the old joke goes, nothing says professional like a gmail address. If you have something like "hotstuff79@gmail.com", it's time to update it to your custom business domain email address.

- Add a phone number. For some people, they are okay to have their mobile number in here, for others they get a generic landline that they use for this purpose. You can adjust your privacy settings so that only your first-level connections can see your email and phone number, if you are concerned with your privacy.

- Add your address. If you plan to see clients and have an office, it's useful to put this here. If you work from home, you can simply put your suburb or city so that potential clients at least know if it's possible to meet you in person. I have clients all around Australia and the world, and sometimes they like to meet, so they must know I am based in Melbourne.

- Add website/s. Adding your main website is important once you build your personal or business sites. But you can add three sites, so consider adding any social media you feel will help your clients get to know you better. It could be a podcast, interview with you, your blog site or YouTube, if you have videos.

- Birthday. You can add your birthday if you desire, but I would suggest it's not important and can be a potential security risk in these days of high cyber-crime, so best to only add a day and month, if you choose to include it.

- Instant messaging. There is a feature to include IM functions such as WeChat, important if you do any work with China, but not required.

As mentioned, your contact information is a small detail, but if it helps you get one new account, then it is worth it.

Number of Connections

17,924 followers · 500+ connections

Figure 19. An example of how many followers and connections a particular LinkedIn profile has.

There are three main reasons why having a high number of connections is important. It makes you seem credible, it helps you to connect to others and others to you, and it shows your mutual connections.

Firstly, it is a signal to the market of your activity on LinkedIn. Whether you like it or not, you will be judged by your online brand. If you are not active and have an outdated profile, you will be perceived as out of date and not digitally savvy. Likewise, if you are posting every day and pushing unsolicited messages out regularly, you might be seen as desperate. It's a fine line between being active and being in demand. More about this in the Leverage phase of the program.

Our recommendation is to have a lot of connections. How many you need will be decided when you do the e-ttraction sales process, as we will map your revenue to your number of desired customers and work back towards how many you will need at each phase of the sales process. With an average conversion rate, you will need 16,000 connections to equal one customer. That's a lot, I know, so don't be put off by this figure, as there are a lot of variances in our conversion rates based on how we like to go to market.

Another very good reason to have more connections is that you can find and connect to new people only if they are second-level connections. It's not impossible to connect to third-level connections, we just don't recommend it. So, the more people you know, and the more people they know, the more easily it is for you to search and find people. Consequently, it's also easier for people to search and find you, as LinkedIn works both ways. If your perfect clients are a third-level connection, they won't be able to see your profile even if they search for you.

Finally, having a lot of mutual connections with anyone you want to connect to helps them feel like you are trusted. If you know people they know, it appears like you are in the same network, which makes it more likely that they will connect with you and start a conversation.

We will cover connections in detail in the Leverage section, but this is a prelude, so you are aware that the overall number is important to be high. Therefore, until you do that part, keep networking!

Featured Section

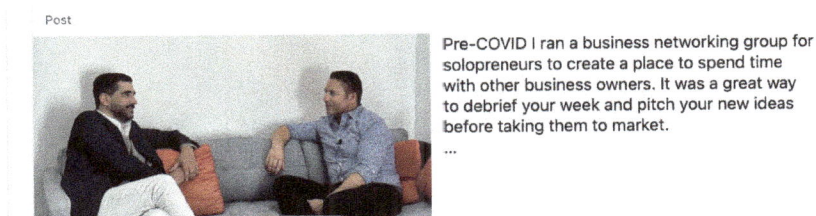

Post

Pre-COVID I ran a business networking group for solopreneurs to create a place to spend time with other business owners. It was a great way to debrief your week and pitch your new ideas before taking them to market.

...

Figure 20. An example of a featured section.

The featured section is relatively new to LinkedIn and is a great addition, in my opinion. It is a large visual banner right under your main profile before your biography.

It was brought into being so you can highlight a few key areas of your brand easily. This could be a blog or podcast you have written, a link to an article or an image you want to display. They make it super easy to put it up and change it regularly. You can list dozens of posts here, but it can be quite effective to just have a few, or even one if you have something big to share.

The way we like to use this section is to highlight your first blog when you launch your portfolio business. As you will see in the Leverage section, we will always start with a foundation blog of your origin story to kick-start your brand to your network.

The foundation blog goes in your featured section to ensure those who missed it on the newsfeed have an opportunity to see it. This might seem like a duplicate of your biography and in some ways it is. But they operate in different parts of LinkedIn and will be written slightly differently, so you need both. Never miss an opportunity to tell your story!

This can raise a particular objection with some clients when we go through this process. They feel they are bombarding their network with information when they post something in different mediums or repeat a post. I would argue that to get anyone to read and engage with your material is quite difficult, so you need to have your story on several different mediums and multiple times. People are smart enough to ignore it if they have seen it before, but if they don't see it at all, we miss a huge opportunity. More on this topic in the Leverage section on content.

About Section

Your biography is an important section as it tells your story and can add personality to your profile rather than a list of facts about you. The way we recommend it to be structured is as an origin story. That means you tell the reader how you arrived at starting a portfolio business via your history and why you are the perfect person to solve the problems of your target market.

The structure will be like the pitch process that you will go through in the Leverage section. I have included a quick reference chart below to get you started.

One thing to remember with the current format of the biography is that only the first few lines show on your profile, unless the reader clicks to reveal more. This should be your tease line that encourages them to want to read more. This line is an extension of your tagline but with more detail or a small summary of what you do and for whom.

To give you an example, I have included my biography, at the time of writing, to give you an idea of how the tagline and biography relate. Like all your digital assets, you should be updating these regularly as your business changes, so mine could be different when you read this part of the book. You can see some examples on the Social Star website to guide you through the process.

About

Hi there, I'm Andrew Ford. I am the CEO and Managing Director of Social Star and CampusLife, where I share my digital marketing expertise with individuals and businesses looking to develop their brand, and with students, who I mentor to become future digital marketing leaders.

Whilst some people may call me a digital entrepreneur, an innovator in channelling passion into corporate success, and a dedicated mentor of young people with great potential, my friends just call me Andy.

My mission is to formulate effective and profitable business models which combine a unique personal brand with your passion. By harnessing digital and social media strategies, Social Star is your number one destination for unleashing your inner personal brand and launching the next step in your career.

My success can be attributed to over 12 years of industry education, more than 15 years of experience in corporate before launching my own business and my ongoing desire for self-improvement and to learn from others. As a lecturer and an industry mentor for several interns at Social Star over the years, I have a passion for helping students. I believe that university does not always provide students with the industry experience they need to feel career-ready once they graduate. This is where I come in...

At Social Star, I mentor interns, who evolve into marketing coordinators, account managers and team leaders, working directly with clients to achieve success. My unique approach harnesses the creative power of today's youth on their home turf, social media, to ensure our digital marketing strategies are modern, relevant and effective. As a team, we deliver measurable results to our clients, growing their social media presence and digital brand to facilitate corporate success.

CampusLife strives to help grow businesses by matching them with talented university students looking for internships before or just after they graduate. I believe that student interns have a lot to offer: they are the most motivated, dedicated and hard-working employees I've had, and I feel that given the right opportunity, they can unleash endless potential and talent for other professionals too.

So, why me? I've worked in the personal branding space for over 10 years, helping individuals achieve targeted corporate success. The key is authenticity. Businesses don't make deals, people do. Therefore creating a digital presence that represents you and your values accurately is crucial to your success.

I'm happy to connect if you need brand advice or marketing work from my team. Cheers Andrew

Top skills
Marketing Strategy · Content Marketing · Digital Marketing · Public Speaking · Social Selling

Figure 21. The author's biography as of early 2024.

There is often a debate whether to use first- or third-person point of view for the biography, and this depends on your brand and the culture in the industry you operate in. LinkedIn has become much less formal and so first-person biographies have been our standard recommendation. However, this differs for some of our clients, such as surgeons and others who want to be held in high esteem and write more about their accomplishments rather than their personal journeys. It's much easier to promote someone with a third-person bio compared to a first-person. Just imagine walking on stage to do a speech and someone else reading your bio, compared with you introducing yourself. You can imagine how others might talk up your personal profile, as opposed to the more modest way we might do it for ourselves. However, these clients are not the target market for this book, we are writing this for people wanting to start a portfolio business and, for you, a first-person biography is preferred.

Experience

Experience   +   ✎

Digital Marketing Strategist
Social Star Pty Ltd · Self-employed
Aug 2011 - Present · 12 yrs 11 mos
Melbourne, Australia · On-site

Social Star is a marketing agency that assists services businesses to do the marketing that they don't have the time, skill or inclination to do. We can help you with your digital marketing - from strategy pla ...see more

♡ Brand Management, Brand Development and +5 skills

Personal Brand overview by Social Star
We help people and businesses attract opportunities by creating powerful online brands. We love LinkedIn but we work with all social media sites. Check out if you fit our services...

Keynote Speaker
Andrew Ford Speaker · Self-employed
Nov 2000 - Present · 23 yrs 8 mos
Melbourne, Victoria, Australia · Hybrid

After a decade of leading the digital marketing strategies for some of the world's largest companies, Andrew turned his attention to discovering how people could best use social media and digital technolog ...see more

♡ Articulate Presenter, Public Speaking and +2 skills

Andrew Ford Speaker on personal brand e-ttraction
Well known and respected in the industry, Andrew is the strategies behind many high profile brands. He splits his time between helping business people build their personal...

Sessional Lecturer - Digital Marketing Strategy
RMIT University · Freelance
Feb 2016 - Present · 8 yrs 5 mos
Melbourne, Australia

Lecturing to Undergraduate students in Digital Marketing and postgrad MEA and MBA (Exec) students on personal branding.... ...see more

♡ Marketing Strategy and Digital Marketing

Founder
CampusLife · Part-time
Jul 2021 - Present · 3 yrs
Melbourne, Victoria, Australia

CampusLife is a platform for university students to connect to like-minded people, assist with university studies, finding jobs and help them live a better life. ... ...see more

Chief Sipper
Tequila Straws · Part-time
Sep 2022 - May 2023 · 9 mos
Melbourne, Victoria, Australia

Tequila Straws is a new business helping bars, restaurants and cafes to remove their plastic straws and give customers the gift of a straw that is durable, taste free and sustainable. Perfect for that next froz ...see more

Tequila Straws.jpeg
Available for order now www.tequilastraws.com.au

Show all 16 experiences →

Figure 22. An example of how to list your experience.

159

Your experience is quite self-explanatory, it's your work experience. There are several parts of your experience that we need to add, so we will review these step by step to ensure we have consistency and optimise these for your portfolio business.

Some people choose to change the parameters of this section to do more sales-oriented entries, which are not your past roles. However, I feel this cheapens your profile and would not advise this. Just put in your full work history.

LinkedIn truncates the experience section at a certain point in your profile, depending on how much content you have in there. For my profile, it's the first five positions that show before you must click a button to see more.

The first question people ask is what to include and exclude from your work history.

I recommend starting with your very first job, even if it is menial and has nothing to do with your current portfolio business. Many people advise not to do this approach and only to put in roles that impact your current business. However, I disagree, because putting in your full and diverse history helps people understand your full journey. Even working in a fast-food place or retail outlet says something about you and helps form your character. It's all part of what makes you unique, so use it.

As an example, I started my work life in my family office products business, straight out of high school. I worked in the warehouse for many years before graduating to more senior positions and into sales and then management. When I speak to small family-owned businesses, I relate stories of working for my grandparents, which creates familiarity and connection between us. They feel

I understand their situation because I have worked in a family business.

We can't foresee what will impress a potential client or stories that will be relevant, so add them in. It's another 1% that could be the difference for some people. Plus, it takes a small amount of time, so there isn't really a downside, so why not include it?

Once you have this starting position, work chronologically forward to your current portfolio role.

A few tips on adding these entries. When you add the position, it will ask for a title. Make this descriptive for the role and not just the position title the company gave you. For instance, corporations often have complicated position roles so internally people understand what division you are in and the level you are on. This is irrelevant outside the company, so just say what you did in plain language.

Each role should feature the company that you worked for with their logo. The logo will appear automatically if you type in the company name, but only if that company has a LinkedIn company page. If this is absent or they haven't added their logo to that page, then this will not appear.

Before there was the featured section, one of the key places to put images in your profile was in each experience area. This isn't used as much anymore, but you can still add this information. You can see from the below screen grab that I have included my hero video for my own portfolio business, which focuses on my speaking. You can add several images, but it can be more effective to just have one because it includes the written description of the asset.

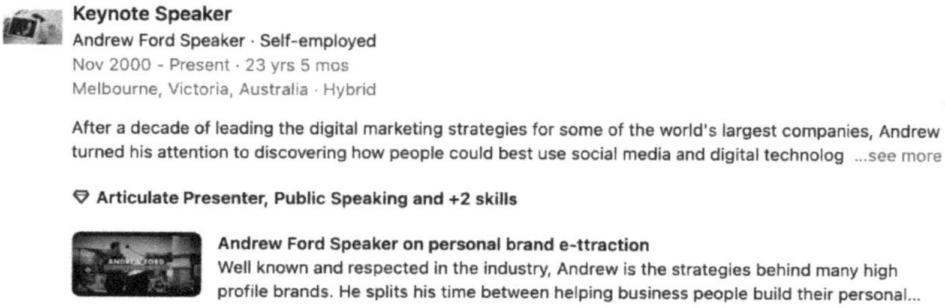

Keynote Speaker
Andrew Ford Speaker · Self-employed
Nov 2000 - Present · 23 yrs 5 mos
Melbourne, Victoria, Australia · Hybrid

After a decade of leading the digital marketing strategies for some of the world's largest companies, Andrew turned his attention to discovering how people could best use social media and digital technolog ...see more

♡ Articulate Presenter, Public Speaking and +2 skills

Andrew Ford Speaker on personal brand e-ttraction
Well known and respected in the industry, Andrew is the strategies behind many high profile brands. He splits his time between helping business people build their personal...

Figure 23. An example of focusing on a particular area of experience on LinkedIn.

The format of the written contents can be quite varied, but thinking back to our chocolate-cake recipe analogy, we will provide you with a basic recipe and you can change it to suit your specific requirements.

The usual format we recommend is to start with a description about the company you worked for. You can usually find this on their website or company LinkedIn page. Don't presume that your potential customer will know who the company is or the exact parameters of the organisation.

For instance, I had a client who was Human Resources Manager for Australia Post. Most people in my country would know who Australia Post is, but it sounds more impactful if you include the detail that they have 63,000 employees! That's an impressive statistic to include. This is only a few sentences to give a high-level overview of the company.

Then add what you did with them. What your role included and how it helped you be great at your portfolio business. Write in plain language, just as if you were sitting in front of your prospective client telling them about the role. This isn't your resumé, so avoid lots of text, dot points or key achievements. Don't sell yourself, explain yourself.

A relatively new feature in this section is the ability to attribute skills to each role. You can see this in my example, and it can be a nice finishing touch on each role.

Education

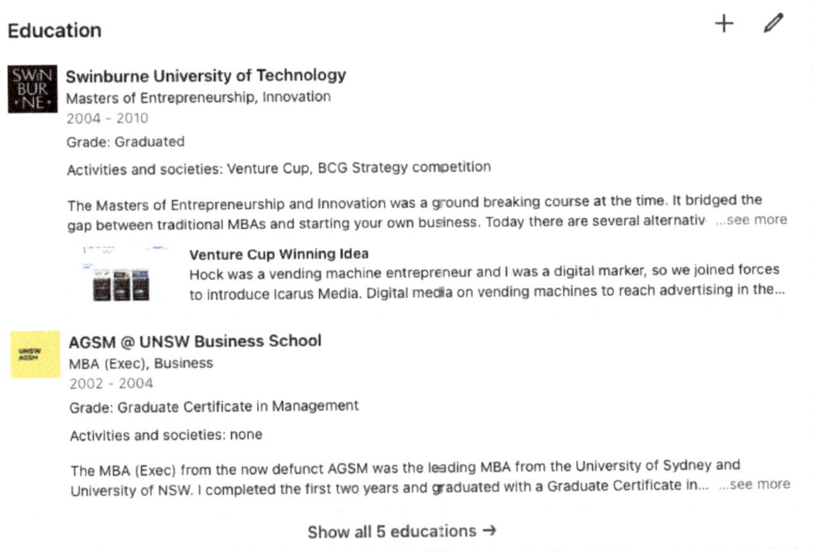

Figure 24. An example of listing formal educational qualifications on LinkedIn.

The education is also self-explanatory, but a very important one to do. If you are claiming expertise in a particular area, it's important to demonstrate how you arrived at that position.

Many of my older corporate escapees grew up in a time when getting a university degree wasn't as usual as it is today. Consequently, many don't have degrees and prefer to highlight their work experience. That works too, it just changes the focus of the biography and means we need to demonstrate external validation of the experience with more testimonials and skill endorsements.

I recall one client who was leading a very high-profile global company in a senior role. He was being pushed out and was considering a portfolio business but would not work with us on the process. He engaged and paid for our services but wouldn't listen to any of our advice and recommendations. He refused to promote himself and whittled down his biography to four lines of text. He also didn't want to include his work history or education. It was a battle from start to finish. I discovered through the mutual connection who referred him to us that he was embarrassed to have never completed any after-school qualifications, so didn't want to highlight his LinkedIn profile at all because people would discover his "secret".

Of course, this was only his perception, and he was going through a hard time, as it turned out, so I could understand his reluctance to participate. He was torn between his perception of being the big-time corporate executive, when he was being rejected from his business, going through a divorce and wanting to disappear from life, not put himself out there.

I have had other clients who only have their high school certificates, and we put this into your education if that is what you have. If you come from a humbler school, that's okay too, this demonstrates your grit and determination to build your career through hard work and smarts. If you went to a private school, we could use that to connect to the alumni from your school, which can be quite powerful. It doesn't really matter what the circumstances are, it's all your story and makes up your journey, we just need to explain it in context and use it where we can.

I recall an entrepreneurial event that I was invited to, which involved me joining a panel discussion around personal branding for entrepreneurs. One audience member raised his hand and asked me how he could possibly position himself when his life had been so complex. I asked him to explain his journey to the room, which he did in about two minutes. Then I asked the audience if they understood how he had arrived at his current position, and they did. Not very complex after all. People are smart and can figure out your story when you tell it honestly and provide all the information.

The worst thing to do is to skip things or not tell the whole story as it creates distrust, particularly if they find out after. Elements of your profile are conspicuous by their absence. Education is a big one in this area.

Note that education is for the *formal* studies you have completed: high school certificate, University or TAFE qualifications and so forth. There are other areas for certificates and skills.

When you format your education section, you have some room to expand on the degree and add more content, just like your experience section. You can add text and images, which isn't necessary but can be useful, particularly if you have a complex degree or made changes along the way.

For instance, I started an MBA (Exec) at the AGSM (Australian Graduate School of Management), a now-defunct institution that was a joint venture between the University of Sydney and the University of NSW. At the time I was enrolled, it was the highest-ranking MBA in Australia. I completed two years of this degree or four units, but then my company stopped paying for it and I decided to change course.

I graduated with a Graduate Certificate in Management and used those credits to start my Master of Entrepreneurship and Innovation (MEI) at Swinburne University, much more aligned with my values and personality. If you read my LinkedIn profile, I describe this course of events because it shows the journey from one to the other. It's not necessary for me to explain this transition. However, if I don't, some people might make their own assumptions and think it was too difficult for me to complete or something else happened. You never know what people will do to fill in the blanks, therefore, it's better to provide the content so they don't have to.

I also included some of my major achievements in the MEI degree – winning the Venture Cup pitch competition and also the BCG strategy competition, beating every MBA program in Victoria – as I am quite proud of them, and they reinforce my current brand position as a strategist helping people start their own businesses. It's one thing to tell someone you have done something and another thing to show them a photo of you doing it. So, a great addition to my education profile for the MEI would be the winning picture of the two competitions – how I wish I had these! Capture these moments when they happen because it's too late when you want them years later.

Licence and Certification

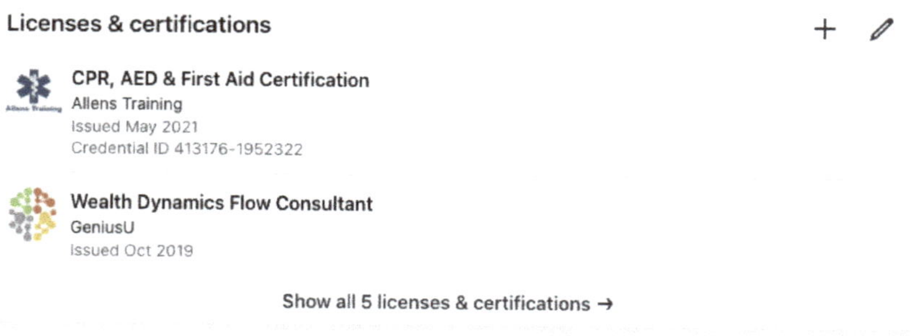

Licenses & certifications   +   ✎

CPR, AED & First Aid Certification
Allens Training
Issued May 2021
Credential ID 413176-1952322

Wealth Dynamics Flow Consultant
GeniusU
Issued Oct 2019

Show all 5 licenses & certifications →

Figure 25. An example of licences and certifications on LinkedIn.

This is an important section for those clients who have formal certificates for their profession. I work with a lot of finance professionals and there is a high degree of rigour to ensure they are legally compliant. Accountants can be certified by the CPA, CA or other group. Financial advisors need to be diploma-qualified and medical professionals have memberships in their related colleges.

Projects

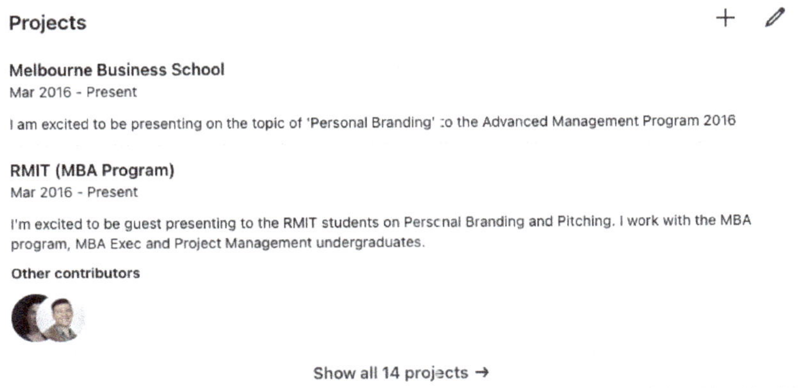

Figure 26. An example of projects listed on LinkedIn.

Projects are further down the profile and are only relevant when you have important ones in your history. For example, I have a client who introduced himself to me as a builder who wanted some support developing his profile to return to Australia after many years working in Asia. He was far more than a builder, as the projects were worth billions of dollars and exceedingly complex. He also had a master's degree and was an absolute global expert in his field. He had worked on several high-profile projects during his career, and we documented them using this part of LinkedIn, as well as through his experience section, ensuring we added images of the scale of the work he did, which was impressive to see.

Other project-related areas could be useful for architects, IT consultants, designers and more.

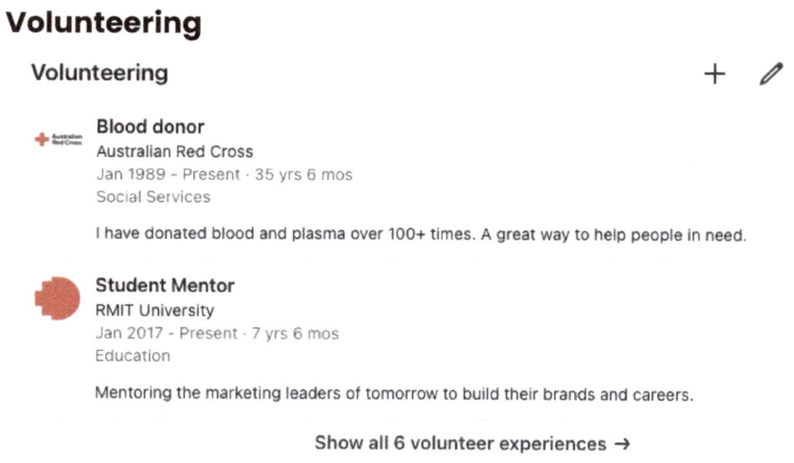

Volunteering

Volunteering   +   ✎

Blood donor
Australian Red Cross
Jan 1989 - Present · 35 yrs 6 mos
Social Services

I have donated blood and plasma over 100+ times. A great way to help people in need.

Student Mentor
RMIT University
Jan 2017 - Present · 7 yrs 6 mos
Education

Mentoring the marketing leaders of tomorrow to build their brands and careers.

Show all 6 volunteer experiences →

Figure 27. An example of volunteering listed on LinkedIn.

Adding areas that you volunteer provides a balance to your business-oriented profile. It provides some heart to the head of LinkedIn. Most people I work with have causes they support and work they do pro bono; however, they are sometimes reluctant to share this as it makes their charity work feel commercial. I understand the concern, so let me tell you a story of a wonderful CEO of a charity I worked with on her brand.

This lady was head of a charity helping the most disadvantaged women in Africa and doing remarkable work empowering them with entrepreneurial ideas and methods to raise them out of poverty. It was heartbreaking and heartwarming to hear these stories of women abandoned by their husbands and society, starting a business by saving a handful of rice a day for months to buy something small, then eventually trade up to owning a cow and possibly make a sustainable living. She also didn't want to promote herself because she perceived it as showboating and didn't want the focus on her, she wanted it on her charity. However, after some work, she realised that raising her profile could shine the light more strongly on her charity work and help even more women in the future. When the *why* is big enough, the *how* works itself out.

The same can work for you. The more you grow your brand and profile, the more you can shine a light on the causes you support. It could be the cancer charity you feel personally related to, the sporting team that needs volunteers, or the event that needs more donations. Whatever it is, be a real person and show some of your heart to your audience.

For me, I have a high value on being a dad, so I support my kids' football and basketball teams. I also have donated blood over 100 times, as I am fit and able to do so, where others can't, and I know some friends who rely on this to survive their afflictions. Finally, I have a high value on education, so I mentor many younger university students through the RMIT program and independently. I always feel I can do more, but with the time I have available, I do the best I can.

Skills

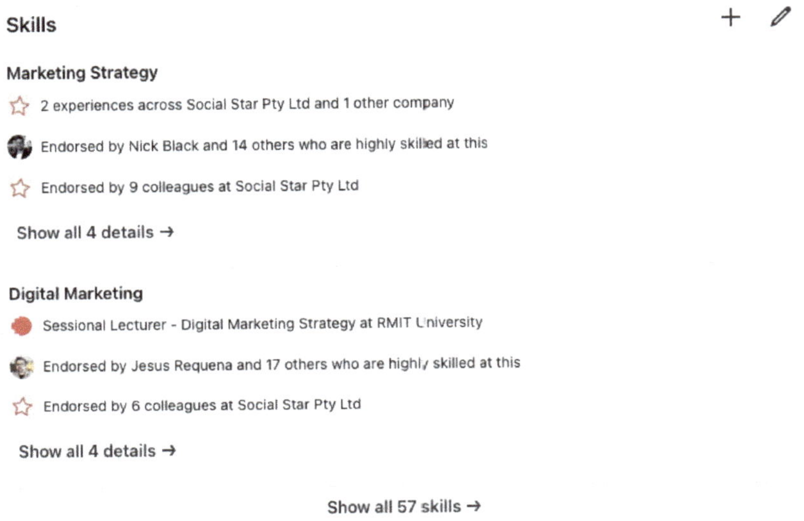

Skills   + 🖉

Marketing Strategy
☆ 2 experiences across Social Star Pty Ltd and 1 other company
Endorsed by Nick Black and 14 others who are highly skilled at this
☆ Endorsed by 9 colleagues at Social Star Pty Ltd

Show all 4 details →

Digital Marketing
Sessional Lecturer - Digital Marketing Strategy at RMIT University
Endorsed by Jesus Requena and 17 others who are highly skilled at this
☆ Endorsed by 6 colleagues at Social Star Pty Ltd

Show all 4 details →

Show all 57 skills →

Figure 28. An example of skills listed on LinkedIn.

The next two sections are about how you gain *social proof*. That means other people verifying your credentials instead of you just listing them. You can choose your own skills. It used to be the case that others would recommend you for skills, but now you can self-appoint them. Others will be asked to endorse you for these skills, and they usually do so when you have created content that they have enjoyed and found useful, or you have worked with them directly. Another reason why sharing long-form blog content is so powerful.

Being endorsed for skills doesn't make or break your content but it's another 1% item, and I would rather have hundreds of endorsements for the skills in the area I work in than none. Remember, only first-level connections can endorse you, so the more connections you have the higher the chance of having more skills endorsed!

Another relatively recent addition to this area shows that someone who is highly skilled in your field has recommended you – presuming that experts recommending you is more valuable than regular people. However, LinkedIn has been experimenting with this area quite a bit, so this could change by the time you read this.

Recommendations

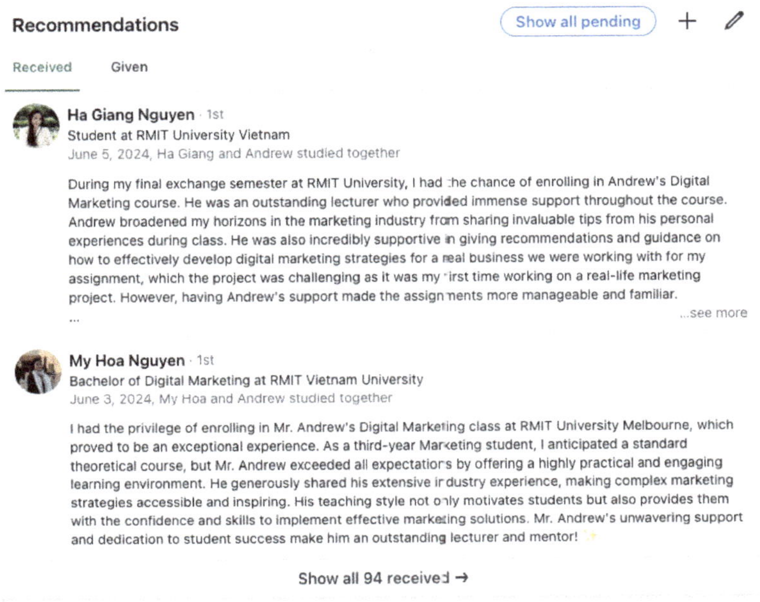

Figure 29. An example of recommendations on LinkedIn.

A more valuable form of social proof is to have people go to the effort of writing a recommendation for you.

This positions their face, current job title and words of recommendation on their public profile for the world to see. Because this is in the public domain, you can use this for your other marketing materials, such as your website, brochures and proposals. But it's always respectful to ask before doing so.

Unlike skills, you will have to ask for these recommendations because LinkedIn will not prompt your audience to provide them. Our advice is to act when a client or other stakeholder in your business proactively sends you a message thanking you for your great work. This could be verbally, in text message, social media or email. These messages are wonderful to receive but not that useful unless they make their way into your profile for your prospective clients to see. Therefore, ask them to do so.

The process is quite easy. Just go to that person's LinkedIn profile and click on the "More" button under their photo and select "Ask for a recommendation". LinkedIn will guide you through the process, ask how you are related and then provide a spot to write a message. If they have sent you something digitally, cut and paste it in here and make it easy for them to press a few buttons to complete the process.

It doesn't matter if the recommendations are for your current workplace and not for your future portfolio business, it's a reputation-building tool. I also suggest asking others in your network to recommend you, as you never know when you may need these. For instance, I lecture at a university and mentor a lot of students, so I ask them for recommendations. I have been doing this for years and then I started CampusLife a few years ago and these became very handy for our marketing. It takes a while to build your recommendations, so get them while you can!

Publications

Publications   + ✎

Our Infinite Power to Heal: 101 Inspirational Stories of Profound Healing from Within
Gower Publishing · Sep 20, 2019

(Show publication ↗)

Sharing 101 inspirational stories from everyday people, Our Infinite Power to Heal will show you that profound healing is possible. The stories in this book include healing from physical illness, bipolar disorder, depression, div ...see more

Build Your Own Business Podcast
iTunes · Feb 1, 2018

(Show publication ↗)

Andrew Ford is a corporate escapee turned entrepreneur. After years working in large global businesses and assembling a mountain of knowledge in the digital, marketing and branding areas, he decided to follow hi: ...see more

Show all 5 publications →

Figure 30. An example of publications listed on LinkedIn.

Yet another area designed for certain specialists. This can be used to list the journals, media contributions or books you have written. Writing something that gets published is a big deal, so it's worthwhile adding to your LinkedIn.

This can also include other new media such as podcasts or an application, if you think it's relevant to your audience.

Courses

Courses   +   ✏

Edward DeBono
6 Hats Thinking
    ⟳ Associated with Hewlett Packard

HubSpot
Inbound Marketing
    ☆ Associated with Social Star Pty Ltd

Show all 5 courses →

Figure 31. An example of smaller qualifications listed on LinkedIn.

This also relates to businesspeople with micro-qualifications they may have achieved. In the IT industry, where it's difficult for universities to keep up with the pace of change, these smaller qualifications can really help prospects see that you are upskilling and have credibility in your chosen area. Add the ones that are relevant to your field.

Honours and Awards

Honors & awards   +   ✏

Presidents Club
Issued by Hewlett Packard · Nov 2000
    ⟳ Associated with Hewlett Packard

Top 1% of sales people in Australia.

Figure 32. An example of honours and awards listed on LinkedIn.

Dust off those trophies and put them in this section of LinkedIn! Include work awards, so people can see that you were successful in certain areas, honorary awards for volunteering and more.

Test Scores

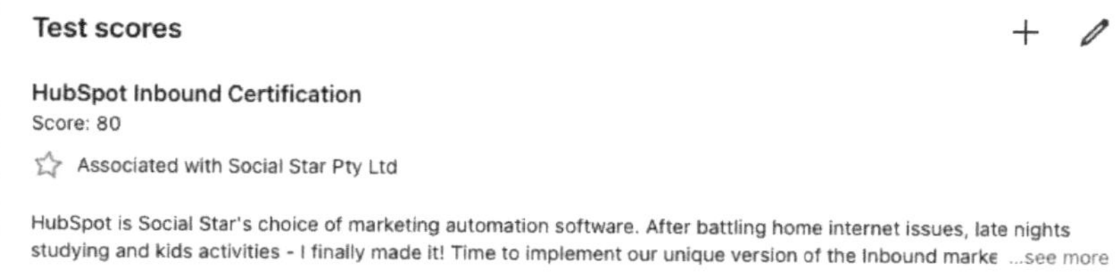

Test scores   +   ✎

HubSpot Inbound Certification
Score: 80

☆ Associated with Social Star Pty Ltd

HubSpot is Social Star's choice of marketing automation software. After battling home internet issues, late nights studying and kids activities – I finally made it! Time to implement our unique version of the Inbound marke ...see more

Figure 33. An example of test scores on LinkedIn.

Test scores are an under-utilised area of LinkedIn, but this is a useful area if you want to add something you are proud of that is relevant to your industry. I added my HubSpot score in here as an example, but this could be your English test if you are from overseas, an IQ score or something that makes you stand out from the crowd.

Languages

Languages   +   ✎

English

Figure 34. A listing of the languages you can speak.

This can be a powerful section if you are fortunate to be multi-lingual. I only speak English, but I put this in anyhow. For those with more language skills than myself, this is the time to shine!

One thing you could consider if you do work with multi-language areas is that you can have a mirror profile in different languages.

I have implemented this for a few clients who work between Australia and China, and it works well because LinkedIn is the only Western social media allowed there. So, it's a useful bridge to this nation. If you think the Chinese don't use LinkedIn, there were over 6,000,000 Chinese users at the time of writing. Not many compared to their population, but they would be businesspeople wanting to work with Western businesses, so a high-quality bunch.

Organisations

Organizations   +   ✎

Lenovo
Brand Ambassador · Sep 2014 - Present
☆ Associated with Social Star Pty Ltd

With the amount of time I spend online I need awesome technology. I am moving off the Apple bandwagon to Lenovo now as you can read in my blog https://www.linkedin.com/pulse/article/20140916132732-4042960-apple ...see more

Figure 35. An example of organisations you have been associated with.

This section refers to companies you have been associated with. I wouldn't put your employment record in here, rather organisations that don't fit in any other category. For me, I used this for the influencer work I did with Lenovo many years ago.

Conclusion

As you can see, there are so many areas of LinkedIn to explore and more coming out all the time, so keep an eye on the LinkedIn official blog https://www.linkedin.com/blog/member or your favourite LinkedIn specialist for updates.

To finish the LinkedIn Step, I want to talk about a few last areas of LinkedIn that we get a lot of questions about. The first of which is whether you should go Premium.

Premium

To go or not to go Premium, that is the question. To poorly paraphrase Shakespeare, this is one of the most common questions we get. The answer depends on your goals, which is why the first part of the Understand section is so important!

Most of the features of LinkedIn are available to non-paying members, so if you are using it to create content, connect to your network and in a business-as-usual manner, you don't need Premium. However, if you are in a growth phase and want to substantially build your network and conduct a lot of searches on people, then you will need to upgrade. We recommend the smallest business plan for our portfolio business clients.

LinkedIn will guide you through the process if you tell them what you hope to achieve. At the time of writing, the Business Premium was approximately A$74.99 per month, if you pay monthly or A$545.35 per year, saving 39%. You get a free one-month trial to see if it's worthwhile for you. Job seekers, salespeople and recruiters have their own Premium options.

I have been Premium multiple times during my business career, mostly when I was launching a new part of the business or looking to expand. Then I revert back to being a regular member.

Business Page

Another under-utilised area of LinkedIn, which is rising in prominence, is the business or company page. The culture of LinkedIn is about connecting to people, not following organisations, so it makes sense that this hasn't been the place users spend their time.

However, LinkedIn is trying out many new features in business and company profiles, which makes being present and active here worthwhile. Especially with the advent of being able to publish blog content and newsletters on the company page. The only issue is how to get people to follow you.

At the time of writing, LinkedIn allows you to have 250 credits per month on each company page to invite people to like it. So, if you send 100x credits out to people to like your page and 50x of them do so, you will get another 50x credits that month. But before you start doing that process, it's recommended that you first have a base level of really good content your followers might be interested in. Plus keep regular content flowing. That way, if they follow the page, there will be a reason to keep engaged. We recommend setting up your portfolio business profile on here, as it means you will have a nice logo next to your experience entry for your new company.

Once you have established your business and have regular content flow, then you can start to invite your network to like the page.

Showcase Pages

These are parts of the company profile that allow you to provide additional context on a product and service. These haven't proved to be super useful yet but, as we always say, better to have one and not need it, than not have one and need it.

If you fill in all these sections, you will be well on your way to a great LinkedIn profile. As much as I like LinkedIn, you don't own that platform and they can take your profile down at any time. Therefore, it's advised to put all your content on your own website, which you can control.

Step 6: Websites and SEO

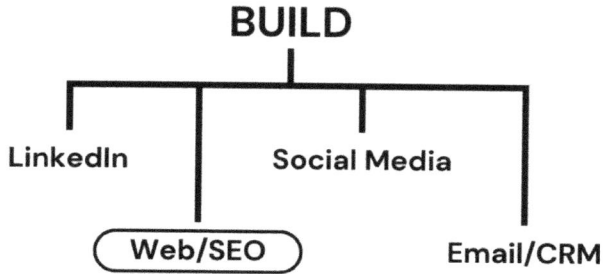

BUILD

LinkedIn   Social Media

Web/SEO   Email/CRM

Figure 36. Web/SEO is the second step in the Build section.

Websites are a necessary part of having a business. SEO is inextricably linked to how search engines rank them, so we will cover both in this section.

Websites

At one stage I remember social media pundits saying that you don't need a website, only LinkedIn and other social media. I didn't and don't agree with this at all. If you understand how Google SEO works, you will know that this is an important part of your strategy so you can be found online.

But as discussed, it's the digital medium you can own. If a social media channel decides to retract your profile, there isn't much you can do about it. This has happened several times to my clients, so it is a genuine risk we need to mitigate.

One client I had was travelling overseas to an Eastern Bloc country and being active on his profile, at the same time we were also doing LinkedIn Outreach for him and the bots at LinkedIn decided that he was being hacked and completely removed his profile. No warning, just removal with an email to notify him that there was a potential hack and to contact them for more information. It took quite some doing to get it back online, as he had to provide enormous amounts of identification and information to validate his profile, but we did it.

This was a good reminder that when building a social media presence, you are building a house in a rented space, and you can't totally rely on them for your business. Hence the need for your own personal website containing all your blogs, news articles, reviews, and a newsletter subscription so you have a database of your clients, your biography and photos, business services and more. Plus, you can do e-commerce transactions and make money from your creation.

Building a website is part of the business portfolio process and we use Squarespace as our primary platform. The reason we chose this platform over more traditional technology like WordPress is that it's global, secure, has great support documents, is easy to use, automatically updated and packed with built-in features. It's far from perfect, but we have yet to find something better for our clients.

We don't have the scope to teach you how to build your website in this book, however, we will talk through the key elements you should include and why it's important to your brand and portfolio business.

Personal v Business Websites

We make both personal and business websites for our clients. The difference is in the focus of the business we set up. At the end of the Understand section, we decided if you were going to start a cash or asset business. Sometimes this is enough to lean towards a personal website for a cash business and a business website for an asset one. But this doesn't hold true all the time.

Some businesses require the distance and protection of a company brand and website. Others are very personal in nature and feel more appropriate to be a personal website. We often start with a personal website and then, if the business progresses to more than the founder, we add a business website too.

A good example of this is our friend Andrew Baxter who I have mentioned before. We started with a personal website www.andrewbillybaxter.com.au and then, as his brand built and he added the 24 Hour Business Plan to his business interests, he built a company website. But importantly, he kept his personal website because it's his home base for all his past work and current interests.

If the focus is on you as an individual working as a consultant, speaker or coach, you may consider setting up a personal website. The URL would be www.yourname.com.au or similar.

It would contain a Home page, an About page that has a biography in the first person, a Services page that features what you do, a Blog for your content and a Contact page. This is the basic construct, and we often add a Podcast, News, Media or other pages as relevant to your business.

A business website has a similar structure, but the tone of the content is about the business, not the person as much. It will still contain all the founder's information in the About section and on the Home page, but it will also have a story on what the company is and how it helps the target market.

Domains

We don't want this book to be too technical since we suggest you hire experts to do most of the heavy-lifting of building your online profile, so you can focus on what you do best. It's inefficient to learn how to do everything yourself and you also will likely not get the best result. But you need to understand enough technical information to manage those suppliers, so it's time to tackle how domains work for this purpose.

A domain is the address for your website. It is the www.yourdomain.com.au that you need to own to set up a website. Without this domain or URL (Uniform Resource Locator) your website doesn't have a home.

We buy our domains from GoDaddy as they have reasonable prices, good business practices and great phone support. But there are literally hundreds of providers out there, so do your own research.

Once you choose a domain provider, ensure you write the username and password down somewhere safe! I have numerous clients who forget where their domains are registered and how to access them. They call me when their website goes down and they don't know why, and then we must spend a while figuring out where their domain is registered, where their website is hosted and how to access them. If this has happened to you, one way of finding where the URL lives is by using one of the "Who is" providers. This search feature can tell you with which company the domain is registered and who purchased it. The only challenge is if you have set the domain to private, which restricts this information from being public and me finding it for you!

Once you have a domain, you need to decide how to build the website. As mentioned, we use Squarespace, but there are dozens of website technologies and hosting platforms around. My only advice is that if you are not technical and your website builder is, ask them what is required to manage it after it is built. I have had many clients who have a WordPress website that is unmanaged and has issues, because they don't have the website builder on a retainer, so the site's plug-ins go out of date, causing a security vulnerability, and the website itself is not backed up regularly.

The bottom line is website builders like the freedom of complex software, but it's not a great solution for my type of clients because they can't run it after it's built. Hence, we use Squarespace.

When the website is ready to go live, we connect the domain to the website. If you use Squarespace and GoDaddy, the process is simple and very quick. If you use other providers, it can take 24 to 48 hours to process.

A fun fact about Squarespace websites is that you can have several domains pointing towards one website. So if you wanted to have www.yourname.com.au and www.yourbusinessname.com.au all pointing at the same website, then you can. But you must choose one domain as the primary or vanity displaying URL.

Another question we often get is regarding alternative domains like: .physio, .guru, .biz, etc. These are an alternative to the .com.au or .com addresses that are most common. People often choose these if they can't get the one they want in the more common .com.au or .com variety. Then they ask me if they will rank on Google as effectively. My response is to ask them to conduct a search on Google for the search terms most common in their industry and see if any of these alternative addresses show in the results. Usually, the answer is no, which tells you that these alternatives don't beat the traditional .com.au yet. It's always best to do these tests before you purchase your domain.

My recommendation is to get the traditional .com and the .com.au domain. I recommend using the .com.au as the primary domain for my clients who operate predominantly in Australia. It informs Google that you are an Australian company, which is important for geographic SEO, as we have already discussed.

Website Content

Once you have decided on what type of website, personal or business and have purchased your domain, the next step is to assemble your content. We will review several of the specific items separately, but this section will give you an overview of the process.

If you imagine building a website is like building a house, this is an analogy that might assist you in thinking about the process. You are super excited and optimistic at the start of the process. The desire is to get stuck in and build! But of course, there are lots of things to consider before you get to that part of the process. For your business, we call this the Understand process you have already read about. For a house, you will need to do your research on areas to purchase, cost per square metre of land, schools and facilities in the area. Having your vision, mission and goals documented will assist in the decision-making process. It's important to think long-term about your business and property as they are expensive and time-consuming to create.

Once you have this sorted, you need to think about the details and understand what the parameters for the house are regarding how big it will be, what materials you want it to be built from, the layout and who will build it. Similarly, for your brand, you need to know your target market and the type of business you will run, which will help you decide what type of website design and structure you will need, and who would be a good partner to build it with you.

I specifically say build *with* and not *for*, as you will need to be heavily involved in the process. After all, it's your brand and business, therefore the copy, image selection, colours and so forth should represent you. It can't be fully outsourced, so allocate time to be present during the process.

Then you get to the exciting part of breaking ground for your new house, and you see things progressing quickly. From a business perspective, this is when we start doing photo and video shoots, creating logos and brand guidelines, writing copy and doing wireframes (rough schematics or blueprints).

When you start to make the content for your website, you will use a lot of the assets we have created for LinkedIn, which is why we start with it first. You will have a photo, biography, key positioning statements, and a foundation blog. A website is a place to put content, so content creation is the key to a good site.

Then we create the menu structure and wireframes, which are diagrams of how many pages you want to have on the site and how each one will be set out. You can sketch this on a notepad yourself to get an idea of how you want your site to be created. We have a website brief document that we get clients to fill in to ensure we capture all these details well in advance. This will ask you to share websites you like the design of, so we can get an indication of your style and preferences.

Once we have a good feel of your desired style and structure, we choose a Squarespace template. There are a hundred to choose from, so our website team will choose this based on your brief and our experience with similar clients.

Logo

A logo is normally the first item on the list of assets we create. This could be for personal or business websites, as we can do both. The logo sets the tone for the colours, style and fonts that will be used on the website. We create a brand guideline document to capture this in detail, which informs the design of the site. On Squarespace, you can select the fonts for the entire site and colour palette and then it's all automatic when you add a new page.

Structure

Once the template has the logo, design parameters and menu structure, we can start to flesh out the content. We like to use a tree system for most websites. This means the Home page contains elements of each sub-page that link to that extra material. For instance, the Home page would have a short biography of you and possibly an image, then click out to the Biography page for a different image and full biography.

This means that a visitor to your website will be able to get a good sense of your brand and how you can help them from just one page, without having to click on multiple tabs. Since the advent of smartphones, people don't like to click and wait for the page to refresh.

Key Words

For most clients, they don't have any of the content for their portfolio business because they have worked in a company and haven't kept these assets up to date. We will build them step by step. It's best if you are fully involved in creating the words on these pages, because it's your intellectual property that we are positioning and the more you are involved in the process, the more it will accurately reflect your brand.

Every client has different skills and personalities. Some clients like to start writing content and get us to edit and refine it. Others prefer us to write the content, and they provide feedback and edits. Either way, we work back and forth to hone the words to be just right.

Chat GPT and other AI services can assist with the start of this process, but it will need to be reviewed and refined by both your agency and you. There is nothing like well-thought-out organic content with personality and real-life examples.

Images

The images need to come from somewhere too. For LinkedIn, we usually do a photo shoot of your headshots, which can work well for your About page, but we usually will require more images to flesh out the feel of your website.

I recall a client we worked with who was a business coach and we needed images for his personal website. He did most of his work face-to-face with clients in boardrooms and small team presentations. Not having any suitable images, we did a second photo shoot with him in a boardroom talking to clients (which was me and my staff). It was him presenting to us on a whiteboard, conducting a meeting in a nice building foyer and so forth. All the images on each page of his website came from this one half-day shoot and brought his brand to life.

Diagrams

Clients often have their own unique processes and ways of working. We work with clients to create diagrams for this, which work well on websites. These unique pieces of intellectual property will have names that can be trademarked and protected to ensure their uniqueness. An example of this would be from another client for whom we published a book. Andrew Phillips published *CEO-Led Sales* in 2023 after working with us on his brand for over a decade.

The key asset for his brand was his process diagram, which was central to the entire book and his consulting methodology. We must have created over a hundred versions to get it just right for all the different ways he ended up using it. Once we had this, it helped to create the structure of the book, and all his other materials came to life. You can see the diagram below and Google him to see his website for more information.[31]

THE RIGHT MODEL

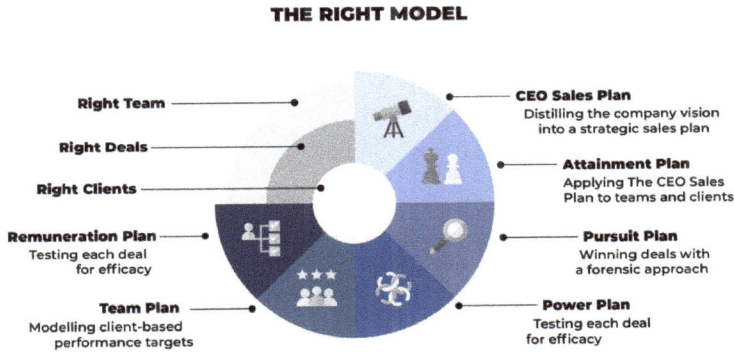

Figure 37. An example of a business model that a client created in collaboration with Social Star.

Icons

Figure 38. An example of icons used to visually represent elements of what a business offers.

---

31   https://www.ceoledsales.com.au/

Another useful item we use regularly is icons. These come in sets, so once we have a few we like, we can use others throughout the site and assets. These can be particularly handy for the services section. This is where we like to list three options for how to work with you. Three is a good number for websites and you will see us use this odd number of assets in a lot of areas. This could be three tiers of price points, three different types of services like speaking, consulting and board positions, or three ways of working like e-courses, group classes or 1:1 consulting.

Icons are a handy way to visually represent these different elements and make it easier to identify from a client's perspective.

Header

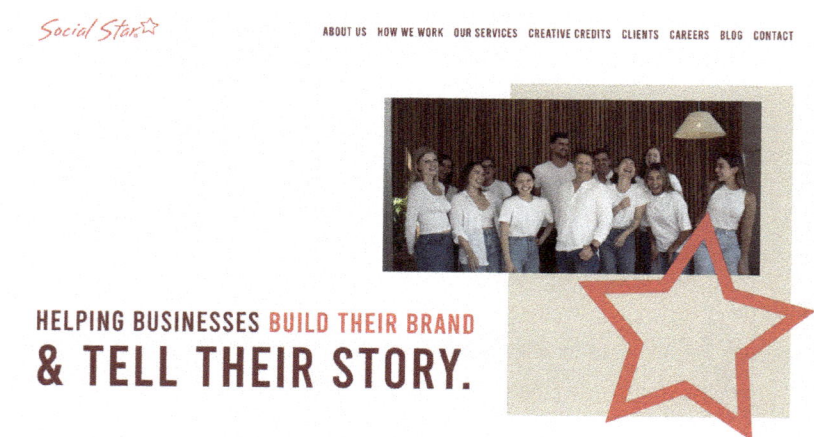

Figure 39. An example of a website header.

The header is the top part of your website and there are a few options for how we treat this area. It is usually visually appealing with an image, or series of images, or video to catch the reader's attention. When we first started building websites, we used to use a three-section image header that told the story of the business. Then we started to do a lot of video headers and now we are doing a lot of single-image headers again. This section always changes based on the trends of the time and technology. The increase in mobile search changed the way we optimised websites for this medium and reduced video usage. Whatever the strategy you choose, it's always better to use organic content rather than stock images or videos.

We often start by using one image we took from our shoot and then, if we get a better image, say of a book launch or large keynote speaking gig, we change it. Remember, we just need a basic site to begin with and can add more content as we work with more clients and collect more content from them.

Footer

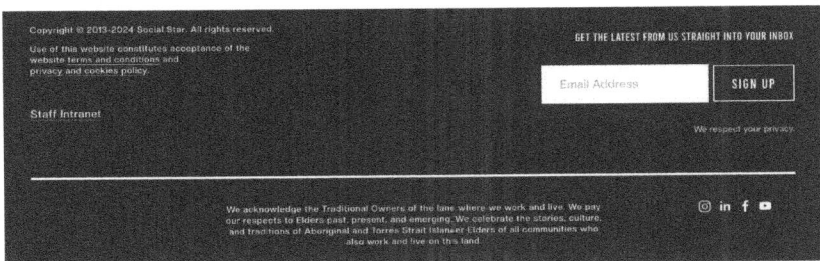

Figure 40. An example of a website footer.

The bottom of the website has a footer and has a few key mandatory elements. Your terms and conditions and privacy policy are important, as is your copyright statement. From there, a few other options can be used, such as a link to your social media, links to other website pages, email subscription and anything else you want to highlight that isn't in the main body of the website or header.

Calls To Action

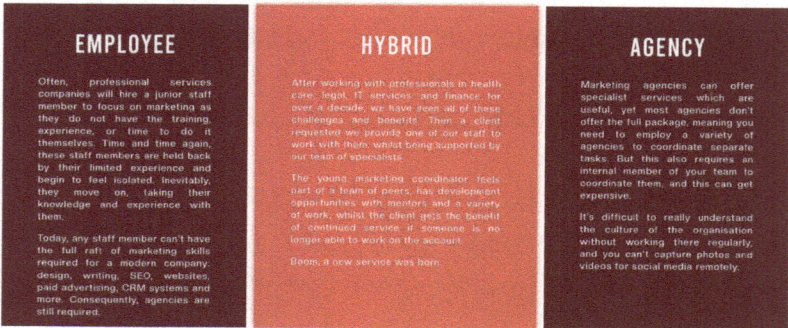

Figure 41. An example of Calls To Action on a website.

It is important to give due thought as to what the next step in your process is for prospective clients. If they are on your website, they are likely interested in what you do and if they want to know more, let's make it easy for them to find out.

Having CTA (Call To Action) buttons on your Home page is a good start, but where do you want them to go? We will cover this in more detail in the Close chapter of the Leverage section. The easiest link to take them to is your Contact page. We often start here on launch, but then work to create a more sophisticated offering for your clients. This could be a quiz, ebook, problem-solving video, webinar or many other options to get the prospect to spend more time with your brand. The goal isn't to sell anything at this stage, as we are looking to engage the person to see if they are a good fit with your definition of your perfect client. Our goal is to find long-term clients who refer you, so don't rush the process. If they are a good fit for your brand and business, then they will buy from you – you don't need to sell.

Mobile v Laptop

HELPING BUSINESSES **BUILD THEIR BRAND**
& TELL THEIR STORY.

TAKING CARE OF YOUR BUSINESS IS OUR BUSINESS

Social Star is a branding agency that works with business professionals to build their personal and business brands.

Figure 42. An example of optimising a website for viewing on a mobile phone.

One thing we often get asked is whether clients should optimise for mobile phones. The question depends on your target market and if they are more likely to look at your website from their phone or laptop. For most of our clients, they are the opposite of the current general norm, and our website stats show that the majority review their content on laptops. We still optimise the site for mobile, but it's not mobile first. There is a difference in how you lay out the content for mobile, so it's worth considering before you start the process. However, if your stats change over time, the website can be altered to be more mobile-friendly.

E-commerce

Squarespace has an advantage in that it has e-commerce capability out of the box, we just need to turn it on. You only need this if you want to sell something online and we usually don't have this on launch. However, as we develop systems and content, we can add this feature. For example, a lot of our clients have the first step in their sales process being a paid workshop or assessment. It can be more convenient to have this as a paid option on the website, rather than send invoices and chase payments. Particularly if you are going to be part-time and don't want to set up accounting software to do invoicing.

Other things we sell include books, group coaching subscriptions, courses and more.

Going Live

When the website has gone through the entire build process, and we have enough content for a minimum viable product, we will go live. We can continue to build draft websites in the background and keep updating the pages as required. But it's important to go live to get Google to start crawling the website as soon as we can. It's also important to communicate with your close network as early as possible, with your first version of the brand and website to gain feedback and start the revision process.

A lot of our clients are perfectionists and want to delay the website going live until they have the best content. But the best content comes from working with real clients, which we attract from the first version of the website. So, we encourage them to go live early and refine over time. We take this approach from the IT Agile methodology of "do, learn, revise and update", which you can infer from this diagram from The Association for Project Management.[32]

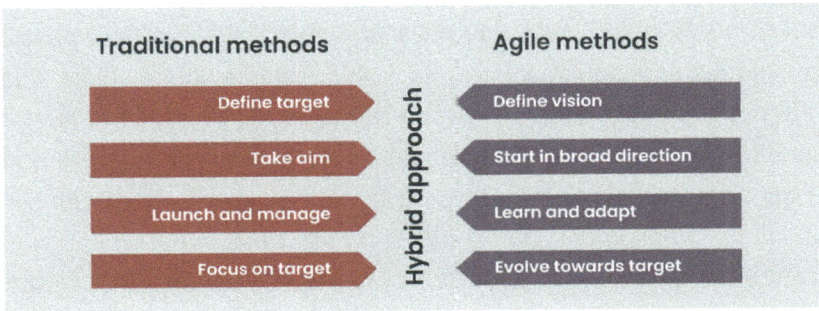

Figure 43. The IT Agile methodology from The Association for Project Management.

Things change as you run your business and so you will need to continually refine who your target market is, your offering parameters, and develop different assets.

The technical process of going live is very simple. At first, we will have the website in private mode. You will then need to put your credit card into the website to pay for the hosting and connect the domain to the site. Once this is done, we just flick a switch and – *voila!* – it's on the web.

But don't panic that everyone in the world will see it straight away. It will only go to people when you promote it, so you can share it with your close network first, then your LinkedIn connections, and eventually use paid mechanisms to get it to your ideal target market.

32   Association for Project Management (2016). *Agile project management.* [online] apm.org.uk. Available at: https://www.apm.org.uk/resources/find-a-resource/agile-project-management/.

Ongoing Maintenance

If you have a Squarespace website, you don't require any back-end maintenance. It is fully self-maintained for updates with technology and changes to SEO, and so on.

I recently had a client come back to me after we built a website for her six or seven years ago for some updates. The website was still performing extremely well, with her blogs bringing in lots of new traffic and it was ranking well in Google. We hadn't touched it for over five years, and it was still adding value to her business.

That said, you will require the occasional version update and change to content in order to ensure it meets the needs of your brand as well as changes to the newer styles of content. A once-a-year review and update would be advisable.

Now we know the basics of how to create a website, it's time to optimise it in search engines so your target customers can find it.

Search Engine Optimisation (SEO)

As mentioned, a website is important for SEO. For those uninitiated with SEO, this refers to Search Engine Optimisation, or how you can be ranked in Google and other search engines like Bing, Duck Duck Go and Microsoft Edge. For this book, we will focus on Google, as it's by far the most dominant in Australia and most of the Western world.

Google is the other master of the internet alongside Meta. It was first set up as a search console in Sept 1998 by Larry Page and Sergey Brin while they were PhD students at Stanford University in California. It was a very different internet site at the time. There was Yahoo and other search pages, but nothing as technical and easy to navigate as Google. It was the first to categorise webpages and decide how to rank them according to a user search. The other search sites had pages of links that they manually updated, which meant crowded screens and less opportunity to find what you wanted.

Google's strength was their investment in their algorithm, which made them the go-to search engine for the world. They also invested heavily in so many other cool things like Google Earth, Scholar, Maps, email, docs (replacing Microsoft Word, Excel and PowerPoint), Chrome browser, Android phone software and more.

These additional services, which are mostly free, keep you in their universe so you always return to their search page, which makes the most revenue for them (57% at the time of writing). Their other revenue comes from (approximately) YouTube 10%, Google Network 10%, Google Cloud 11%, and the other 10% from other products that include developers paying for software and users paying for the Google Workspace (formerly G suite) of professional email and related services.[33]

In October 2015, Google had a branding issue like Facebook and created Alphabet as a parent company to hold all the Google brands. This didn't change how it works, but it is interesting to see how brands grow organically and require a refresh of their brand frameworks.

Google is important to understand as it impacts a lot of the work we do with setting up a personal brand and portfolio business. A vast majority of people in Australia, 94% at the time of writing, use Google as their primary search engine, with Bing at 5%, a long way behind, in second.[34]

---

33   https://www.doofinder.com/en/statistics/google-revenue-breakdown
34   https://gs.statcounter.com/search-engine-market-share/all/australia

Now that we have reviewed a bit of the history of Google, let's dive into the key parameters for SEO that we need to be aware of when running our business. There are whole books on SEO, so this will be a summary of the relevant topics that will be useful in building your brand. Furthermore, the Google algorithm changes regularly so covering too much detail would make this out of date quickly, therefore, we will start with a high-level view.

Time

Google loves old content, it's a part of the algorithm that the longer it has been around the more Google knows about it and puts it forward for search results. This is one of the downsides of SEO, as it takes time to rank. Luckily, with a few ninja moves, you can help your content rise to the top of searches quite quickly.

Distance

Google did several large releases and named them with cute animals, perhaps to soften the blow to all the SEO agencies out there who based their work on the current version of the software. One of the larger ones was Panda in February 2011, where they sought to remove the "black hat" SEO techniques. Black hat refers to content farms that were creating websites that had huge amounts of content with keywords in them to gain a search advantage. The outcome of this change was that people started to create websites for the client's benefit with genuinely useful content and not just content to increase their rank and get sales.[35] This was the start of the *user journey consulting* or UX design that you might have heard from your agencies.

Next came the Penguin update in May 2013 to stop another black hat SEO technique of creating links in the back end of your website

---

35   https://www.searchenginejournal.com/google-algorithm-history/panda-update/

to gain a search advantage. This is when quality and genuine links from other websites became important. They also refined the fight against excessing content with more ways to stop keyword stuffing.[36]

In August 2013 Google quietly released Hummingbird. It was described as a total rewrite of the search algorithm to make it more precise.[37] This meant that instead of the search results being based on keywords, it now examined complete phrases to assess the websites based on their overall tone and context. Pretty advanced stuff!

From there, Google focused its attention in July 2014 on location-based search and they called this update Pigeon. This was partly in reaction to the advances in mobile phone technology, led by the release of the iPhone in 2007. The implication of local search meant that *where* you are when you do a Google search matters to your search results. Not just *what* you search.[38]

Since these four cute animal updates from Google (or would you believe three cute animals) there have been other updates, but none with names as nice and not as impactful to the overall search experience. The reason I put some history in here is so you can see the way Google works. They want users to have a quality experience and have relevant results. So, the way we work to gain SEO is to make your website useful for your specific target market! It's not rocket science, and many agencies overcomplicate the process. Our strategy is that there is no use having people who are not part of your tribe coming to your website, it's a wasted effort. This is why the target market and buyer avatar sections are

---

36   https://www.searchenginejournal.com/google-algorithm-history/penguin-update/

37   https://www.searchenginejournal.com/google-algorithm-history/hummingbird-update/

38   https://www.searchenginejournal.com/google-algorithm-history/pigeon-update/

important, as we need to understand what they want to read on your website so we can produce it.

The bottom line is don't try to trick Google, just work with them to produce meaningful content for your audience that they will find useful and are likely to read and share with others. Partners will refer people to your site, as it's valuable and they feel confident you will look after their customers, and these referrals are called *backlinks*.

Backlinks

When SEO became an industry, some of the leading providers created a thing called *domain authority*, which ranks your website against others in your space to measure which one is more credible. Moz was the first one to do this and Semrush followed soon after.[39] This isn't a Google solution but a way to analyse what happens in Google, so it's a useful indicator.

One way to build your authority is to have more links from other credible sites to yours. For instance, if you were a physiotherapist and you wrote an article for the Australian Physiotherapy Association and published it on their website and linked back to yours, that would be a great backlink.

Content is the key to getting more links and we can provide links to websites and ask for them in return. You can check your own website authority by searching one of the main SEO providers like Semrush or Moz.

---

39   https://www.forbes.com/councils/forbescommunicationscoun cil/2021/07/30/a-guide-to-domain-authority-and-how-to-boost-it-in-2021/

Activity

Being active on your website matters. Having regular content, like blogs, podcasts or videos, helps Google understand that you care about your website and its users. Plus, it's great for your customers!

Website Optimisation

It goes without saying that your website needs to be optimised for Google. Squarespace does a lot of the heavy-lifting here, with clean code and constant back-end updates. It also offers a suite of easy-to-use SEO features like page descriptions. We will ensure your headings and content are on point and your image's metadata tags are named correctly.

This is the tip of the iceberg for SEO suggestions and, if you are curious about learning more, there are plenty of great blogs and guides out there from HubSpot, Semrush, Moz and many others.

Getting an SEO Agency

SEO is one of the most misunderstood parts of digital marketing, which is why I wanted to break down the basics for you, so you have a general understanding of the key parameters. I wouldn't recommend you manage it yourself long-term, but having a certain amount of knowledge will ensure you don't get ripped off by unscrupulous SEO salespeople. There are a lot of people out there who promise the world but don't understand all the elements of marketing well enough to get the best results. For instance, it's all good and well to be found in Google, but if you don't have a clear target market and website that communicates your value explicitly to them, they will not convert. Most, not all, SEO agencies don't do this type of work. They presume you already have this figured out.

When the platforms are new, there is no rule book for these agencies, so they make up their strategies from trial and error. That's a natural way to learn a new space. The platforms don't provide access to their algorithm, so we can only interpret how it works by their guidance and through experimentation. After a while, it becomes apparent what works as the latest version of their algorithm gains currency in the industry. Google and other search platforms are quite mature, so there is a lot of data around about what works and doesn't.

To come up with a strategy, it's important to understand that different styles of businesses need different strategies. Product businesses require an outside-in marketing strategy, as discussed, this means they focus on the products first, then the business, and lastly the people. These products are often low-value purchases and people can make their choices based on the products themselves, as these provide the value they are looking for.

For example, I worked with a company in Melbourne that manufactured and sold meal replacement shakes and bars. These are high-protein, low-calorie products to help people lose weight. They had their own e-commerce website to sell directly to consumers, and had many pharmacy and other retail partners. Consumers would compare the product value based on the ingredients, price, taste and who recommended the product to them. It was a high-quality product, so many pharmacists and dietitians would recommend the product to their customers.

Therefore, the strategy for Google was to focus on searches like "meal replacement shakes", "weight loss shakes" and so forth. These are product searches. The first search category in the outside-in strategy.

Clients might also search for the product name or the business, which was Formulite, therefore it's important to purchase these words, so we can direct these searches to the right place too. Competitors can buy your name in their search and direct your traffic to their websites, so it's important to ensure you buy your brand search names, which is the second search category in an outside-in strategy.

The third, or last search category is the people in the business. This could be the founder, key staff or brand ambassadors. This is often not part of a product business strategy, as they don't feel it's required to sell a product, but it can give you an edge if you do it well. Founders who do this well are people with large personal brands, for example, Richard Branson. He is a very well-known brand, so when he launches a new division of his empire it grabs people's attention. Virgin Cola, for example, might be a great product, but people in the UK are only aware of it because it has the company name of Virgin and has the associated endorsement of Sir Richard.

Other companies, which don't have such a well-known founder, use paid actors as their company representatives. The AAMI Insurance lady has been a different person since the advertising strategy went live 12 years ago and has changed to keep up with the times.

Nespresso took a different tack and hired famous movie star George Clooney to advertise their coffee way back in 2012, and this consistency in their approach means he is always associated with the brand. This can be risky as you can't control your ambassador's behaviour, success or what else they endorse once you stop paying them.

For product businesses, the SEO focus could be product 70%, business 20% and people 10%.

For our purposes in starting a brand-led business, this style of SEO strategy is the opposite of our approach which, as I've said previously, is inside-out. Being a service offering, you are the only "product" and your potential clients need to compare you to the market to make their decisions. Therefore, your personal brand is the most important part of the mix, and we need to promote your name as the first search result we find on Google. If you Google your name, where does it come up? What would you like to appear? These are the first questions we ask clients when we are going through the Build phase of the program.

For most of our clients, we want their website to come up first and LinkedIn second. Other links to come up could be articles they have written, media appearances they have attended, awards won, podcasts and videos they have created. This is why we produce content as our main SEO strategy, as it works well for people-based marketing.

It's easier to own your name in Google search results than a product. This is the advantage of going with this strategy. For instance, if you are a mid-size accountant in an outer Melbourne suburb, then getting a search result for "tax return" is tremendously difficult because of the other 1,500 accountants that also provide that product (1,500 is the number of accountants I got from a simple search on LinkedIn of "accountants Melbourne").

Furthermore, when someone completes that search and sees dozens of search results, what will stand out for them? How will you convince them your solutions are a good fit for their problems? The truth is that most business for professional services comes from referrals. This removes the difficult and time-consuming research phase of the process, as you can get some trust from the person providing the referral. When referring these professionals, the vast majority will be to an individual name rather than the business name.

This makes sense as services are variable and so one person's delivery is different from another, even in the same company. If you had a good experience with your accountant, you might refer your friend to that person. From there, most people will then do a Google search on that person to see what they are like before contacting them. This is why you need to control, as much as possible, what those search results are.

However, it takes years to get your company and product names to mean anything to your target market. Unless you have had a hundred clients through the process, it isn't worth marketing because it's so new and isn't tried and true yet.

Those clients building an asset business will start hiring other people to run their business, which means their business and product names become more compelling and important, which changes the SEO strategy.

But at the start, your focus would likely be: 70% your name, 20% company name, and 10% product name. The opposite of a product-based business.

In the previous section, we reviewed some key elements of what Google looks like when ranking content for clients. Now we will review some of the other social media that can be useful to communicate with your target market.

Step 7: Social Media

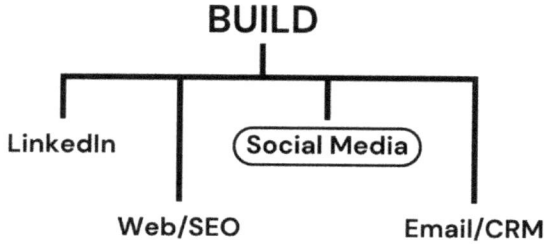

BUILD

LinkedIn   Social Media

Web/SEO   Email/CRM

Figure 44. The third Step of Build involves optimising your use of social media.

Social media is our next digital asset to tick off the list and it's a doozy! There are so many areas to explore that we can't possibly review all of them, so we will take the point of view that if you were building a personal brand for a portfolio business, what are you required to pay attention to? You might not need all of them, but these would be the ones to be attentive to, as they should be useful.

Some social media networks are too far out of our target market, so we will only refer to them in passing. There are also many new entrants to social media appearing every year. But the best ones are the long-standing ones, as they have the most people on them and the best tools.

Of course, we have already discussed the best tool to use for your personal brand, LinkedIn, at length so we will move to other social media networks.

For most of our clients, this section will be of interest, but not for direct use, as they will not require any of these to run their brand. For those clients, LinkedIn and their website will be sufficient.

But for others, one of two of these may become important. If you start to produce videos, then YouTube will become a factor; if you want to run paid advertising, then Facebook and Instagram can be relevant; podcasts require audio channels, such as Spotify and Apple.

Let's start with the biggest social business in the world, Meta, which owns Facebook and Instagram.

Facebook

Facebook is one of the oldest social media networks now. I'm sure you have all heard of Mark Zuckerberg and maybe seen the movie about his rise to fame and fortune called *The Social Network*. He has been at the helm of this network since the site went live on 4 February 2004, originally called "The Facebook" before it dropped the "The" to be known as Facebook forevermore.

I remember seeing it for the first time when I was in software marketing at Hewlett-Packard way back in 2005. It was only available in Ivy League universities in America at the time, and one of my technical pre-sales colleagues had been to the US on a business trip and had seen it. It looked less than impressive back then, but I followed the software with interest as I am always curious about new things.

Another interesting step in Facebook's journey was its Initial Public Offering, which is when they listed on the New York Stock Exchange, on 8 May 2012, for US$38 per share.[40] It didn't have an advertising platform back then; it was a free site that people used to connect and look at each other only. It set the value of the company at US$104 billion – yikes!

---

40   https://www.investopedia.com/ask/answers/111015/when-did-facebook-go-public.asp#:~:text=The%20company%20was%20founded%20in,around%20half%20a%20trillion%20dollars.

I chose not to invest and thought I was vindicated when the stock plummeted over the coming months. I'm so smart, I thought. "Where is the revenue model?" I would smugly ask my friends. At the time of writing, the stock price for Meta is US$530 per share. Oops ...

Another brilliant strategy honed by my MBA training was refusing to invest in Ponzi schemes. I was offered a chance to be a millionaire in about 2012 when a loose connection on Facebook offered me this crazy thing called Bitcoin for about $100 each. Ridiculous, I thought. "Where is the revenue model for that? You can't even spend them!" Glad I dodged that bullet as 1x Bitcoin is now valued at A$100,000. If I had trusted a few new things that I didn't understand, then I would be writing this on a gold-plated Mac right about now and enjoying my ivory back scratcher.

Alas, life is a fun journey of hits and misses and we must enjoy the rollercoaster of the process. Growing up through the digital revolution provided some perspective on the booms and busts of any new industry. I also saw many a friend lose a bundle on new tech ventures and start-ups. It's not all roses, they are fertilised on the soil of many a misadventure and ruin.

I have digressed, back to our old friend in social media: Facebook.

Zuck, as his friends call him, for many a year has overseen Facebook's growth from a way to connect with friends in college to the dominant force in online advertising. Many social media experts, me included, feel Facebook has had its peak and is in decline. But it is still the best advertising platform in the world and for my e-commerce clients, it outperforms anything else. It has the most data and allows you to target people very specifically. With almost 3 billion active users, it's a powerhouse and should be considered if you need to reach a lot of people.

However, be aware that it can be a divisive platform with many people using it to vent their frustration at life. They often take out their issues on unsuspecting businesspeople or advertisers. An example we had recently was a specialist doctor who created a podcast for general practitioners to educate them about particular conditions and issues. He makes no revenue from this process and he does it as a purely educational pursuit. He has a high value on Education over Money, as he must fund it.

The Everyday Medicine podcast by Dr Luke Crantock is followed by many medical professionals. They are traditionally very hard to reach in any digital realm, so we promote to them on LinkedIn and Facebook. The podcast came into being at the end of COVID, when there was still a lot of resistance to the COVID vaccine, and Facebook blocked all our podcasts interviewing expert scientists in the field. Then other podcasts that were not even related to the COVID vaccine were targeted by anti-vaccine advocates, who would write nasty comments directed towards the medical profession in general, like they were all in cahoots together.

Our approach to handling negative comments is to leave them if they are factual and a difference of opinion, but remove them if they are defamatory, personal or in any way offensive. Our clients are strong enough to manage a debate online, but not with people who are not willing to engage in a reasonable discussion and instead have the motivation to vilify a particular person or group. This raises a meaningful point: if you are going to create any social media site, you need to monitor it. It's easy to create social profiles, as they are free and simple to do, the challenge is to use them effectively for your benefit. Creating regular content, keeping it up to date and monitoring it is required to ensure it doesn't damage your brand.

Facebook has a few great features you can use, and I will cover them from a high level, as they are likely to change in the future.

Facebook Profile

The first is the basic Facebook profile, which most people would be aware of. This is your profile based on your personal brand. It has your photo and you would likely be sharing interesting information like what you had for breakfast and your latest holiday snaps. You need a personal profile to set up a business profile or do any form of advertising. This is how they know you are a real person and Facebook has tried to remove fake profiles.

We have had a strategy for some years of creating a fake personal profile for a business to manage all the company profiles and advertising that doesn't depend on one singular person. We do this because let's say the marketing person left your business on bad terms and had the company business page connected to their profile. They should have invited the business owner to be the administrator on the page, but let's say they didn't and left acrimoniously and wouldn't give you permission on your page, then it is very difficult to wrestle control off them.

This has happened to us with various clients, and it's best avoided by having generic company profiles that manage everything.

Facebook Business Pages

Once you have a personal profile, you can set up a business page. This is a page dedicated to your organisation and enables you to do advertising. One person can have many pages that they manage, and a page can have many managers. A frequently asked question is: If I set up a business profile and add other managers, do they have access to my personal profile? The answer is no. There is no connection between the two profiles. These profiles are free and relatively easy to set up.

The main reason to have a business profile is so you can boost posts and use the advertising features. This is one of the most useful features of Facebook, as it's still the best advertising medium in the world. Not for everyone, but it has the most reach, data about people and tools to target them.

To run a useful page, you need to post content. That means blogs, videos, pictures and so forth. The only people who will see this are your followers. Most pages don't have many followers so we can boost your posts to all the people on Facebook by spending a little bit of money. For between $50 and $100 you can usually reach thousands of people with your posts. It takes a lot of time and money to create content, so you might as well get some people to see it!

To do this, you have to be an administrator on the Facebook page and you will see a button on the post you have already made live. It will say "Boost" and take you to the options for how to boost your post. I recommend making it simple, select the cities you want to talk to clients in, and then either their professions or job titles. Don't get too tricky and add too many filtering options because people don't always have their full details on Facebook.

It's a volume game, so you want to spread your message far and wide in your geographic area. Please note that it doesn't mean they will see the post and consume the contents, it usually means they have an opportunity to see it when they scroll. That's why it's cheap to advertise. Think of it like a digital billboard on someone's phone. They may see it but could be distracted and not pay it any attention. Which is why we need multiple ways of reaching people.

Meta Business Suite

As Facebook grew their business and started acquiring other businesses, notably Instagram in April 2012 for US$1 billion, their branding didn't work anymore.[41] The product and business were both called Facebook.

So, in October 2021, Meta was created as the hero brand of the organisation. This made sense as it allows Facebook and Instagram to be stand-alone businesses. Meta runs each company's advertising businesses separately while it focuses on the "metaverse" – another business I don't think will go anywhere, but you never know!

Meta advertising accounts are full of features, and you can target people quite well because Facebook allows you to target someone based on anything they have ever put into their platform. I don't recommend this for our clients as it's mass advertising and is expensive due to the complexity of running the software. For personal brands and portfolio businesses, this isn't a fit. Boosting your posts is all you need. For e-commerce product businesses, Facebook is a great tool.

Facebook Messenger

This is one feature of the platform that the kids love. It's a super easy and free chat network that is keeping the product alive. I believe a lot of the user statistics Facebook sprouts is people using features like Messenger, in addition to Marketplace to sell products and events, rather than people scrolling their newsfeed. This means there are likely fewer people paying attention to your messages and advertising than they say. But there are still a lot of

41   https://www.business-standard.com/article/international/
      mark-zuckerberg-bought-instagram-as-it-was-a-threat-to-
      facebook-120073000324_1.html

people, mainly older people, using Facebook so it's a good option if that is your target market.

Facebook Groups

Another useful reason to be on Facebook is the group's feature, which is still very popular. It's free to set up a group and they have a lot of useful features, plus they were early to market with this feature, so a lot of people set up groups a long time ago and it's difficult to move them. As we discussed with our Mornington mortgage-broker mum, she used this feature to e-ttract all of her customers. However, be aware that to join a group, most don't allow you to market your services or target specific customers. This is *push* marketing and not the best way to engage the audience. Our way is to e-ttract them to you via referrals by answering their queries and questions with very friendly and relevant advice. That way people will see this and want to recommend you to their friends, a much more effective strategy.

Instagram

The jewel in the crown of Facebook is Instagram. Since they spent that lazy billion in 2001, it has continued to grow and be one of the most influential social media platforms in the world. It has a bent towards fashion, food and people showing off their holidays and other highlights of their lives.

The advent of Meta means you can create a post on Facebook and automatically share it with Instagram, which is a handy time-saving feature. The boosting of posts works similarly so you can do two platforms and target markets with one effort. Just remember that the content doesn't always translate, so ensure you match the requirements of that platform. Instagram started as a photo-sharing application for phones and has remained a mobile-first application. Remember the original logo of a Polaroid camera?

Facebook is a desktop application designed for computers that have multiple phone applications, so remember the shape of your photos matters. Instagram is portrait orientation and Facebook prefers landscape. It also means that to manage your Facebook profile and pages, it's best to do it on your laptop, not your phone. The opposite on Instagram.

Instagram has several different ways to share content. There is the *grid*, which contains the pictures you post and this remains on your profile. Then the *reels* are short videos that you post and can save, which are like stories but slightly different as they disappear after a certain period. Stories have a button on the application, so they are easy to find.

Instagram is incredibly popular with Gen Y and it can be very competitive to get ahead on the platform. We don't use it much for our target market as it's easier to use content marketing on LinkedIn, your website and email marketing to build your referrals. However, for certain clients, it can be useful too.

If you are targeting people on Instagram and want to build your brand with the younger generation, then I suggest you do some specific training on this, as it's changing frequently in order to keep up with TikTok and other competing platforms.

TikTok

TikTok is the choice of a new generation, as Pepsi famously sprouted in the cola wars. TikTok is a hugely popular phone application that took the world by storm in 2018 and has been pervasive since 2020. Owned by Chinese company Byte Dance, it's caused controversy as it's the first Chinese social media to challenge the USA's major technology companies.

Used by very young consumers, it has been criticised for its unregulated content and addictive properties. However, all social media applications have been initially adopted by younger consumers since Friendster and Myspace created the first online social networks in the early 2000s. As the platforms mature, they attract older and broader audiences and become useful for advertising. TikTok is no different and can be used to great effect for certain companies.

I don't recommend it for my clients unless they have a specific reason to create content on here as it requires a lot of personal effort. What I mean by that is my company can meet with a high-profile expert, record their videos in four hours and produce content for six months or LinkedIn, their website and even Facebook. Whereas TikTok requires the client to be in the videos and post far more frequently to gain some traction with the algorithm. Some influencers advise posting four times a day, which is a significant effort, as they also say that posting via the TikTok application and not via automated programs is best. This is beyond the ability for most businesspeople to achieve. This is also far too personal for most of my clients because you need to be in the videos, and they don't want to be so active in their marketing. But if you are a Star personality profile and love being in front of the camera, then this could be a niche strategy for you. Just ensure the platform suits your target market.

Twitter/X

This is another hungry medium that requires a lot of attention. This platform is good for certain sectors, such as the media, medicine, technology and influencers. It is more of a messaging platform than just content distribution. You share a tweet on your profile and others respond. It's expected that the person posting will engage with the responses to create the conversation.

The challenge for our clients is that it is difficult to respond to those questions or comments in an authentic way. It's also tough to outsource, so it's only recommended for people who like to use the platform themselves.

YouTube

Owned by Google, this is the world's most popular place to store your videos. It is a major player in the social media world and one that is more useful for distribution of content than engaging with people specifically. We do a lot of videos with clients and usually store them on YouTube – it's free and secure – then post these videos on their website, LinkedIn and other social platforms.

Unless you are a professional creator, it's unlikely you will get a lot of views on your YouTube channel directly. However, it does give you a chance to appear in Google searches because your videos can rank quite well if they are put onto YouTube with SEO in mind.

SnapChat

For the kids. You don't need to bother with this channel.

Pinterest

This could be useful for some of our clients, if they have a very visual brand. However, its history was founded in storing and sharing images on boards so you could create a vision board for things like weddings. It has expanded its offering but the majority of its content is fashion, food, holidays and other visual areas. Not quite a fit for information professionals unless you work in those industries.

Other

There are literally hundreds of other micro-sites that are competing for your attention. From gaming-specific platforms like Discord and Twitch, to chat boards like Quora, Reddit and Tumblr, plus many more – the list is endless.

We could also bundle in chat sites like WhatsApp and Telegram, but we must be practical in our social media offering and consider the big picture of how we best connect to our target audience without becoming overwhelmed by too many channels to think about.

As I said previously, a quality LinkedIn profile, website and regular content shared on these platforms in a way that Google will effectively rank you in your niche is plenty of digital for most people. Focusing on quality content and becoming well-known with your small group of clients is better than spraying the world with your mass content. We call this strategy *inside-out marketing*, and we will go into depth on how to do this in the Leverage section. For now, let's examine Email/CRM.

Step 8: Email Marketing/CRM

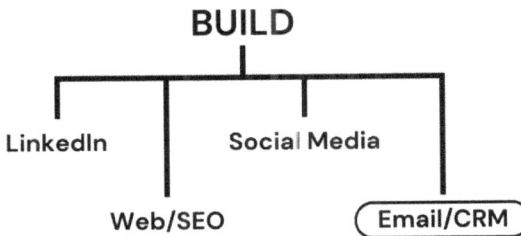

BUILD

LinkedIn   Social Media

Web/SEO   (Email/CRM)

Figure 45. Email and Customer Relationship Management are covered in the fourth Step of the Build section.

Email marketing is an effective way to keep in touch with your community who are in your hot zone and current customers who have purchased your products. It is a very versatile and low-cost way of sharing your message, but is often an under-utilised tactic of marketing for people running a portfolio business. Let's explore how this solution can be used effectively and some tools and techniques that are required to run this well.

Email Marketing

Most people get far too many emails and do not like to be messaged unnecessarily, so be wise with your strategy. Think to yourself, what emails would your customers value? How does it help them? Will it add value to your brand? Apply common sense to your strategy and treat your database like they are real people in your network – because they are!

There are many strategies you can use, depending on your business type and size. Product businesses are very different from services businesses and our recommendations are all on the latter, as that's our focus at Social Star. Follow these steps in our process to set up your CRM (Customer Relationship Management) and get your database working for you.

Action 1 – Choose a Strategy

For most of our clients, email is a small part of their overall marketing strategy. They are looking for more referrals from people in their network, so email forms one way of contacting your existing network. With email open rates ranging from 20–50%, you know only a portion of your network will read them. That is why we publish the same content in multiple places – LinkedIn, Facebook, Instagram and email – so people in your network have the best chance of seeing the content in a place they like most. This is the number-one strategy to communicate to your current network, who are likely to be current customers or trusted people in the Hot zone. The secondary strategy is to collect new subscribers who visit your website. They will be Warm, as they are on your website already, and you want to add ways for them to learn more about you so they can form trust.

Action 2 – Choose a CRM

Having a quality CRM is a must for any business. If you are starting your business, many companies offer a freemium model, which means you can use many of the features for free. They bank on you keeping their product for the long-term and upgrading to additional services when your business grows.

Social Star became a HubSpot partner many years ago and we have been recommending their software to our clients. It's highly secure, easy to use and has great training and support. However, it can also get quite expensive to use, depending on the number of people in your database and the range of features you want to utilise. It is also complicated to set up and you might need some expertise to help with that.

There are many great CRM platforms to use, depending on your budget and requirements but, whichever one you go for, ensure it has good reviews and great support services to help you through the process. Some focus more on email marketing specifically, others are great for sales management, and others for tracking social media results. Do your research and do a trial before you fully commit to integrating it into your website and business process.

Action 3 – Create an Opt-In Process

The recommended way of getting Warm people to choose to be part of your database is to set up an opt-in function on your new website. This can be done many ways, depending upon how you structure your website. Some websites have dedicated landing pages for valuable content like an ebook and, if a person wants to download it, they need to give you some of their details and subscribe to the database. Others produce regular content and choose to have an opt-in at the end of the page so, if the content is liked, then people can opt-in to get it emailed to them. Another way is to have a pop-up window that encourages people to opt-in for some type of benefit, like free content or a discount on the customer's first purchase. Some have all three!

Whatever your choice, it's important that you have a way for customers to take the next step in the buyer journey by telling you that they want to hear from you. People on your email list who are actively engaging in your content are far more likely to purchase from you than social media followers, as an email is seen as a more personal way of connecting. They are trusting you with their information, and we should respect that and add value in our content. Part of this is having a fair and reasonable opt-out process.

Action 4 – Clean Opt-Out

There are specific laws in each country that apply to this form of marketing. Unlike social media or websites, which have less regulation, email marketing has very specific and serious legislation attached to it, which we will review in the following section. The most important of which is the Spam Act.

In Australia, the *Spam Act (2003)* is the law you should read and understand.

Specifically, it says: "The Spam Act prohibits the sending of commercial electronic messages via email, SMS, multimedia message service or instant messaging without the consent of the receiver."[42]

The *Privacy Act (1988)* is also something to review because it has related items to consider in your communication. "The definitions of 'consent' in the Privacy Act and the Spam Act are broadly consistent. The Privacy Act provides that 'consent' means 'express consent or implied consent'. Under the Spam Act, however, consent can be express and inferred, although it may not be inferred from the mere publication of an electronic address."[43]

I am not a lawyer, but I will paraphrase how I understand these sections – and you are free to get your own advice. In essence, you can add to your database anyone who has opted into your communication specifically or has/had a commercial relationship with you. So, if they buy something from you, attend one of your events and provide an email address as part of the registration, then you can email them.

Alongside ensuring you use a quality CRM system, you should always have a clear and easy-to-see "Opt-out" button at the bottom of all messages. This should be a one-button opt-out that doesn't ask people to log in to your CRM or anything tricky. I personally hate it when people make the opt-out so opaque to stop you from pressing it. Like making it dark grey text on a black background. Or sometimes they have a convoluted process in a vain attempt to keep you on their email list. If someone doesn't want to be on your

---

42   https://www.alrc.gov.au/publication/
     for-your-information-australian-privacy-law-and-practice-
     alrc-report-108/73-other-telecommunications-privacy-issues/
     spam-act/)
43   https://www.alrc.gov.au/publication/
     for-your-information-australian-privacy-law-and-practice-
     alrc-report-108/73-other-telecommunications-privacy-issues/
     spam-act/

email list, there is no point in keeping them on it. Let them go. The goal is to have a small number of people who want to hear from you and want to read your information because they are true fans.

Overseas the laws differ, so if you have an international client base, then you need to get some advice on each country. Europe is known for having quite strict legislation on spam and privacy, so be extra careful operating there. Your CRM will provide some level of guidance on each geography that is helpful.

Action 5 – Email Content and Frequency

Once you have a few clients on your email list – either through opt-in directly or customers who have a business relationship with you – then start by sending one email a month with your blog. This will keep your database clean because those who don't want to receive this email will opt-out. That's okay, don't take it personally, just realise that it's feedback and not everyone wants your information.

Once you have established a regular cadence, we advise monthly emails to your whole database and then more niche emails to specific audiences as required. As your emailing list increases, you can segment your database into groups. This can be to different target markets who want different information or are interested in different services. For instance, you might have people interested in your board roles and advice around that part of your business. A different group might be interested in your advice and services around speaking opportunities. An example of this is a specialist surgeon client we have who wanted to better communicate with his target audiences. He split his database into two groups: GPs who refer to him; his patients. Using the same CRM software, HubSpot, in this instance, we created two different lists. Then we created one email newsletter a month. The template was designed the same and some of the content was the same, which enabled the team to build one newsletter, then duplicate it and modify the content for each target market. This saved time and still made it relevant to each list.

Action 6 – Automation

When you have a few people in your database and are used to the software, you can try some automation to save time. I advise my customers to do this slowly and carefully, as it can lead to customers feeling like your emails are impersonal, if done poorly. A lot of marketing agencies that are used to dealing with product companies will want to send emails very frequently and start pushing sales. This isn't appropriate for professionals, so keep your automation light.

Our recommendation is to automate standard processes first, not sales promotion. For instance, when someone subscribes to your email list send them an automatic email saying thanks and letting them know the frequency of your emails. If you have a book and someone orders one, then you can email them saying thanks and inviting them to join your database. After you do an initial call with a client, you might have a three-email sequence that provides them valuable content such as a relevant blog, podcast episode or ebook to prepare for their next steps. Finally, before you conduct a strategy session, you could send them an email with preparation for the meeting.

When I mention automation, this doesn't necessarily mean that they happen without your involvement. It could be that these are pre-written emails that you can easily send with one press of a button. You might modify the email slightly if the circumstances permit, or your CRM can personalise the name only. Once you have used this process for some time, you can set up automated emails like the sequences I mentioned. This is more advanced and it's important to keep an eye on this, because I have experienced many issues when you forget the sequence is unfolding after someone has opted out, changed circumstances or drifted off the normal course. This unveils that these emails are not personal and could reduce your brand trust in the eyes of the customer.

There will be an organic evolution in your database list as your business grows and develops naturally. Remember that your tribe are your customers and the lifeblood of your company, so treat them with respect and add as much value as you can. If you take this approach, you will build a valuable resource in your database and email marketing will be a very useful part of your business.

CRM Sales Process

A good CRM can be very useful to store notes and details about your clients during the sales process. It is secure, more so than a spreadsheet, and has a bunch of good features that can keep your sales process on track.

When we refer to sales in this way, it's more about tracking the people who want to work with you through their buyer journey. A great investment for any early-stage business is to do a client-journey mapping session to understand your client's experience. This is only useful once you have been running your business for several years because you have to have real experiences with your clients.

At the start of your business, we set up your CRM matching our e-ttraction four-step sales process. The four steps are Cold, Warm, Hot and Sale, which we touched on in earlier sections. At each phase, there might be several subsections of the process, all of which can be programmed into your CRM so that when a prospect does an action, you can move them through the journey. The 10 steps we use are all listed in the Hot section below. This is useful because you will see the progression of your deal flows and get to better predict your revenue. You can also track your win/loss ratio and document why the prospect became a client or not. By understanding at which stage they dropped out of the process, you can make improvements to your systems. Understanding your sales is vital to the success of your business because without clients you don't have a business – it's a hobby.

A common sales flow we set up for clients would look something like the following.

Cold

At the Cold stage, your paid advertising, social media, and website SEO are tracked by Google Analytics, social platforms, your website software or CRM. There is a lot of data you can access and it's hard to put it all in one spot to know what's working and what's not.

As these are Cold prospects, we don't track them individually because we don't know who they are until they directly engage with our content. You get a great overview of what works and what doesn't, but no specific information as privacy laws mean we can't identify any specific individual. We get an IP address only, so we report to our customers the total views of their content on social media and advertising reach.

Warm

At the Warm stage, you can see how often the prospect interacts with your website and which content they are engaging with. For example, if they read your blogs and download your ebook, then you can see this data. Your website analytics can also provide many statistics that are useful and complement your CRM statistics. Specifically, what we report on is how many people liked, commented and shared your content on social media, and then those that clicked on your links to visit your website.

When they get to your website, I like to use the built-in Squarespace analytics because they have heaps of data, which are very well laid out and easy to access. The three most important data points are: how many people visited in total, where they came from (which social media or other content), and where they went (which pages of the website were they most interested in).

Hot

The Hot zone is where your CRM adds the most value. When a customer subscribes to your email list, buys a pre-product or enrols in a course or webinar, you know they are keen. This is the representation of trust. They like you and think you are credible. Once they have taken this step, you can see a lot more of their intentions. The data moves from an IP address hitting your website to a person interacting with your website.

For instance, we can see if a real person has opened an email, and how many times. We can see if they clicked on any of the links and which pages on the website they visited and how long they spent on each page. Very useful to gauge their intentions. We can also see when they come back to the website, if they engaged on our social media content and more. It brings to life our data, as it relates to a specific prospect, and we can categorise these into groups of customers related to our target markets.

Only when a prospect books a meeting, or you receive a referral, do we start to track them in the CRM. The stages of the tracking process are:

- 20-minute introductory call

- 1-hour understand call

- Quotation

- Closing call

- Quote accepted

- Invoice sent

- Invoice paid

- Onboarding meeting booked

- Onboarding completed, or

- Deal Lost.

I like to see these in a table view, so I can easily see how many people I have in each column and the total value of deals in each stage of the process. As they move through the stages, the details become clearer, such as the amount of money the deal is worth, timing of the start date, and specific solutions to deliver.

Sale

Finally, in the Sale zone, when they are a customer using our products, it's much easier to measure their engagement over time to ensure they keep connected to us. This measurement helps us produce content that is relevant and useful to them. Our customers are our most valuable resource, so it's important to keep them engaged and connected. Which is the main purpose of the email list, to keep our current and past customers up to date with the developments in the business, so they can keep using our services and refer others as well. To review how the entire build process works for a real customer, we will review one of our long-standing clients and their journey building their brands.

Case Study: Dr Luke Crantock

Building your personal brand requires time, effort and persistence to create a range of online assets that will accurately and thoroughly represent who you are. There should be enough content in a range of formats so that your prospects can get to know, like and trust you. One client who exemplifies the Build process is Dr Luke Crantock. I met Dr Luke many years ago when he was introduced to me by a client I was working with at a different hospital, Dr Stephen Nutter. I had recently completed Dr Stephen's LinkedIn profile and when Dr Luke mentioned he wanted someone in marketing, Dr Stephen thought of me.

I had an initial phone call with Dr Luke to assess his requirements and fit for our process. His goal was to improve his brand and that of his company GI Health, a gastroenterology practice in the outer suburbs of Melbourne, for an eventual exit sometime in the foreseeable future. He had his own day-procedure facility to do scopes called GIH Access Endoscopy, so there were a few brands to work on. We followed the usual Build process of LinkedIn, websites/SEO, social media and email marketing. From a personality perspective, we hit it off immediately. He is very creative and outgoing. Quite the entrepreneur, he had a lot of innovative ideas on how to grow his business and it was clear he worked hard at whatever he focused on. We had a lot in common from a lifestyle perspective: we liked to exercise, travel, learn new things and enjoyed our non-work conversations.

Please don't underestimate how important it is to enjoy the company of your clients. When you work for yourself, you can choose who you work with and that's a blessing and a major difference with a self-run business, compared to working for others. It's joyful working with people you genuinely appreciate.

One colleague described it to me as the beer-and-puppy test. If you would have a drink with your client on the weekend and trust them to look after your puppy, they are a good client.

Once I had the commercial arrangements clear with Dr Luke, we started working on his brand. To kick-start the process, I worked with him on his LinkedIn profile, as it's the best collection of assets and gets the most SEO of any social media when you search for a person. He didn't like his headshot, so we arranged a photo shoot, and it made sense to capture all of his doctors since we were going to set up for a shoot at his practice. So, we started working on all the LinkedIn profiles of the doctors at his clinic, which led us to revamp the clinic's website too. Once you have improved assets of photos, biographies and graphic design, you might as well utilise them across all of your digital assets. We consistently updated his website with new content as new staff were employed and left the business, new procedures were implemented, and content was created.

Dr Luke is creative and isn't afraid to try new things, so we experimented with some different formats of content to engage his audience of GPs. Some projects worked well and some experiments didn't. We first published some blogs to position him in his industry. This was followed by the launch of his podcast *Everyday Medicine*, alongside face-to-face events, videos and regular posts.

Of all the work we did together, the podcast was the most successful. Dr Luke has recorded over 150 episodes at the time of writing and each one is thoroughly researched and professionally interviewed. He has a gift for finding interesting medical professionals and exploring topics of interest to himself and his fellow doctors to make learning interesting. The main audience is doctors, but patients also listen to the podcast. As it is medical-related, some patients aren't able to understand all of the information but, even so, it still develops the perception of him being friendly and an expert at what he does. Even if a GP or a patient doesn't listen to the podcast, just having one sets a certain appeal of standing out from the crowd and being good at what he does. Just like writing a book provides weight to your brand, a podcast has equivalent value when you have produced over a hundred episodes.

The videos we worked on together have taken many different directions. From recording patient information videos for his GIH Access Endoscopy website – which saves staff time explaining certain aspects of the treatment – to recording commonly asked questions and now short TikTok videos. We are regularly creating different content for different purposes. The goal is to save staff time and add value to clients, so they have a better experience in his practice. This is one of the key benefits for professionals in their branding – saving time is sometimes more important than attracting clients. The future of our work together is now moving to writing books. Dr Luke has several concepts to explore, from diet and cooking, to understanding digestion and how your body works, to lifestyle books.

The books will have an audience due to his work on the podcast and videos. Having built his brand over the years, he can now launch new businesses and know he has a willing audience who already like and trust him to deliver quality information that is easily digestible. One thing is clear, Dr Luke epitomises the content creator who truly builds his brand for future benefits. He now has digital assets that anyone who wanted to buy and run his company can easily take over. The websites are modern and up to date, he has a significant amount of content that is useful in differentiating his business compared to others, and he has implemented a CRM database in tandem with a range of social media profiles. It's exit ready.

Furthermore, if Dr Luke wanted to then set up a portfolio business by sitting on boards, doing consulting, speaking, writing books and so on, he has the personal brand already set up to do so. It would be an easy transition to move to the next phase of his working life.

After spending time Understanding yourself more deeply, deciding what you really want and Building an online set of assets to help you position yourself in the market for your services, it is time to Leverage that work. The Leverage process is where the real action starts with your personal brand and portfolio business. It is where you put yourself out there to clients and get your hands dirty, if you like. To use the NASA analogy, we've counted down 3-2-1 and it's time to launch!

PART 3: **LEVERAGE**

e-ttraction® Method

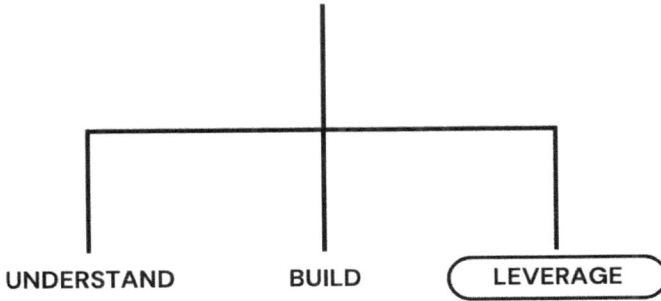

UNDERSTAND BUILD LEVERAGE

Figure 46. Part 3 of the e-ttraction Method is Leverage.

`used to run this whole process (Understand/Build/Leverage) face-to-face in a university format. It had online videos as lectures and a three-hour tutorial each week for the 12-week semester. It was a good test of the whole format, and what was interesting is that, depending on the personality of the attendee, they all had a favourite section. Scme preferred the Understand section because they enjoyed the introspective nature of that stage. Others liked the Build section because they enjoyed technology and digital creation. Some preferred this last section, Leverage, as they enjoyed creating content and networking. Extroverts like getting to face-to-face, whilst introverts prefer to network from their offices. There is something here for everyone.

As with the Understand and Build sections, the Leverage section has four Steps: Content, Connections, Pitch and Close. However, before we get started, I want to alert you to some of the risks of getting out there that I have experienced during my decade of coaching people through this process. Up until now, the work has been theoretical, but here we are talking to real people and making the whole experience real.

Risks of Getting "Out There"

The Leverage section is when people can get nervous about putting themselves "out there". It can be quite a departure from our client's previous roles of leading organisations to being the lead of your own portfolio businesses. Writing content from your point of view and asking people to connect with you is quite different from your marketing department writing for business- and sales-making connections with people. It can be confronting because there is nowhere to hide.

If your content is criticised or people don't want to be part of your network, many people take it personally. It's hard not to when it's all about you. I encourage my clients to consider it from a different point of view. In the context of your portfolio business, it's not you, it's the business avatar of you. We need to establish a brand separation in your mind, so we can progress the work without the ego getting in the way.

When you have been around a while, you learn to put up shields to protect yourself and place barriers between your business persona and your personal life. It's a porous shield because we still need to show our vulnerabilities and authenticity, which helps us connect to our audience. But it does protect us with some Teflon, so the negativity of others doesn't stick to us. I coach people to see the reality that when others are critical of your new portfolio business, it's often jealousy that they are unable to build the courage to do it for themselves.

If you launch something new and interesting, others will compare themselves to you and feel triggered emotionally that they are not doing as well in their lives. Some will wish you well and pretend to support you, but they are neutral toward your brand. They will support you by buying your book, recommending friends to use your service or coming to your presentations. Strangely, these are often the people closest to us like family members, siblings or good friends. Even partners can be negative towards your change in lifestyle, because they see growth in your life and feel that it's a risk towards the relationship if they are not growing equally with you.

I have seen many relationships have a shift in dynamic after someone has gone from a dependent job to an independent self-employed business owner. This is more common for less prominent corporate escapees who may be more dependent on their partner for emotional support, income or time. As they become more independent and don't require these crutches, the partner feels less needed, and it changes the relationship dynamic. Instead of thinking of this as a threat, it's an opportunity to reach a new level with your relationship. Bring your partner on your journey and help them face their own internal challenges and prepare them for an overall better relationship. Having been through this change myself and not managing it well, I know how difficult it is to redefine yourself once you have set expectations and habits in a relationship.

One particular client comes to mind whom I was coaching through this process. She was much younger than her partner and was living and working for him. Therefore, she was dependent on him for her income, accommodation, emotional support and identity. She had recently moved from overseas when they met and didn't have a strong network apart from their mutual friends.

When she reached out to me and wanted to start her own independent brand, he was initially supportive because he thought it was a good way for her to take a large lead in his business.

However, when we did the Understand section, she realised that she really wanted to be independent of his money, brand and control. We built a strong online profile, a personal website, social media and more. But when it came to the Leverage part and he suddenly realised where it was going, he felt threatened. He was a huge guy, trained in martial arts and very scary. She was a petite, much younger girl. When it turned violent in their house, she lent on me for accommodation and advice. This was far outside my scope, skillset and professional parameters. But when someone like that is in need and has nowhere else to go, you help if you can.

She had an opportunity to move on from that abusive relationship and start a new life and business. However, it wasn't a fairy tale, and she retreated to him and his business and abandoned the work we were doing. This is the challenge of the Leverage section. It's a chance to change your life, but change is difficult for most people and particularly if those closest to you are secretly hoping you fail and come back to the comfort of your old life.

Another more positive example was a lovely older lady in the human resource industry who was so nervous about posting her first blog that I literally had to hold her hand and press the Post button on LinkedIn, since she was too nervous to do it herself. Obviously, as soon as I had pressed the button all hell broke loose! Kidding – nothing happened at all. Our minds build these moments up far more than they are in reality. Your network isn't hovering over their laptops just waiting for your next post; in fact, you will be lucky if anyone even initially notices your brands in the marketplace. So relax and focus on being prolific with your content, not perfect. Over the next few days, she received many positive comments, likes and shares from friends and colleagues congratulating her on starting her own consulting business. All was well and we did her first three posts as part of our package, but then she never wrote another blog again. Without the support to make it happen, her previous fears returned and, unfortunately, it was challenging for her to increase her brand and client base.

As you go through this section, notice the reactions of those around you. There will be equal amounts of supporters and challengers, there always are. Take note of the supporters and spend time with them, surround yourself with the people who are on your side, and you will accelerate your progress.

The Leverage section is the most important in the whole process and all the other work is in preparation for this work. It's vital you take each Step seriously and don't gloss over the activities because the devil is in the detail *and* the practice. The Steps we will cover are: Content, Connections, Pitch and Close.

Step 9: Content

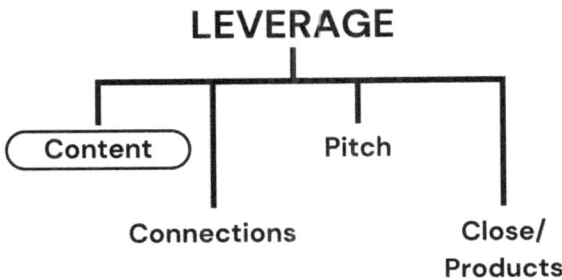

LEVERAGE

Content

Pitch

Connections

Close/
Products

Figure 47. The first Step in the Leverage section is Content.

The first Step of Leverage we start working on is content. This refers to all of the information that we produce and distribute to our target market. Remember, your target market is what determines the social channels you use for content, which then drives the content that is the most appropriate. The reason we start with this is because it takes a while to get this into production so, once we begin this process, we can work on the other three parts of Leverage. The aim is to create content to engage with a target audience and e-ttract enough clients to fill up your portfolio business.

We discussed at length how the process of personal branding is to engage our audience through the Cold, Warm, Hot and Sales zones, so they are either e-ttracted to us or not. The first two steps of this process are where marketing assists in the process and the second two are more sales-related. What we mean by this is when clients are in the Cold zone and don't know us, they can't talk to us because they don't have a connection with us. They check out our digital presence from afar. Then as they cross over to the Warm zone, they review our online assets like websites and social media, in effect, looking at our content.

Once they trust your brand and begin to engage with it, you can tell they believe you are credible because they move into the Hot zone and request a meeting with you. That is when you classify the action into the Sales category. "Sales" has a negative connotation to some, so we classify it into the two stages of pitch and close, which we will review in detail in the next Steps. For now, we will review the format types of content that will help our prospects get to know us and move down the funnel from Cold to Warm to Hot and, finally, to Sale.

Content Format

There are only a few varieties of content formats that you can produce: video, written words, audio or images. Each format suits different channels and can be repurposed to use in a variety of ways. For instance, if you produce a recruitment video for your website, it can be 5–10 minutes long, as potential employees will invest the time to watch this before they make the big step to join your organisation. This would be in the Warm zone. However, potential employees would still need to be e-ttracted through the Cold stage of the funnel. So, we would post a 30–60 second highlight reel of the same video, but in a slightly different style on social media, such as on LinkedIn, Instagram and/or Facebook. To gain Cold audiences, we would boost the post to your target audience and then invite them to view the careers section of your website where the longer video resides. The same video is cut two different ways and used for different purposes.

Another way we use variable content is with blogs. When we write long-form content for clients, we usually post it on LinkedIn as an article because it gets excellent SEO. Fun fact: did you know that LinkedIn blogs are the only social media content where you own the intellectual property? These articles are searched for and listed separately on Google searches, so they are excellent for your Cold audiences looking to solve a particular problem. Furthermore, they appear in Google Snippets, as we discussed in the SEO section of Build. We post these blogs on your website for SEO too. These all e-ttract the Cold audience and once they hit your website or LinkedIn, they are considered Warm prospects.

We can also use the photo from the blog and post it on Instagram and Facebook with a summary of the blog and a link back to your website. Facebook allows a link back to your website, but Instagram currently only offers one link, so we utilise Linktree or other such services, which we covered in the social media section of Build. The point is you can see that one piece of content can be repurposed for many different uses. The adage we use at Social Star is: produce once, distribute many times.

Now we understand the four formats of content (video, written words, audio or images), let's review the types of content to use at each stage of the sales funnel, starting with Cold as you can see from the diagram below.

e-ttraction Sales Funnel

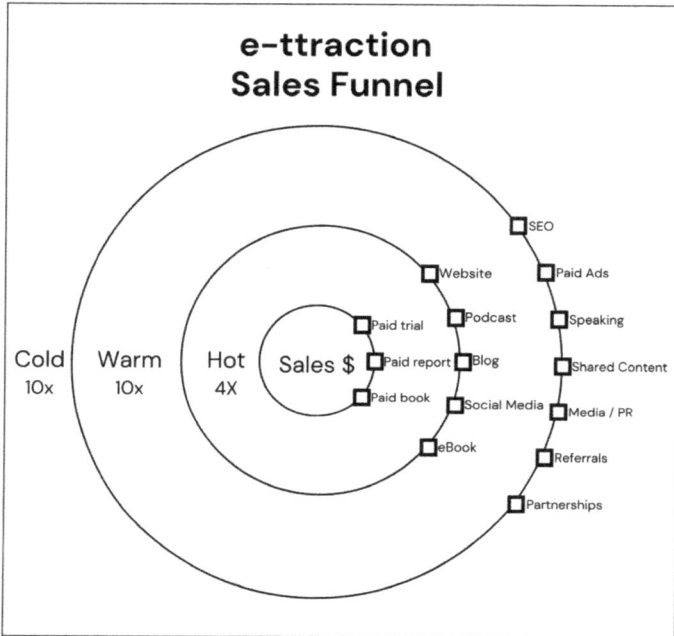

Figure 48. Template for mapping the e-ttraction Sales Funnel.

Cold Content

In the Cold zone, we create specific content to communicate with people who do not know us. As they are strangers to our business and brand, they are not on our social media and haven't visited our website. Therefore, they will spend a very limited amount of time getting to know us, so we must be very impactful with our communication to form trust quickly.

Given these people are not on your channels, we need to use other people's channels to reach this Cold audience. There are a variety of ways we do this, such as through Google search or SEO, which we have previously covered in the Build process, but now we will explore this in relation specifically to content. We can use paid marketing, such as advertising or boosting posts on LinkedIn, Facebook and Instagram. Or we can use appearances on other people's platforms, such as podcasts, as well as events to reach new audiences through partnerships.

The best way to get Cold clients is via referrals from a trusted source. However, all of these areas work in conjunction to assist a Cold prospect in paying attention to your brand and business. We will explore all of these in detail.

Search

When someone has a need, they generally do some research. This could be by asking people they trust in this area, utilising a search engine like Google, or paying more attention to advertising for that area. Depending on the size of the purchase and the urgency of the problem, they might spend quite a while in this search phase. They might collect and collate data on possible solutions over a period of time. That's why it's important to continue to share content regularly, so you keep in the prospect's awareness zone during this phase.

Let's use a real example to help us understand how customers search.

I was working in our Collingwood office doing a paid workshop with a client. Halfway through the two-hour session, I had a phone call that I answered. I don't answer calls with a client who is paying for my time, except for my kids and school. This was my youngest's school calling to tell me he'd had an accident and had broken his arm. It was quite a shock to find out your 10-year-old boy had fallen off a swing and broken his arm and the ambulance was on the way to take him to the hospital and his mum was en route.

Faced with this situation, what do you do? Continue the workshop because the client has paid for it, and his mother can manage the hospital? Or leave immediately and go to the hospital? Considering my clients have similar values, they completely understood that I chose to end the workshop and reschedule, so I could go immediately to the hospital. They respected me more because I made that decision, as it would be how they would choose to react. Same values, same decisions. I wonder if I had decided to stay, would they have thought less of me because I didn't go? We will never know, but likely they might have.

But let's continue the story. The ambulance took my son to the local hospital, which was the protocol. I called my brother and sister who both work in medicine and they suggested we take him to a private hospital and seek a specialist to fix his arm. Not having been through this situation before, I really didn't know what to do. We chose to let the public hospital do their job, as we didn't know how we could move him to a private hospital and get a specialist so quickly.

When the doctor arrived to set his arm, I didn't feel confident in his ability immediately. Why? Not sure, to be honest. I looked at his face and he didn't seem confident. He seemed unsure of what to do and didn't fill me with assurance that he could do the job well. He was likely in training, and this is understandable. But we decided to trust him because he is a doctor – right? He wouldn't be there if he couldn't do something so simple as setting an arm in plaster. Wrong.

In the middle of the night, my son's hand turned purple and was twice the size it should be. We had to rush to emergency and get the cast cut off as it was too tight and restricting his blood flow. Once the cast was off, and he was in a temporary brace, we decided to take my family's advice to go private and find a specialist. How do you research doctors? Being me, I started with a Google search of paediatric orthopaedic doctors in the private system in Melbourne.

I found about half a dozen and went to their websites and LinkedIn profiles to review if I liked them and if they were a match for our needs. There was one lady I researched who said she was a specialist, but then she listed a whole range of other services that she did, which didn't make me feel comfortable, as a specialist doesn't do plastic surgery on adults, kids and many other things. They just do one thing, which is why they are a specialist.

I ended up choosing the doctor I liked the best, who felt credible, and he only did orthopaedics but worked with kids as well as adults. His website was forthright with his expertise, and he seemed quietly confident in his ability, which I observed from his photos. On attending his office, I noticed that his practice did a lot of work on AFL footballers, which reinforced his credibility. We met him and he was very likeable, and we hit it off immediately. He was great with my son and the operation went well. I recall sitting in the waiting room and this specialist came out during the surgery to let me know that they had to insert a pin in his wrist because both bones were broken clean off, and he asked me whether that was okay.

Everything went well and I'm pleased to report that my son made a full recovery. On reflection, what was interesting from this experience, that I wasn't conscious of at the time, was how I made all these decisions. We all make decisions when we choose to work with people, often it's through trust, but sometimes we simply don't know what the factors of this e-ttraction are. We are strange creatures. I remember one client saying he couldn't work with another supplier because she had the same name as his ex-wife! As I said, we are complex, but trust is the number one indicator of a client wanting to work with you.

In my doctor example, I went to Google because that's what I am used to. Most people my age will rely on the most popular search engine in the world and search using a laptop, as we like the larger real estate. That's when the SEO you adopt counts. We have covered this previously, so we will not delve into how SEO works, but suffice to say that this is where it truly matters. Remember, that if a client gets a referral from someone they know, then they might search for your name or company name or, if they have a general need, they will be searching for a solution for their problem.

I was searching for an orthopaedic surgeon in Melbourne who specialised in paediatrics. So that's what I got. I didn't have a name or clinic to refer to, so I did the unknown search and had to filter through the results. It's much faster and easier to have a referral and that's what most people would prefer. Note that the search results on a laptop will be different from a mobile phone. Phones have a GPS chip that knows exactly where you are and have recently been, so the results are much more geographically based. A voice search on a phone also produces a different result from manual typing, because it usually only provides one result since the AI tool reads this out to you, rather than providing a long list of results. If you have ever used Siri, you will be used to her speaking to you with your search result.

Kids today use social media for search, and I know my kids use TikTok as their main source of information. Scary but true.

From the Google search for a doctor, I reviewed websites first, since that's usually the best source of information about services provided. So, your website needs to be clear and specific on who you are, what you do and for whom. We have discussed websites at length and it's important to know that this is a constant throughout the whole sales process. It's the gateway from Cold to Warm through a Google search. Then you can move people to Hot via booking a call from your Contact page and even into a Sale with an e-commerce booking of your services.

But I digress – back to the Cold zone and the ways to get clients to your brand. Another way is by utilising paid advertising. I use paid advertising sparingly because if you do the connections and content process well and have a clear and specific value proposition, you should get enough clients. However, if you have a limited network to start with or you are pivoting into a different business territory from what you have done before, you might need to boost your efforts with some paid marketing.

Paid Ads

The first area to set up is Google Ads. These are the links at the top of a Google search result that are paid to get to the top, rather than being the best fit for the search words. Google works on a few different systems, but to keep it simple you pay per click. Each time a potential client clicks your result you pay a fee. Each cost per click (CPC) is an auction system between whoever wants to buy it, so the price varies for each word and at different times.

This gets your brand to the top of the search results for your main keywords, whilst your natural SEO through your content gains traction. As we mentioned in the SEO section, Google respects how long content has been on the internet since it can measure its quality more accurately. Therefore, the longer the content has been around, the more SEO it can achieve. Newer content doesn't get as much reach, so using paid ads can be helpful when you first start your business.

This is faster to set up and will give you some early feedback on your messaging and pitch, so we recommend you use it if you are in a hurry to build your business. Some of our clients aren't in a hurry and are happy to wait for the organic, inside-out marketing to take effect. It all depends on your goals and resources. The way we do Google Ads is a bit different from other agencies. We follow the three-brand rule we covered at the start of the book. For example, for our company Social Star, we could buy the keywords "Social Star". But that would be a bit redundant because we get organic links for free, especially in our home base of Melbourne. But if we wanted to advertise in a new city where we are not yet strong, say Brisbane, then we could pay for Google Ads whilst we create more of a presence there.

We know that most services referrals are for a person so, following on from this example, we could also buy an ad for "Andrew Ford". This would ensure we are getting these clicks if someone is searching for a person. We could also buy our other staff members' names, if they were customer-facing, so clients could be talking about them.

Finally, we could buy "personal branding", "starting a business" and brief descriptors of other services that we provide. This is called an *unknown search*, as the prospect doesn't know anyone in the industry and hasn't received a referral, so they are searching with a blank sheet of paper. This is the hardest prospect to convert, as you must build a lot of trust with this person via digital means before they are likely to convert. This can be expensive because you need to have a significant repetition of clicks, and you are paying per click. Plus, you need to have a lot of these prospects to filter out the ones who are not suitable, so there is a large wastage of clicks on people who will not be a good client for you. This is why we highly recommend to our clients that we get referrals for you or your company name, since it's much more efficient and economical.

Often clients ask me what sort of budget they should put into Google Ads at the start. Of course, the answer depends on your goals. Most of our clients require low volumes of clients at a high value, between 2–10 clients a month. They are also super niche, so we buy what's called *long-tail keywords*. This means we are not buying "accountant Melbourne", if that was their field. That is a waste of money and time. We would hyper-focus on a niche that they have a speciality in and produce a great digital asset like an ebook, podcast or blog series on that topic. Then buy keywords like "Payroll tax for doctors", which was a big issue at the time of writing.

This is an important concept to understand. The more specific you make your target market, the better your conversion rates are at the Cold end of the funnel. For "accountant Melbourne" we would expect the cost to be high, perhaps $1 a click or more. The conversion is low, say 1 in 1,000, which is the current rate on the e-ttraction sales model to go from Cold to Warm, so you might move only one prospect into Warm, which is not usually enough to land even one client. For $1,000, that's not a very good result.

The answer is to focus on the niche, as we can purchase these keywords cheaply and they convert at a higher percentage, so we only need a very small budget for this program. If you allocated $500 a month that should be sufficient to drive 1,000–2,000 clicks to your new website at a CPC of $0.50 to $0.25, and if we use our conversion from Warm at 10%, then we have 10 prospects using our system.

For this to work, it's important that when the link is clicked the prospect lands on a page that is dedicated to the search they conducted. It should answer their question and provide enough rich materials that they start to form trust. Remember, trust is a derivative of likeability and credibility. Therefore, photos and videos of the team talking are great, alongside meaningful information on how to solve the problem. This is mandatory. Don't worry about giving the answers, the prospect will not solve the problem themselves, as they usually want someone to do it for them. Give your best advice for free. Client reviews, testimonials and awards are also useful as social proof of your credibility in this area. This is why we get LinkedIn testimonials early in our branding process, as your new company is unlikely to have any of these yet, so we will use your personal testimonials.

There is strategy, technicalities and design work in setting up Google Ads, so I recommend you get someone to do this for you.

Boosting

Another useful process to fast-track your business-building is to boost posts on LinkedIn, Facebook, Instagram and TikTok. Boosting is a way of advertising on social media that is low cost and less complicated to set up than other forms of paid marketing. The way it works is you choose a post from your business page that you have already done which is getting some interest from your community. Remember, this can't be done from a private page, only a business page. This could be a blog, post about a podcast, or event you want to run. It's useful to boost content that is meaningful to your target audience or makes money for your business. Then press the Boost button at the bottom of the post and choose the people you want to target by demographics such as age, location and interests. Allocate a budget and a timeline for the boost to run. We advise about $50–$100 per post to get it out to 5,000–10,000+ people over a 7–10 day period. The exact price and reach will be determined by each platform on a case-by-case basis.

The platform will then push your content to people whom you have selected in your targeting that are not following your page to see if they are interested in the content. The more people who engage with the post, the more it will be sent out for the allocated budget. That's why it's important to make it of value to your target market, so you get more reach for your dollars. Each platform is a bit different in the way they run boosts, and they change the features over time, so the main point to remember is that you can boost a post with very little knowledge of paid digital marketing. It's low cost and low risk, so it's a great way to see if pushing your good quality content out to more people would be useful for your business.

What we normally do at Social Star is boost the video, blog or podcast posts because they cost the most to produce and add the most value to our audience. We focus on LinkedIn, Facebook and Instagram with a nominal budget of $50 per post per platform. We don't have a big presence on TikTok, as it's not where our audience hangs out, so we don't boost there. The analytics of these posts show that the organic audience engages with the post far more than the people we reach with the advertising boost.

This makes sense, since those who already follow your page and know your brand will more readily like, share and comment on your content. They are already in the Warm zone. The boost of the post pushes your content into the newsfeed of people you don't know, who are in the Cold zone. So they might see the post but, as they are unfamiliar with you and have no trust, they are less likely to engage.

If you are considering a paid marketing campaign on social media, advised by an agency or a friend, we recommend boosting your content yourself first to see how it performs. If you get a positive result, then you could explore doing a more substantial paid marketing campaign on that channel. Paid marketing is very different in that it takes time to set up, is far more complex software-wise and requires an ongoing budget to maintain the ads. Expect to pay $1,000 to $3,000 for the management of the advertising campaign and a budget of $2,000 to $10,000 for the ads themselves. Plus, the cost of any significant creative content like a podcast or video series. These sorts of costs are usually reserved for larger companies with e-commerce business structures.

For information professionals, we recommend boosted content as the only paid ads on social media. Google isn't a social media, it's a search engine, so isn't included in this analysis. We recommend paid Google Ads as they are *pull* not *push*. The key difference is that a prospect is voluntarily searching for a solution to a problem and is driving the engagement. They want to find someone like you. On social media, you are interrupting their scrolling of the newsfeed with your advertisement, they are not actively searching for you or your solution.

Speaking

Speaking is by far one of the best ways to promote your brand. If you are the one at the front of the room with the microphone, it's likely that you will be seen by others as an expert. Being invited onto other people's stages is a big compliment and one we should say *yes* to more often than not. This could be a panel interview, a keynote speech, a breakout room workshop at a conference, a boardroom event or a training session with a team. I have done a lot of speaking over the years and I enjoy doing them because it hones my skills, refines my pitch and creates brand awareness for my name and topic.

I have had a lot of clients come to me years after a speaking engagement to tell me they remember key parts of the presentation. It's quite interesting how deeply you can impact people if you put your heart and soul into your speech. I find the more that I authentically share my story and examples, the more it resonates with the audience and the longer they remember me.

Sometimes these speaking gigs are paid and sometimes they are free. It really depends on the circumstances and where I am at in my business journey. For instance, I was on the panel of speakers for Certified Practising Accountants Australia for many years. I enjoyed the engagement with these small business owners, and they really appreciated my efforts. But after doing these presentations for free over many years, I can only recall securing one client from them. This was despite many people saying they loved my presentation, it really helped them and they were very keen to work with me. I decided that they were not my target audience and now I charge to do these, so that it's fair value for me and them.

My perfect audience is professional services, so you would imagine that accountants are a direct hit, however, when we drill more into the exact buyer persona or avatar of my clients, they are entrepreneurial professionals. They might be accountants, but only the ones who are more growth-oriented and see the value in marketing. Not the ones who enjoy a free talk and are stimulated by the discussion, but don't really want to put themselves out there or achieve anything new. They don't have the drive to pursue new areas of the market and, thus, don't really need my services. This is a good example of getting a prospect into your Hot zone but no Sale. They will not convert because they ultimately don't have a strong enough need and you will end up frustrated in your business or going broke. That's why it's so important to drill into your target market and understand them intimately. Plus, test your material on the market early to understand who buys and who trusts you but doesn't transact.

When I was teaching in the MBA program at RMIT University, I used to do a presentation to every class about personal branding to advance the students' careers or businesses. I would always pick up a client or two from these engagements as the audience was progressive and entrepreneurial. You don't spend $50,000 on an

MBA and all that time if you are not motivated to do something in your career. A bonus was that they would pay me for my time, so it was a win/win. I got paid to pitch to my perfect clients, so I put in my A game and they got the best results from me.

I recommend to my clients who are new to their business to do as many speaking gigs as possible, as it's a very fast way to see if your pitch resonates with people and to practise your networking. Plus, you might get a client or some referrals from it. You don't need to be a proficient speaker to start this process as the practice is what makes you better. If you are speaking about your core topic, you should have the knowledge and experience to do the speech well. Then it's a matter of learning to make it interesting with stories and examples.

Many speaking opportunities are now online via Zoom, Google Meet or Teams. This makes it easier to get to more places in the world without travel; however, it's harder to engage the audience and chat after the presentation, which is where the real opportunities to get clients are. I always like to spend time at the end of the presentation to talk to those who are the most motivated to talk to me. They are in the Hot zone, so I make an appointment with them to talk further and better understand their requirements.

I don't speak to the RMIT MBA classes anymore, as during COVID they recorded a video of my presentation and that is now in the curriculum. It's the same content but less impactful as I am not there to engage the audience. I still get a few leads from that work but less than before. If you have the choice, I would make the effort to go there physically and network with the audience.

Media

Another similar format to speaking is getting on podcasts or blogs. If you have ever run a news publication or your own content channel, you realise that you constantly need new talent to keep the show turning. Therefore, there's many media platforms looking for knowledgeable and credible people who can speak effectively to give value to their audience.

Many clients want to be guests on shows and ask me how I get them for my podcast. Of course, like all podcasters, I only want the best ones, so the first thing to do is to present yourself as an expert in your industry. This is where your personal branding becomes important. Having a quality LinkedIn profile with recommendations and endorsements, plus a personal website with examples of you speaking, the topics you cover and your perfect audience, will all help. This significant investment at the start of the branding process pays off when you apply the Leverage section.

Your challenge is to find shows that are the best fit for your brand and offer as much value as possible to the person who has the media platform you want to appear on. Remember, it's not your job to sell yourself in these formats, your job is to make the interviewer look great, plus engage and teach the audience. Most interviews are pre-recorded, so if you are not good, they will edit out parts, such as self-promotion or, at worst, may not use you at all. Plus, if you want them to promote you on their show, best you promote them too. The better your content, the more their audience will want to engage with you on your social media, which automatically moves people down the funnel from Cold to Warm. If they are interested, they will visit your website and social media proactively, not because you told them to.

A good way to find the best shows for your brand is to think about your perfect client avatar and what services they would need to complement their outcomes. You are looking for service providers who help these same clients but don't overlap with your brand.

An example is an accountant client of mine, Sevan, who runs a podcast called *The Bottom Line* to promote the firm. I was referred to him as a potential guest by another client, Darren Bourke, as he was also a guest on the podcast. When I met Sevan to discuss the podcast, we ended up talking a lot about his business. It was such an engaging discussion that we met a few times and it led to us engaging with him on one of our marketing retainers. A great outcome for both of our businesses, which all started with a discussion regarding the podcast.

Another benefit from this discussion was that once I had done the podcast and it was released, some of Sevan's clients heard it and liked the strategies I discussed for professional services marketing. They reached out and we did some business with them too. As a reward, I invited Sevan onto my revitalised podcast BYOB, so he could benefit from the exposure of his brand to our audience. This is part of the benefits from creating content for these platforms – it helps create strong relationships with clients and exposes you to new audiences.

One point I would like to highlight in this story is that when you seek people who have similar values, you tend to get along well with them and many opportunities arise for business because you want to find ways to work together. Not *reactively* when a need arises, but *proactively* looking for problems to solve together. This is why we use LinkedIn Outreach to seek out people to add to your network who are like you, even if they are not clients right now, because they could be one in the future. Take a longer-term view of your relationships. They might have the potential to be a client, partner, referrer or share content one day. If you connect on a deep level, you will do many things together, so seek to engage, not just to sell your services.

Partnerships

A partnership can come in many forms. There are business

partnerships where you run a company together, partnerships where you share clients, and ones for marketing only.

Once again, look for those who have shared values with you but offer a different product to a similar audience. Some examples of the different partnerships we have at Social Star are firstly a business one with Social Video. Adam, who runs Social Video, and I have been working together for over a decade and have always liked each other's company. We would go for drinks regularly through my BYOB networking group and have similar friends. So, when he approached me to do more work together, I was very interested. His offering was video, photography and creative work for people similar to those we work with. He needed my marketing and sales skills, and I needed his creative skills. The timing was great, as we were looking to expand and make video a key component of our offerings. Our partnership was so fruitful, we started doing a lot more work together and now we run the business as a true partnership.

Another example is Ephraim from a company called WDM who is also in marketing. However, his speciality is paid Meta Ads, something we do on a very small scale but isn't our speciality. So, when I was working with a client in an advisory capacity that was in fast-moving consumer goods and they wanted a new provider for this service, I brought him in to help. This was a shared client as they invoiced him directly, not via Social Star, so it was more of an arm's length partnership. Interestingly, I had also known him for a decade, since he is one of Adam's friends, and I always thought he was smart and a good guy. His company did a great job and is still helping the client long after I finished my advisory work.

The third example is a marketing partnership where you cross-promote each other but don't work on the clients together. For

Social Star, one example that stands out is Gareth Benson, our go-to intellectual property lawyer. We have been friends since we met through my Master of Entrepreneurship group over a decade ago. We hit it off immediately and have helped each other out many times. I refer all my clients to him for trademark law and have had him on my podcast a few times. He invites me to his events and sends good contacts my way too. Right now we are in the process of buying and recommending each other's books on Amazon!

In all these partnership examples you will see a commonality in the circumstances. The partners have known each other for a long time, enough time to develop trust. There is no money changing hands for referrals, as we want to promote each other's services because we believe they are high quality. Plus, we like to spend time together and so our communities become intertwined. This is a wonderful way to build your business, as it's fun and great for your bottom line.

So how do you get started with partnerships? Slowly is a good process. Start with one form of engagement and if it turns out to be mutually beneficial, then it can turn into a partnership and become a more formal relationship. A good way to form a partnership is to run an event together. Once you have been on your potential partner's media, or them on yours, you will see if there is a communication fit. Then you can arrange a dual webinar or face-to-face event where you both commit to bringing clients and educating that audience on a particular topic. This is mutually beneficial and can be used to great effect to source leads on both sides whilst sharing the cost and work to run the event.

At times people run multi-speaker events and these can also be a useful way to find new Cold Connections. I have participated in a few of these and sometimes there is a fee to be on the same stage as someone with a larger brand than your own. They bring the audience for you, which is why you pay for access to their people. I don't normally do this, but I know some people who have used this to great effect. I prefer to have a mutually beneficial arrangement of shared audience and shared cost, as it feels more organic to me, and I can be assured that the audience fits my brand.

Social media

Let's imagine that you are a guest on someone else's podcast. They are likely to promote it on their social media, which is a great way of getting exposed to new people. Furthermore, when you post content and others like, comment and share it, then you are being exposed to more new people in the Cold zone. This is why regularly publishing content is so valuable. It doesn't just warm up your audience, it can add new people to your audience. As we discussed previously, if you build your brand specifically around your niche, then your connections and friends will be similar to you and actively like you online because you are similar.

Remember, social media isn't just about promoting your brand and services. It should be social, which means talking to people and engaging on their social media too. Let's use an example to elaborate. Let's say you want to be on someone's podcast. The first step is to listen to some of their episodes and like, comment and share them to your audience. This will build awareness of your brand to that person. Creators of content definitely pay attention to those who help promote them. Connect with them on LinkedIn by saying you love their podcast and, once they accept, you can then approach them to be a guest – it's a warmer introduction if they have seen your recommendations.

Furthermore, I would make the effort to have a pre-meeting before the podcast and preferably in person. Take a photo of both of you together at the meeting and post it on your social media to give their business a shout-out. This is a good personal post on LinkedIn, Facebook and Instagram. The purpose is to drive some attention to your new partner, so tag them and their company in the post and communicate their value offering.

When you go in for the podcast, take some photos before the recording and share parts of the conversation in the post. Then when the podcast is released, promote it on your channels too. It might seem like an overkill, but this process usually occurs over months, so the posts will appear as occasional. They are also hugely beneficial for your brand. It shows that you are a great guest for podcasts, which makes others consider you for their show. It creates gratitude with the host because you are making efforts to promote them, and they are more likely to reciprocate. Plus, they might form a stronger partnership in the future, if the episode goes well. All these are benefits to you and your brand for a relatively small effort and no cost.

Referrals

Let's review an example of this to explain why referrals are so valuable. We always ask our new clients how they heard about us, and one example was quite interesting in the strange way we received this referral. Mitchell is a CEO of luxury brands in Asia and sent us an email enquiry via the company website to assist him with some work with his personal brand. In our first call, I asked him how he came across our business, and he mentioned that his neighbour had recommended us to him during a conversation. His neighbour is the business partner of one of my long-standing clients, so he knew about our services. However, the referral was to me by my name – not to Social Star, but to Andrew Ford – which is very common. I think the exact phrasing was: "Fordy is a good guy, you should give him a call." That's all it takes to get a new client ... plus the 20 years of brand-building before that statement.

What are the chances that I would come up in conversation? Lucky for us it did, since Mitchell was a fantastic client for us. You can hear his journey from luxury brands CEO to running his own portfolio business in our BYOB podcast on our website.

The point about this referral is that he didn't require a tremendous amount of warming up to convert to the Hot zone. He had a need, told a few trusted people what he wanted help with, and his community gave him a few referrals. Upon researching these few referrals online, he must have liked something in our branding and contacted us to take the next step in the process. Referrals like this form trust from the referrer and, therefore, they don't have to spend as long establishing trust in the Warm zone from consuming your content. In other words, you only need a small number of these clients to generate a lot of business in the Sale zone. This is why, for our style of clients, referrals are the best form of marketing.

Outreach

Compare your desired number of Warm or Hot contacts with your current accessible database, you might be short a few. Then you need a strategy to increase your numbers over time. Frequently we rely on LinkedIn as our way to increase Cold connections, as it's one of the most convenient and appropriate channels to increase our database. As discussed in the LinkedIn section, it is one of the only business-oriented social media channels. It's part of the culture that you can reach out to Cold connections and ask them to connect for potential future collaborations, just like you would do if you were at a business conference.

Our preferred method is to reach out to your second-level connections, which means you have a mutual connection in common. LinkedIn has a built-in function called InMail, which is a way to connect to people you don't know. We tend not to use this function, as it doesn't appear in the normal inbox area for messages but in a different section called Other, which many people don't check often. It basically says that they don't know you, but want to sell you something.

We prefer to add the person as a connection. It is the direct approach and I like it better, as it has several benefits over an InMail. Firstly, they will see that you want to be connected to them, which alludes to a longer-term relationship, not just making a sale. They can see you have at least one person as a mutual connection and might review who else you have in common. On the strength of our profile and the network you have, they will decide if they want to connect with you. In this way they are faced with an instant judgment of your profile. Do they like you and feel you are credible, or not?

Not everyone will resonate with you or what you do, and it's best to know at this early stage, rather than waste time and resources trying to convince them to come along on your journey when they just don't vibe with you. It's exhausting and energy-zapping to try to work with people who don't appreciate what you do. You should rather focus on those who understand you and feel connected to you for some reason.

The truth is, we don't really know why someone likes us or not. In the Understand process, we have come up with some strategies to match our target market to our brand, but there are so many deep environmental and psychological reasons why people either relate to us or don't. If we had a perfect way to match people, we would create a dating application and be instant billionaires!

How we solve this problem is to use our Values section to provide a basis for the connection and likeability. People with similar Values often relate well together and will have common ground. For instance, many of my clients have similar Values to myself, which is why they are attracted to work with our organisation. My top Values are Family, Business, Health and Education. Therefore, those people with those same Values would like to do similar activities and talk about the same things. We chat about kids – and I understand the pressure of running a business whilst looking after children – and we share books and podcasts that we are enjoying. It's a tough balance when you are passionate about both your family and your work, so people with these shared Values are often more compatible.

I recall a potential client who was referred to me by one of my long-term referrers. He has sent me clients consistently over the last decade, as we see eye-to-eye on many things. He has two kids, works in marketing, plus his name is also Andrew! One client he sent me was a woman who was considering leaving the corporate world and starting a portfolio business. She entered the sales funnel as a Warm contact and came to visit me for our first meeting. We had a nice chat for 45 minutes, and I learnt more about her situation and, whilst it was a pleasant chat, we didn't have a strong personal connection. She didn't work with me and later I found out she went with a female-led agency in Sydney where she was based. That was her preference, which was absolutely fine. What I found interesting about this was that she referred one of her friends to me – a male corporate escapee who we are still working with to this day. She wasn't a match for me but developed enough trust to refer a friend, which was pretty cool.

The lesson from this story is that you are not for everyone and not everyone is for you. Don't take it personally because you don't know why they do or don't like you. Similar Values are a clue, but there are so many other factors at play that it can be hard to build a business around trying to please everyone. Don't do that, just be you. In fact, be *more* you!

We find that the more specific you are with your branding, value projection and style of work, the stronger others can either resonate with you or be repelled by your brand. Done well, your brand is a filtration system for the market, so you only receive well-qualified people based on them seeing a fit with you as a person. Some marketing people would argue that we should get as many people as possible into your funnel, as we might miss out on potential clients. This might be true for businesses that have a different model, like selling products or generic services, for instance, but, for a knowledge-based business or any speciality professional service where you are providing the product directly to a client, this doesn't fit. When you have to directly interact with the client, they need to like you first, and think you are credible second.

Both are important to move from the Warm zone into Hot, but no one who doesn't like you will buy your services over and over and recommend you to their network, no matter how good you are at your service. The only exception to this is if you have a monopoly on that service. Let's say you are the country's best brain surgeon, then a patient might not like you but will use you because you can best solve their problem.

Warm Content

Once someone has been exposed to your brand and decides they like you, they may want to explore your work in more detail to decide if you are also credible in your area of expertise. This is the Warm zone, where they start to develop trust. Your website, your social media and the content you have created, such as podcasts, videos and blogs, are important at this phase of the journey. The main difference between the Cold and Warm zones is that in the Cold zone prospects are not on your digital media, as they are unaware of you, they are on their own spaces. The job of all the work we did in the Cold zone is to help them get to your digital areas that you can control more effectively.

Google

There are several ways to get clients from the Cold to Warm zones, of which search engines like Google play a big role, as do social media. But these are channels of distribution for your content, so we need to understand how this works to use them effectively. We will review a few of the ways we can get your content in front of your perfect client, using an example to illustrate this process.

I have a few mortgage-broker customers and, let's say, they have a perfect target customer of Double Income No Kids (DINKS) in inner-city Melbourne. We would start working with them to Understand themselves, to refine this target market into a perfect buyer avatar. Then Build a website, social media and content to engage this perfect client. But for those who don't know the broker, they will never see this useful content unless we can grab their attention in the Cold zone. So, we publish blogs on LinkedIn and on their website that address specific problems their customers have. For instance, one question might be: "Is an inner-city apartment in Melbourne a bad investment?" This isn't about mortgage-broking specifically, but it's something the target market might be curious about and be searching for early in the property research phase. Our client's blog will be crawled by Google and could be shown in search results and perhaps in Google Snippets, which is the recommended FAQ part of the search results we discussed in the SEO section. The potential client may then click on that link.

Blogs

If the client clicks on the blog and visits the broker's website or LinkedIn, they are now in the Warm zone. They have entered their digital domain, and a few things happen. The client reads the blog and might review more blogs from the mortgage-broker on similar topics that might be useful for their property research. These would gradually lead the prospect towards understanding their finances more and discussing their options with their broker. They can review the credibility of the broker by reading their biography and seeing their credentials and background. Perhaps reviews they have had from happy clients or awards that have been won. These are all elements that will help the prospect to start forming a brand position in their mind of who this mortgage-broker is and if they want to work with them in the future. It's a subtle, slow and powerful process.

Whilst a prospect is in the Warm zone, they are trying to figure out if you have value to them or not. It's a fragile position and easily ruined if you rush out and try to sell them something. It's not the time to sell, it's the time to help. Only when a prospect has already formed trust and entered the Hot zone, can we try to close them. If you push too quickly, you will push them away and break the limited trust you have created. This is why when a client visits our website or LinkedIn profile, we don't immediately message them. Give them space to walk forward in your funnel, don't push them down.

Video

As mentioned, having your content show up in Google searches is an excellent way of getting people into the Warm zone. It's powerful because it seems like Google is recommending you, particularly if it's an organic search result, not a paid one. Bonus points for Google Snippets!

There are other ways of getting into Google search results organically, other than blogs. Videos are a great way of sneaking into the first page of Google, as they own YouTube. This is why we create video content, as it gives the dual benefit of being an additional SEO link in Google. Just like a blog will give dual benefits from LinkedIn and website links, so too does a video hosted on YouTube, because it gives you two chances at Google presenting your content to a Cold prospect. Then you also get the benefit of them following the link to your YouTube channel or website. Of course, there are other video-hosting platforms like Vimeo, however, we like to stick to the main platforms since they usually carry more SEO benefits than the smaller ones that perhaps have greater functionality.

It's recommended to have a video series on a topic, rather than just singular disparate videos because, once you get a client to your YouTube channel, you want them to see the depth of your offerings and spend more time with you. One of our clients creates a short video with every podcast they do as a summary of the material, which is posted on YouTube, creating more short-form content that can be a great way for prospects to see what the material is like before investing time in the podcast.

Ebook

We often create specific longer-form content at the Warm stage to ensure prospects keep moving down the funnel to Hot. An example of this is an ebook or a research report. Some people think these branded documents are a bit old school, but they continue to perform strongly with our clients, particularly when in digital format. We occasionally print these out, such as when we do an Outreach campaign with GPs, since they like printed material. But most clients like to have it digitally for convenience of storage.

One such campaign we did recently was for an accounting client who was targeting GPs because there was a particular issue with payroll tax due to a change in government regulations. This was a serious issue for doctors and the accountant had some particular skills and experience in this area. They decided to specialise in this solution and, to meet more GPs, they booked a booth at a large conference where doctors attended. We assisted them in designing the booth with banners and a branded background to showcase their expertise in this area. We decided to have the senior consultant conduct one-on-one free consulting sessions with doctors in the booth. The assistant accountant would make these appointments for the senior consultant and, if the doctors had to wait, we made sure they could read the printed ebook regarding the solution to their payroll tax issue. Since the doctors were travelling and didn't want to carry brochures, we sent them an email with a link after the consultation to the website to download the digital copy of the ebook when they returned home. This meant the prospects at the conference could visit the website and have another touch point with the accounting firm to build trust with the people involved. It was advantageous to have it in both printed and digital formats, as they could flick through the hard copy on the day to see the value of the content, which would make them far more likely to download it from the website afterwards.

Book

Of course, an upgrade from an ebook is a published print book. This is beyond the scope of some clients, as it's a two-year time investment to write a good quality book and costs a lot of money. Some people promote writing services to create a book in a few months, however, after working with several publishers and very experienced people in the industry, I have a belief that you can write a book in a short period, but to write a great book takes time.

A book is a great resource because it establishes the author as an expert on a topic and someone who has a lot of intellectual property. The books we create with clients are all to support their existing businesses and not to sell as a way to independently make revenue. The amount of book sales necessary to get a return on investment of your time, effort and money to create a book, isn't worthwhile. We make the returns from speaking, consulting and coaching clients based on the materials in the book. The book is a great way to get a client from Warm to Hot, as it builds trust through credibility.

The way we use a book is to give it away to our perfect target client at speaking events, sales meetings and sometimes on the website. Offering your book for free on your website is a great hook because people need to give you some of their contact details to get the book delivered. We want the potential client to read the book because it will solidify your methodology with them and, if they appreciate the material, they are more likely to enter the Hot zone and use you for work or refer you to their community.

Hot Content

If a client is willing to give you their email or phone number, they are interested in your services. It doesn't mean they will necessarily buy anything, as they might not be in the right position to do this at that time. It means they have the propensity to buy if the price and circumstances are right.

These customers find you likeable and credible enough to trust recommending you to others. Giving them a hard asset like a book is great marketing because people can see they have it and they can give it to others. Other marketing that can work to get clients from Warm to Hot are webinars or events. If people are willing to spend time with you, then they are likely engaged in your brand. You need a large Warm audience to run these, and they can be costly if they are face-to-face, so we normally start with an online event to test the waters.

Webinars

Web-based events are making a comeback. People are seeking advice from trusted people in their communities rather than sales-focused ads on social media. Webinars are a great way to get your Warm prospects to invest time in learning about your systems and processes. By the time they get to an event like this, they are on the precipice of becoming a client and will want to know how you solve their problem specifically.

Content Cadence

Now we know what sort of content we need at different stages in the sales funnel, clients usually ask us how often we should post content. The diagram below provides some advice on the cadence for your content, which depends upon how many clients you require.

Social Star ☆

e-ttraction®
5 Step Content Plan

	Daily	Weekly	Fortnightly	Monthly
High Growth 20% utilised	Instagram TikTok YouTube Shorts	LinkedIn Blog	Podcast	Video
Building 70% utilised		LinkedIn Post	Blog/ Podcast	Video
Maintenance 90% utilised			LinkedIn Blog	Podcast/ Video

Figure 49. Template to help schedule the posting of online content.

If you are building your business, you need more content, and we recommend posting once a week on LinkedIn and your website. If you already have many clients and want to keep topping them up with lighter marketing, post once a fortnight and, if you are full, then once a month might be appropriate. This said, it's important you keep content flow at a minimum of once a month, even if you don't need any clients. We have found that if you stop engaging with your community, then awareness of your services will be reduced and, eventually, new clients will stop being referred. Then it takes time to rebuild that network of referrers.

An example to illustrate this situation was a surgeon who recently contacted us for some work. He has had a very successful career at one of Melbourne's major hospitals and in private practice. He is planning to retire in a few years, but enjoys his work and is at the peak of his career, so he wants to keep working. However, his client flow is slowing down, since his regular GP referrers are retiring and he hasn't spent any time building his brand. He has no website, LinkedIn or social media presence and the next generation of GPs doesn't know who he is and are referring patients to the younger surgeons, who do have a brand presence and make the effort to market to them. I advised this surgeon that it will take time to reach these new GPs, as he is starting from Cold. These GPs don't know him and so he will have to invest resources to gain their awareness and build trust. Times have changed and no longer is it acceptable to ignore personal branding in professional services businesses, even for a highly respected and qualified surgeon.

Content Structure

For our style of clients, we have created the Expert Marketing System, which can be seen in the diagram below. It's a quadrant process for content that works well for most of our clients due to its simplicity and clean structure.

Social Star ☆

e-ttraction®
Expert Marketing System
4x4

Video
1 hour shoot = 6 videos

Internal Post
Create likeability from understanding you & your business

Blog
Written content for SEO based on video transcripts

External Post
Create credibility from market and industry insights

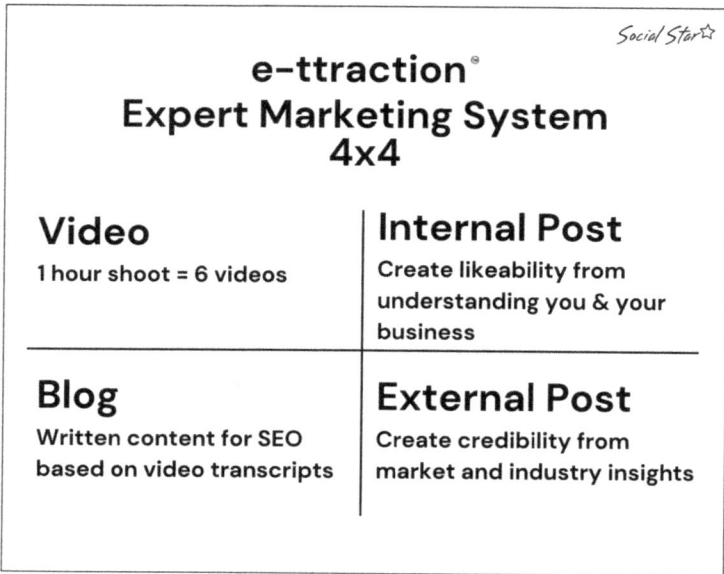

Figure 50. The Expert Marketing System designed by Social Star.

The process is four posts a month or one post a week, enough to keep your brand fresh without overwhelming your audience. This works best for a LinkedIn and email strategy plus getting SEO for your website. But we can also add Facebook and Instagram to this mix. It doesn't work with other mediums like TikTok or X, because they require more content than this process creates. However, you can still post the same content on these platforms with some adjustments. As we have mentioned before: produce once, utilise many times.

To produce this content, we start with a half-day video shoot to capture the authentic brand voice of the leader. Then we cut this into one key piece of information per month. We like to use video, as it's the densest information content format you can get. It represents your brand authentically because it captures your words, tone, facial expressions and body language. From this video, we can write a blog on the same topic, which gives us another solid content post that is valuable for SEO cn LinkedIn and your website. As mentioned, LinkedIn articles have their own ranking in Google, so it's a great content strategy. We finish off the month with two posts: one internally focused on your life or your business activities; one externally focused on the environment or industry you work in.

To start this process, it's important to have a marketing plan in place that captures your overall strategy. We then work on a six-month sprint with a key focus, which is usually building more clients, staff or partnerships. Drillirg down on exactly whom we want and in what numbers, will give us the cadence and content pillars. We use this information to come up with six key post ideas that can be used for the sprint. Then we create questions that the target market would like the answers to, in order to engage with your content and use that as the script for our video shoot.

This makes the process very easy because we know what the next six months will look like. For example, one of our new clients is a veterinarian hospital and we recently kicked off the Expert Marketing System with them to help them recruit more highly qualitied staff. There is a shortage of experts in their sector, so it's their top priority to get more vets and nurses. After creating their marketing plan, we did a video shoot to capture their six core messages and we are posting them each week as per the plan. They already had good quality content posted before they engaged us, but it wasn't as coordinated and focused as our system. The Expert Marketing System provides a framework to ensure everyone in the organisation is focused on the same goal for that period.

We usually post this content on the company's social media and then ask the key staff to like, comment and reshare the posts on their personal social media. The 4x4 posting schedule of one per week doesn't mean you can't post anything else on your social media. It's the base requirement for your company brand. If you are doing something interesting, like speaking at a conference, you can do an additional post and not clog up your social feeds. These posts on your personal social media can then be shared onto the company profile, if suitable.

Content Length

The length of your content can be different depending on the industry you are working in and your target clients. If you work in a highly technical industry, you might need to write longer-form content to demonstrate your credibility.

I had a client once who was a specialist in carbon-trading analysis and reporting. The only issue was that the government of the day had discontinued their carbon-trading scheme, so there wasn't a lot of consulting business available at the time. He contacted me to assist with his marketing and we worked on his brand and business presence on his LinkedIn profile, website and blogs. His style was to be very technical and detailed in his approach, as that was what his consulting was based upon, so it made sense to match this style in his content.

Furthermore, he wasn't growing his business due to the uncertainty following the government's discontinuation of carbon trading. So, he produced one blog and one post per month, which was enough to maintain his brand, and this approach reduced the time and money invested in the process. This worked quite well, and he received some high praise from the CEO of one of the largest energy companies saying it was one of the best blogs he had ever read on that topic. The fact this CEO had read it and commented on it was a great testament that our client was gaining traction with the right people in his network. He mentioned at the start that he only has 100 potential clients in Australia and this CEO was one of them.

The industry was lying low during our time working together but, months after that, I discovered that the government had changed their posture on carbon emissions and there was talk of a new scheme. Companies raced to get some analysis and advice, thus, my client suddenly became very busy. Due to his branding and blogs, he was well known amongst the potential clients and was first in line for this new business. In his industry it was important to have more detailed and longer blogs delivered less frequently.

Content Discipline

Once you choose the frequency, style and length of content that is appropriate for your industry, write out your content plan. For those who are doing this yourself and not getting an agency like ours to produce the Expert Marketing System, you will need to plan how and when to get your content created. Otherwise, it will be the last thing on your list and you will keep pushing this task out, because although it's important it's not urgent. That's one reason to have an agency doing the work for you, if you can afford it, because it provides the discipline of weekly meetings and production assistance to reduce the barriers to you getting this done.

If you are doing it yourself, one great way to make sure you follow through on your content is to schedule the time in your diary and the place you are going to be when you write it. For instance, if you are going to get up early and blog at 6 am, then schedule an appropriate amount of time and choose your spot, like the home office, kitchen or go to a café. Ensure people in your life know that's your plan so you are not disturbed.

Visualise yourself doing it and make a point of going to that place and starting whenever it's scheduled. Even if you don't produce your masterpiece that day, it's important to lay down the basis of a habit. If you skip the session or wake up and start thinking of where to go, it's easy to not do it. Once you skip it once, it's far easier to skip it again and again. Try to keep your discipline up.

When I started writing this book, I realised that this would require a significant effort to get started. I was motivated and wanted to get stuck in straight away. My work and home life are hectic and it's hard to find more than a few hours to get this deep work done. So, I booked a trip overseas to a place where I knew the layout, I wouldn't be disturbed, and I could focus. None of the daily chores or pressures were present and, as I had taken time off work to be there, I had the time and space to make sure I did the work.

What was interesting for me is that I booked a large suite with a proper desk and kitchen, so I could work from the room undisturbed. But as an extrovert, I felt like I was missing out on the people interaction and wanted the energy and white noise of others. So, I sought out cafés and bars to work in. I would do two- to three-hour sprints of writing during the day, take a break and go for a walk, swim or go to the gym. I've always found exercise is a great way to refresh your brain. Then I'd do another sprint. Later in the day, I might do an activity like visit a friend, play some pool, then do another writing sprint whilst having a few drinks and listening to a band or music. It may sound a little strange to write a book in a pub whilst a band is playing with a few people milling around for happy hour, but it worked well for me. I was travelling alone, so having the disassociated company of strangers made me feel like I was enjoying myself whilst I was working. Rather than forcing myself to stay in my room whilst life goes on without me, which is what I could have done in my home. But I knew if I spent the money to travel and write, then I would get it done as I would have the pressure of the investment and time off work to produce a result!

Everyone is different, but by understanding your own personality and how you best work, you can make up your own rules. You don't have to be like everyone else, be yourself and you will keep in flow. If you are keen on seeing my pictures of my writing trips, then look me up on social media as I have a bunch there.

If you are going for more advanced content, such as videos or podcasts, I highly recommend hiring a professional to assist you. It will ensure it actually happens and is of high enough quality for you to be proud of the result. I recall my first efforts at video over a decade ago and they never saw the internet! They were quite average but a good practice for my future work. The issues were that the lighting and sound were very average, so you couldn't see or hear me properly. The content was good but the production was not. But remember, they don't have to be perfect, and your first of anything isn't the best you will ever do. So let people see your vulnerability and get your message out there. Just ensure it's produced well enough for people to be able to hear and see you clearly.

Long and Short Content

There is a subtle but important difference between long- and short-form content on social media. As I've explained long-form content is the credibility piece. Short-form content tends to be the likeability piece.

Let's review the differences and advantages of long-form content. We will start with LinkedIn as it's the best place to put your content. When you post on LinkedIn, it's important you know the difference between a post and a blog. They call a blog an article, and you can see this as an option when you start adding content. When you press the Article button, it opens a new window on your computer, and this is a different piece of software from the newsfeed. This blog area provides a lot more functionality, which we discussed in the LinkedIn section. Videos, quotes, more images and increased number of words are all key differentiators. A post can be up to 3,000 characters (about 500 words) and a blog 120,000 characters (about 2,000 words) at the time of writing – a substantial difference.

It takes significant effort to put together a quality blog of 1,000–2,000 words, but it only takes a few minutes for your client to read it, which is why you need several blogs for them to read, if you can capture their attention. They could read 5–6 blogs in less than 30 minutes and decide if they agree with your strategies and style. That's based on the average reading speed of 200–300 words per minute.[44]

Aside from a sales-cycle approach, blogs appear in Google searches separate from your profile and this adds significant value to your SEO. But this is the Google rule that says if the same content appears in two different places, then they will only rank one of them. From my current understanding of the algorithm, posting the same blog on your LinkedIn profile and your website doesn't conflict with this rule. Most SEO experts recommend posting your blog on many platforms to increase the chance for visibility and the chance that Google will crawl it. HubSpot provides some great advice on blog length and frequency in their article cited in the footnote below.[45]

When you create your blog on LinkedIn, you can save it, send it for review by others, keep it as a draft, and many other cool features. It's a great place to do your primary writing, rather than a Word or Google document. When you are ready to post it, you will be asked to write a brief description of the blog so that it can appear in the newsfeed. That means when you write a blog, you get two pieces of content, the blog and a post. Once you have this content, you can

44   https://wordsrated.com/reading-speed-statistics/
45   https://blog.hubspot.com/marketing/blogging-frequency-
       benchmarks#:~:text=If%20you're%20writing%20for,the%20
       quality%2C%20kudos%20to%20you!

cut and paste it to your website. This is good for your readers and SEO. I haven't found a way to automatically transfer the content from one to the other, so it's manual at this stage. But I am sure someone is working on this as add-on software.

Another great place to put the blog is on Facebook, if you have a company page. You can put the whole blog on there, as it accepts long-form content on the newsfeed, up to 63,206 characters (a very generous 4,000 words). Facebook allows so many words on the newsfeed because they don't have a separate blogging platform like LinkedIn and want you to post your long-form content there. We have experimented with putting a summary of the blog on Facebook, usually the first paragraph, and having a link back to your website to send prospects from their platform to yours. This strategy will have fewer people reading your entire content but it's more valuable to segment your readers from people who want to go to the next step in your engagement process. Your strategy of posting long- or short-form content really depends on where you want the traffic to end up. If you are building an audience on your Facebook page, you can keep them there or, if you are building an email list, try to get them to your website.

Other long-form content includes videos or podcasts, which we have discussed previously. Both are excellent ways of building connections with your community and can sit on your website and respective social media. Then we use cut-down short-form versions to post on your social media.

In addition to posting long-form content on your LinkedIn, website and Facebook, we also produce specific short-form content for these platforms. As part of our Expert Marketing System, we create two long and two short pieces a month, posting one per week.

The two short-form pieces are usually image-driven with a small text component of 100–200 words. One would be an internal post related to what's happening in your business. For example, the arrival of a new staff member, a client testimonial, a conference you went to, or something personal like a holiday or a reflection on your life. This is designed to build likeability. The external post is designed for credibility and would feature industry news, statistics, market analysis and commentary on the field that is your area of expertise. Having a variety of long- and short-form content with a variety of approaches and content types ensures your material is interesting and suits all types of people's preferences.

Instagram isn't a place for this long-form content, so we post images with a short amount of text that suits our internal and external posts on the grid. The blogs can still be utilised on this platform, as we can post the image and the introduction text and refer people back to your blog on the website. You can only have one link on Instagram so, unless you use a linking feature that has multiple links, you will only have your website linked. We also utilise video on the reel function to post short videos that will appear in your connections feed, on your grid and can be searched easily via hashtags. You can also add stories that disappear after a day and appear at the top of a follower's feed, which can boost engagement of your post.

X is similar in that you can post a summary of your blog, podcast or video with an image but not the whole post. LinkedIn used to have an auto feature to do this, but that went away several years ago. With only 280 characters (up from 140 back in the Twitter days), this provides short and sharp content distribution. As discussed in the social media section, we don't recommend X to many clients as it requires a different strategy from our preferred other platforms. There are other sites like Medium and various blogging sites that can work for some brands, but we tend to stick to the standard business sites because it's more work to manage more sites.

The final place we like to put your blog, video or podcast is in an email to your subscribers. Cut and paste the blog into your CRM system and send it out to those who are interested in being on your list. Even if it's only a small list, it's worthwhile sending it out because, once you set up your template, it is quite a small task. Having people with an email address on your blog can make it easy for them to refer you by sending that email to their connections. It reduces the friction of having to find your blog on social media, copying the link and opening their emails to send it to someone. This is difficult to do from a phone and it's much easier just to forward an email you have sent them.

Step 10: Connections

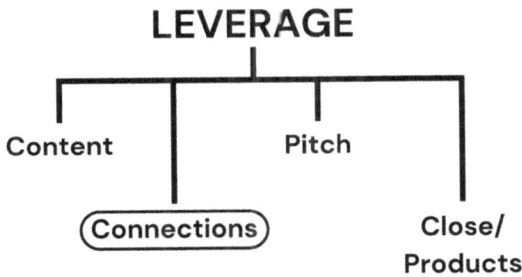

LEVERAGE

Content   Pitch

(Connections)   Close/ Products

Figure 51. The second Step in the Leverage section is Connections.

The heart and soul of any business is customers. Without them, you don't have a business, yet many companies don't spend adequate time on the customer journey process and fail to treat them very personally. They are people, after all, and when you are running your own business the initial customers are people you already know. They are your connections: people you have worked with, people you studied with, and friends of friends. As discussed in the Resources Step, your network is a vital asset to protect at all costs because these will be the source of your customers directly or via referrals. You never know where a lead can come from. I hope you have treated people well along the journey to where you are now!

A lot of the high-profile ex-CEOs, founders, and professionals we work with have extensive networks. Yet they don't have them in a usable form. They have never needed to contact their connections on a large scale. They have their information stored on their phone, in email accounts, various social media accounts and business cards. They don't have a CRM that is easily accessible and usable. The challenge of not having all your contacts in one place is that it makes it hard to centrally communicate with them. As we have already completed the Understand and Build sections, we know which social media channels we will set up and can forecast which places we need your connections to go. The main recommendations are to use LinkedIn, as well as an email list stored in your CRM (as mentioned in the Build section), which is useful as you can also include phone numbers for SMS alerts and addresses for posting materials.

To forecast the number of connections you need in your LinkedIn and email list, refer back to the e-ttraction sales diagram, which we have used throughout your sales process.

The previous Content Step helps us to understand what marketing materials we need to help a prospect move down the funnel from Cold, Warm, Hot and, finally, to Sale. When we review connections, we take the opposite route and start from the middle outward (Sale, Hot, Warm to Cold) to calculate our desired number of connections at each phase of the process. We will review each of these sections briefly and then several of the key principles that will bring clients to you, rather than you having to chase them. These principles are trust, referrals, outreach and niche.

Sale

Start in the middle and take your sales goals from the very first section of the Understand part of the journey. If you did this forecast in annual revenue, break this down into months to get your monthly target. If you haven't designed your products and prices, you will need to estimate your average package value and then divide it by your monthly revenue to understand the monthly number of customers you require. For this example, let's set this at 10 customers for now.

Some clients who have a variety of products ask me which products count as a Sale. A general rule is to use your core product. If you haven't yet created products around your service offering and are charging by hour, we will cover how to create products in more detail in the Close section.

Once you have your number, put that in the middle of the Sales diagram. Then you can work outwards to the Hot section.

Hot

This area is where customers who know, like and trust you reside. They would buy your service if they had the need at that time, and the price and circumstances were suitable. We can work out this number by the conversion rate estimated in the diagram. We have this set at 25%, or one in four customers. Therefore, using our example, if we took those 10 sales, the Hot zone would be 40x Hot customers.

We know they are in this section when you have had several conversations with them and you are quoting them on services, discussing contract terms and start dates. They have chosen you to provide the service over others and are working through the price and logistics parts of the negotiation.

Warm

The next outer circle is Warm. This is where customers are building trust with your brand and new portfolio business. They could be people you know who like you but are still discovering your new portfolio business, and don't yet understand what you do. So they wouldn't yet recommend you to others or buy your services because they don't currently have trust in the business service. This could also include people you don't know at all, who have been attracted to your brand from referrals or your content. These people take longer to go through the Warm phase, as they don't have as much trust in your brand due to spending less time in the funnel.

We will discuss the two essential elements of building trust in just a moment.

The conversion rate at this stage is usually 10% or 1 in 10 customers. Using our example, if we want 40x clients in the Hot zone, then we need 400x in the Warm zone. They would be reviewing your website, reading your content on LinkedIn or by email, and gradually forming trust as they hear and see more about what you do.

Cold

The final phase of the process in our Connections section is the Cold zone. This is where we start the marketing process but finish our forecasting. People at this stage are strangers. They don't know you yet, but have been e-ttracted to your business for one or two reasons, such as they like your brand or they require your expert services.

They will see your brand on channels that are not your own. How could they be on your website, social media or email list if they don't know you yet? So, they discover you from searching Google and your name or business coming up as a result from SEO. They could have seen you on other people's social media or content when you were featured on news articles, podcasts or in blogs. Or it could be from advertising.

The conversion rate for this phase varies, depending on the medium we are using to do the marketing, however, as we need an overall number for a goal, we have a standard estimation of 10% or 1 in 10. Meaning that our 400x Warm leads will come from 4,000x Cold people.

This is your final number to complete the e-ttraction sales forecast and provides you with the overall number of connections you need in your database on LinkedIn, email or another central database.

The conversion rate in this section changes depending on the style of marketing you are doing in the Cold zone. For instance, if you are doing paid Meta Ads (Facebook and Instagram), then we know that you will have a conversion rate of 1% on average.[46] We base our method and metrics on higher-converting activities like referrals, high-quality content, speaking engagements and networking. These activities convert at a higher rate because they promote more trust, as we will discuss in the next section.

Trust Process

Amy Cuddy is a renowned Harvard University researcher, author and speaker. She conducted some research for her book *Presence*, and discovered that people need equal amounts of likeability and

---

46   https://www.wordstream.com/blog/ws/2017/02/28/
     facebook-advertising-benchmarks

credibility to form trust.[47] That means a Cold client will enter the sales funnel with 0% likeability and credibility and, therefore, have no trust because they don't know you. She goes on to assert that Cold people need to like you before they see your credibility – the order matters.

Using our example, you will need 4,000x people a month to engage with your brand. That could be reading a blog, being presented with a paid ad, seeing you speak, listening to a podcast episode you are featured on, and so forth.

These new people don't need to be refreshed each month, as you only need 4,000 each month, which means the same people can be exposed to your brand over time and gradually make their way into the Warm zone when they start engaging with your brand on your own channels. The good news for those who are starting to sweat from the scale of the contacts they require is that most of our clients don't require many clients from the Cold zone. They get their clients mainly from the Warm zone referrals, which means we are working with the 400 figures, not the 4,000 ones.

The second part of the trust equation is credibility. Once they like you, they will move from Cold to Warm, but Warm to Hot requires them to feel like you can do the task required. For most business clients, this means you need to specialise in something to the exclusion of other things. Many clients initially struggle with this part since they are very experienced, have had quite a few different roles, and can help a whole range of people. Focusing on only a few solutions is difficult and they find it limiting to their potential.

The reason we need to focus on a niche is that it provides certainty

47   https://medium.com/marketing-and-entrepreneurship/a-harvard-psychologist-says-this-trait-matters-most-10-ways-to-make-a-great-first-impression-ef377eb97463

for the prospects in the Warm zone to see that you have deep experience and credibility in the exact problem they need solved. Just like my orthopaedic paediatric surgeon, he didn't do plastic surgery or any other type of procedures. He just does bones and has experience with kids. That was my need, and he fulfilled it.

As a funny postscript to that story, it turns out that I bumped into our doctor at our local footy club as his son played in the same team as my older boy. It wasn't a surprise that he was in the same network and friendship group as me, since we are similar in many ways. Like attracts like. We also revisited our good doctor at the time of writing this book as my son injured the same arm with a suspected minor break. He made room in his diary to fit us in and treated us very well because we are known to him and he wanted to get my son back to playing before the finals. Likeability matters!

When you are choosing your niche, you need to focus on the unique combination of skills and experiences that you bring to market. I often draw three overlapping circles for clients and ask them to fill in the big circles with something that makes them unique, as can be seen in the following diagram.

Niche

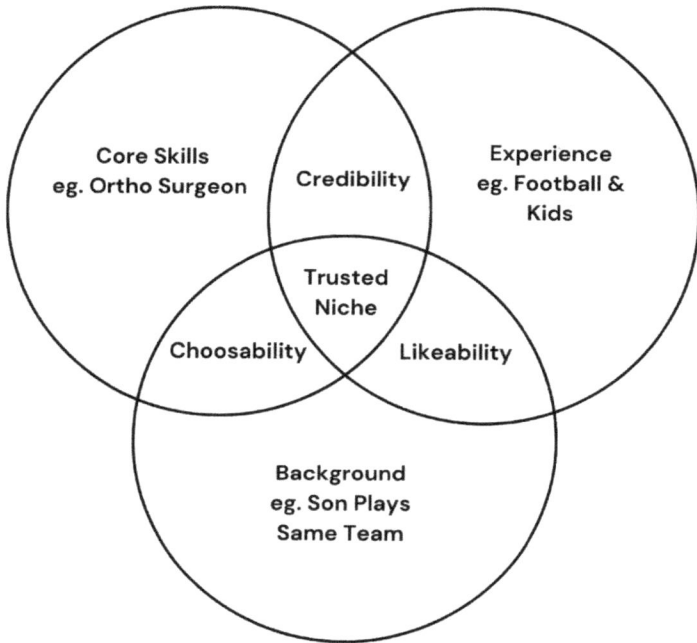

Figure 52. An example of overlapping circles that can help you define your unique niche.

The first circle is usually your trained skills. For our doctor friend, it could be that they are an orthopaedic surgeon. That's mandatory to do the job. For me, it's being a marketing professional. I can prove this with my marketing degree and postgraduate qualifications, plus teaching marketing at many of the nation's best universities. This education is great, but many people also have these qualifications. There are also quite a few orthopaedic surgeons.

Another aspect, in circle one, is applied when I look at my work experience and you can see that I have worked for globally respected organisations in marketing leadership roles. This adds credibility to my claim that I know a thing or two about marketing. My doctor had pictures of all the AFL players he had worked with on his office wall. This reinforced his credibility by referencing a sport that I recognise, since both of my sons play Australian football and this resonated with me. For some, this is enough; however, to really stand out to people, you want to add more to this niche.

For the second circle, we fill in something from our background that makes us unique. This could be where you are from, using it as a cultural advantage. It could be how you were raised or another interesting aspect that makes you who you are. For me, it's my mother's impact on how I was raised. From my doctor's example, his son plays at the same football club, and he fulfills the role of trainer for the team, which means he understands kids' injuries and how to deal with their physical and mental injuries. Often teenage boys want to get back to playing as soon as possible, and he will offer his advice with this consideration in mind, so they understand what's best for them and the team they play for. Essentially, he understands our situation well because he is in a similar position.

As discussed at the start of this book, I didn't have a traditional white Australian upbringing. My mother was a hippy free spirit and had a lot of interest in Eastern religion. I was more Buddhist than Christian, and she took me to a lot of ashrams with courses that exposed me to a lot of different people and thinking. This gave me a very different outlook on life, a strong interest in personal development, and what makes humans do what they do.

One course stands out in my memory. I was about 16 years old and my mum took me to a popular course at the time called Love and Relationships training, hoping to set some strong foundations for my future. I vividly remember doing a 1:1 session with a woman who was recently divorced and discussing her choices of how to raise her kids separately from her ex-partner, alongside her angst at the failed relationship. I hadn't even had a relationship at that time and didn't have a lot to add to the conversation. But I discovered that I could listen well. Funnily enough, that was more important than adding any personal anecdotes or providing advice. She just wanted someone to listen to her without judgment or preconceived notions of telling her what she should do.

This experience taught me how to relate and listen to people. Really see them without judgment based on my experience and not to give them advice from my value set, but help them in theirs. Over the years I have realised that this is a skill not everyone has. Many well-trained marketing professionals haven't had many exposures to personal development and tend to take on a consultant posture of instruction without listening. For clients who resonate with my style and brand, this is an important factor in the equation of why they want to work with me and not others. Not everyone wants this, which is why we are not for everyone.

For our doctor friend, I believe that it was his sporty vibe that was one of the reasons I felt comfortable with him. I have played a lot of sport and am very physically active. This is my Health Value coming out in this decision. I could tell he was the same and not every doctor is like that. To get to that level there is an incredible amount of study that doesn't lend itself to a sporting lifestyle. So many doctors are bookish and less sporty. However, this one was more like me, so I chose him.

In my case, the second circle was personal development. For my doctor, it was his sporty nature. But it will likely be different for you. I have worked with many people from overseas who come from a different cultural background and that can be a differentiator too. One of my favourite clients, whom I coached to great success, came from Syria and was concerned that people would judge him and not like his brand because he was Muslim. I argued that working in cyber-security, he had just the right background to understand some of the threats that Western organisations faced dealing with politically opposing countries creating cyber-threats. He used to hide his background and image from potential clients, but we ended up pushing this to the foreground and his newfound confidence meant he attracted many larger organisations to his company. Often your biggest fear can be your largest asset when used in the right context.

The final circle is for clients you most like to work with. For me, I seem to attract many male clients over the age of 50 who want to leave corporate lives or their own businesses to start a portfolio career. That's me! I left my corporate career at age 40 to do the same – too early, in my opinion. I attract people like me. We all do. It doesn't mean I don't work with women; I certainly have many female clients that I love working with. I also work with younger clients, but not as many as the older ones. I have found the closer they are to me in age, style, values and interests, the more work they do with me and more referrals I get from them. This is key. We don't just want them as clients, we want them to like us enough that they want to send us other clients, to see us be successful. You must be credible and do good work for them, but it's how much they like you which will stimulate the referral mechanism in them. That's why we want to be super niche with our target market and positioning online. The more we focus on that perfect client who will love working with us and has the exact problem we can solve, the more they will enjoy the work, continue as friends and refer their network to us. In our doctor example, he likes to work with football players. They are featured on his wall and, due to his involvement in our local football club, we can see that he enjoys this type of work.

To summarise this section, it's important to have a specific niche service so you are known in your market for solving specific problems. You can build upon that with new services or target markets once you are established, but not before. Amazon famously started only delivering books in areas of the USA that didn't have bookstores. They mastered their business processes and brand in this niche before branching out into other products. We need to build our business in a similar way, so we have consistent clients and cashflow before we look to grow.

A great way to establish your brand in your chosen niche is with a powerful pitch.

Step 11: Pitch

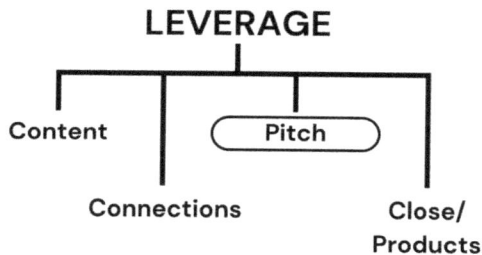

LEVERAGE

Content   Pitch

Connections   Close/
Products

Figure 53. The key Step when establishing your niche is a powerful pitch.

The next section to review is the pitch process. This is the tip of your marketing spear, and is often overlooked and under-practised. The template below is designed to assist you in constructing your own pitch process. You can review this before we explore each stage at length.

e-ttraction®
Pitch Process

Social Star☆

Target market _____

Top 3 problems _____

Tease > **Problem** > **Solution** > **Why You** > **What's Next**

Tease	Problem	Solution	Why You	What's Next
10 words to spark Curiosity	100 words to build empathy	100 words to spark enthusiasm	50 words to position your authority	50 words to create an opportunity to meet in the future
"Interesting, tell me more."	"I know right!"	"Wow that's amazing!"	"How do you do that?"	"Can we meet to chat more?"

Figure 54. Template for developing your own powerful pitches.

We use this methodology for your elevator pitches, formal pitches, written pitches and more. It's a very flexible and simple process that you should be able to remember and modify to suit your personality and business.

The pitch process is as follows: Tease, Problem, Solution, Why You? What's Next?

There are more complex and sophisticated pitch methodologies available. These are also great to learn for more complex situations; however, this basic pitch process has been developed for its simplicity. If you can't do it off-the-cuff when required, then I think the process is too hard. We need to be always pitching our businesses to practise how to do it effectively. To learn what works best and to let people know what we do!

Please don't confuse pitching with selling. Pitching is answering someone's question effectively. We have all been asked the standard warm-up question of: "So what do you do?" or "What are you up to these days?" We can choose to answer these questions with a standard response of "the usual" or "not much", but what a wasted opportunity!

Tease

To test if the person is genuinely interested in an answer or just making small talk, we start with the Tease. You give them a small sample of what you are doing, but without enough information to clearly understand what you mean. We can use an example to illustrate this point.

Let's say you are a physiotherapist. There were 42,098 physiotherapists in Australia in 2022, according to the Physiotherapy Board of Australia (Ahpra).[48] That's quite a few and you would imagine that most of them offer a similar service, with the main differentiator being their location. Therefore, the response to the "So what do you do?" question would logically be "I'm a physio" or "I'm a physio in Camberwell." Not very inspiring and unlikely to warrant a client to provide you a referral to their friends, unless there was a lack of physios in that location. However, let's say you have been working through this program and discovered you can charge a higher fee by having a niche in a specialist area. Say you are passionate about sports and, in particular, triathlons because you compete in them yourself. You know a lot of people involved in the sport, so you speak the same language and understand the intimate dynamics of their training and injuries. There are not many physios in your area who are like this, so you make this the foundation of your brand.

We now answer the question with your Tease: "I help triathletes

---

48   https://www.physiotherapyboard.gov.au/News/Annual-report.aspx

avoid injury and recover faster." Now that's an interesting answer! Most people would be curious about what that means and so ask a follow-up question, such as: "Really? What do you mean by that?" Mission accomplished! They have stepped forward into the conversation and are genuinely interested in your next answer. Or they miss the Tease and say, "Oh, that's nice", and you move on with your conversation. Either way, you have nothing to lose from the Tease.

We modify the Tease to suit different situations and audiences. You must size up your prospect to find the right Tease that you think will interest them. If they are not sporty people, they might not be in your target market. However, they might know someone who is! We all have siblings, cousins, friends, work colleagues, neighbours, nieces and nephews who might be exactly your target market. You never know, so position your Tease accordingly.

Problem

Let's continue with this physio scenario for the content of the pitch: the Problem. They ask the follow-up question: "Really, what do you mean by that?" Then you say: "Did you know that most triathletes suffer repetitive strain injuries? Mainly due to overtraining and imbalance of strength and control due to lack of cross-training. The problem is a lack of awareness of how to train properly and is a major reason as to why injuries occur."

Solution

If the prospect nods and seems engaged, then you continue with the Solution: "Being a physio and a triathlete, I have seen many injuries that could have been avoided with better training systems, such as a more effective bike set-up, and different strength and conditioning routines. I test these out myself and have found them very effective to avoid those repetitive injuries that stop you competing for long periods."

At this stage, the prospect may ask a follow-up question, such as who the best practitioners are, the cost, or about other athletes the physio has worked with. We encourage questions because it builds their engagement. We can also ask them questions during this process to see if they have any personal experience that they want to add to the conversation. "How are your shoulders or knees?" is an obvious one, and they might relate their stories of their own injuries from sports.

Why You?

Then you can add something like the following in the final content piece of Why You? "Because I am a trained physiotherapist and triathlete, I understand the pressure to train all the time to stay competitive. It's difficult to rest and find the time to cross-train. But with a few adjustments to your routine and equipment, my system will enable you to avoid those weeks of recovery where you can't train at all."

Once you have completed the process, the prospect will be left knowing *exactly* what you do. It's specific enough for them to refer you to anyone they know who might be having these problems. You are building your reputation and referral network every time you meet someone. If they are a prospect or know someone right away, they will ask for your business card, location or website details.

What's Next?

This is the final step of the pitch process. It's important that they ask for your details. If they want your services, they will ask, if they don't, it means either the pitch wasn't effective or they are not a prospect, so giving them a card is a waste of paper. Learn the principles, practise your own approach and see what referrals come your way!

Finally, it's easy to *not* do this and just give a standard response. However, when running your own business, you are responsible for the generation of leads. If you want to have the rewards, you will have to do the work. The first time you do this will probably not be your best, but eventually you will get better and more effective. Also, you are doing yourself and your prospect a disservice by being generic – it doesn't help anyone. Once you nail this process and see the engagement of the person in front of you, it will give you tremendous confidence in your business. Give it a try and post your results to the group.

Good luck out there!

Step 12: Close/Products

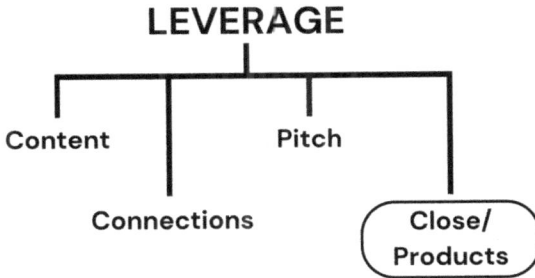

LEVERAGE

Content   Pitch

Connections   Close/ Products

Figure 55. Step 12 of e-ttraction involves closing deals by having clients buy your goods or services (products).

For those new to having your own business, *closing* is one of the most important areas of marketing and sales strategies. It simply means closing the deal, getting the order, and having your Hot client purchase your products (goods and/or services). Without closing deals, you are not in business. The rest of the process doesn't matter if you are not selling your products to your clients.

If you have a business that isn't selling your products, you have a hobby. That's the key difference of owning a business. You need to sell what you make to generate an income. Of course, from your personal perspective, it's not all about the money, but from a business perspective cashflow is the lifeblood of your business. It's useful to start separating your personal perspectives from your business in your mind, so you can make effective business decisions.

Of course, in the early stages, you think you *are* your business. You are the only employee, and you deliver the service directly. You might not have a company structure set up yet, so you operate under your personal name as your brand. With all that in consideration, it feels like the business is you! But it isn't. Remember, the three brands: you, your company and your products. You are the e-ttraction agent for your business, your business is what sells products (even if you are the salesperson), and your products are what the client exchanges for money.

We have reviewed the e-ttraction sales process already, but let's review the product stages, so we understand how to take a client from an initial meeting through a product hierarchy to become a loyal customer.

Free Products

The first products are the free ones. This is offered during the Warm phase of the sales process to encourage a prospect to engage more with your brand. We discussed having an ebook, a physical book, a whitepaper, or some sort of download that is valuable enough for the target audience to want to give you their email address to get it. This strategy has been around a very long time, so it's often overlooked as *passé* in today's super digital times. However, the basic strategies often work well, as they are tried and true. The problem is people don't generally want to put the effort into creating a piece of content that is valuable enough. They get sold tricky marketing re-targeting campaigns and complex sales funnels that don't engage the audience with real content. The issue with these funnels is that they cost a lot of money and take a long time to show their value. With one piece of value content, you can easily see if the audience likes what you have to say. Good or bad, you will get the feedback.

It's better to learn what works and what doesn't with something low-cost that you can create with a little bit of support. Then tweak and refine it as required until you find that sweet spot for your perfect client.

This free product usually sits on your website in exchange for an email address, but not always. It can now be downloaded from LinkedIn or other mediums, but I still prefer your website to be your home base, as it's the only online real estate you can own for the long-term.

Apart from an ebook, a physical book or a whitepaper, this product could also be a workshop, webinar or other interactive medium. Your target audience will give you the answers for what is suitable for that particular industry and demographic. Geography is also a consideration, as it's hard to get people from all over the world to an event, so a download of a web-based event might be the only one you can do at this phase of the sales cycle.

Pre-Products

Once someone has engaged with your free product, they are still in the Warm zone and establishing trust. You will know when they have developed enough trust to be in the Hot zone because they will then pay for your services.

For our clients, this is usually a paid workshop to create a marketing plan. For many others, we do some type of assessment or analysis of their business based on how they help clients. We have set up cyber-security assessments, board of directors' analysis and planning, carbon emission reports, and legal analysis of corporate structures for clients. As a rule of thumb, these pre-products are 10% of the cost of a typical engagement for the full product. If your main product is $100,000, then your pre-product will be $10,000.

It's important that you over-deliver on this pre-product so the client wants to continue the process. If they don't get full value at this stage, it's unlikely they will want to do more with you or refer you to others. I have had some clients complete our Understand workshop and found tremendous value but they didn't have the funds or right circumstances to continue with our full personal-branding project. However, they felt how much effort we put into the process and referred others to us for the same product.

The pre-products should have a few touch points involved, because the purpose is to get closer to the clients and learn more about them and for the client to get comfortable having you consult with them. If you can meet more of their team and network internally in their business, then even better. It will create more relationships that might be influential in the future.

If you are delivering a strategy session, do some research and talk to the stakeholders involved. In the workshop ensure all the decision-making parties are there and, when you deliver the final report, ensure the distribution list is everyone involved and follow up with a presentation. It takes more time and effort but will expand your network and build your brand with new people who can refer you to their friends, partners and their next companies. People move companies regularly and usually within the same industry, so get to know these people who may take you with them on new adventures.

Main Products

These are the main deliverables you will have on your website. Usually, we have three, just to have some variety and not too many to cause decision fatigue. If consulting is your main service, you might have three ways you do this: in person, remote or in a group. You might do speaking, consulting and coaching. Some do board positions, consulting and writing. Everyone is a bit different, and we can usually find these different offerings quite easily.

The pricing for these is a little more difficult. How much do you charge to be on a board of directors or for a speaking gig? How we usually scope these are based on all of the parameters that matter when delivering these services. Then, based on time, we allocate a per-hour cost to these. This can give us the base cost of delivery or the floor price. However, if the service is in high demand and there is little competition in your area or other unique circumstances, you often can price it at what the market will bear. This is your ceiling price or the highest price you feel you can charge and still feel you are delivering full value. You always want to feel you are providing great value, otherwise it's difficult for you to sell the service in the first place.

Once you have a floor price and ceiling price, this becomes your range for the service. I would start off not publishing prices on your website, then deliver the price after you've talked to the client and have decided where in the range you want to price it. Some circumstances to consider are:

1) How busy you are: if you are not full of clients and want to
be, you may quote lower to ensure you get the deal. Or, if
you are very busy, you might quote higher as you are not
seeking the work.

When I first started Social Star and needed to make enough income
in the first two months to replace my corporate salary, I said yes to
all deals regardless of what it was. I needed cashflow and activity
to build my portfolio and referrals. Being active is great for your
energy and makes you feel like you are making progress. It helps
with your sales posture as you are genuinely busy and in demand.

2) Travel: if you must do some lengthy, expensive or difficult
travel, then you have to add the cost, time and penalty for
this.

I have a client whom I helped write a book to help set up his
portfolio business. He had some speaking opportunities and
wanted our advice. He was based in Melbourne and the gig was
in Adelaide. It's a plane flight and they didn't even want to pay
his travel cost, only a nominal fee to speak. It was a loss-making
enterprise and not a strategic client. Our advice was to offer a web-
based presentation for the cost or if they paid his travel costs and
bought some of his books, then that would be worthwhile.

Even though our client had been thinking it was only a one-hour
presentation, it would have been a full two-day exercise and cost
more than they offered to pay him to realise the opportunity. If he
had other clients to see in that city, it might have worked with some
more negotiation, but sometimes you just have to say no.

3) Strategic fit: if the client and their audience are your perfect
fit, you might see more value in the deal than just the

project. It could lead to more work and referrals, so you don't need to make the full price on that one deal.

I have a client who wanted me to fly to Thailand for a conference to speak at an event. It was a three-day event and my session was one hour at most. It's a long way to go for an hour! So, I bundled in some video and photography of their event, which I would manage, plus I would tack on a holiday at the end. They were a very good client of ours, so I only charged them my travel and external expenses. My client wanted to introduce me to his other contacts for potential new business, so I put the whole trip down to pre-sales work.

4) Value-add: you might be able to bundle more work into the deal.

I recall having ANZ Bank reach out to me to do a speaking gig. It was through a friend from my kids' footy team. As they were part of the club, I did it for free. Also, it was a lunch-and-learn for the staff, so there was no commercial benefit to them. I put in full effort to the presentation and made a strong impression – so much so, that they wanted me to speak at their next event for hundreds of their staff. I negotiated to not only speak for a good price but to get paid to take headshots of everyone as a value-add to my personal-branding presentation. I also gave a few boxes of my books to the audience, which was part of the deal. Overall, it was a full two days of work for me and my team, and we established a large database of potential new clients.

5) Reach your target audience: sometimes you will do a deal with a client because they have access to your perfect client.

Teaching at several universities has been a great way to meet potential new employees for many years. Not only do they work with me directly, but they refer their friends to work at my office. This was particularly valuable when the labour market was very tight and good people were hard to find. We had a rich database of staff and never struggled to attract the right people.

6)   It's the right thing to do: sometimes it's just good to help people.

I work pro bono for several organisations to help them with their branding just because I feel it's useful for them and the people involved. I don't publicise this work or seek to get kudos for it, as that would ruin the purpose of me doing it. I do it because I have skills that can help people.

Annuity Products

Once your main products are working well, you may also consider having an annuity product. An annuity product is one that is automated and creates income but doesn't consume a lot of your time. The format of this could be a digital course, a software product you sell, or something else a client would pay a small retainer for, like support.

Most people chase this so-called "passive income" at the start of their branding process. I have learnt from experience that this should come at the end. Once you have a large enough brand and database to have at least 1,000 true followers, you can launch this type of product.

A popular theory by Kevin Kelly, former editor of *Wired* publication, helps define why we only need 1,000 true followers. In his popular essay from 2008 [49] he discusses that a true fan is someone who

---

49   https://kk.org/thetechnium/1000-true-fans/

would buy whatever you have next: the next book, course or product. They will come to your event and refer you to their network voluntarily. These fans are hard to get and keep, so don't underestimate how difficult it is to gain 1,000 of them. But the benefits when you do are enormous. Say you sign them up on a retainer for a nominal price, perhaps $50 a month for a special group to receive content, then that's $50,000 a month income with a very small amount of time to maintain.

The true cost is in establishing these followers in the first place. The years of content delivery, speaking, conversations, work with clients, and so on, is how you establish these followers, plus you have to offer them something of value!

I recently heard of a YouTuber who has a business with a micro niche. He produces content for expats to move to the country he moved to a few years back. He spent many months and thousands of dollars setting up his channel and producing high-quality content to establish a base of fans. It took years to get going, but now he has a large fan base. He offers tours, accommodation and, importantly, a paid member group, which is very small in cost but, with hundreds of people in there, is quite a good earner.

The salient point is that all the hard work is at the *start* of the branding process and all the rewards come years *after*. That is when the annuity product comes in – at the end of all that hard work, not the beginning.

My Leverage Journey

One reason I left sales roles to work in marketing was the boredom of repetition. Sales is a laborious process of doing the same thing over and over again with 100% enthusiasm, even when there is no obvious result in sight. It's easy to get disenchanted and slow down or reduce the effort. It's a vicious downward spiral to self-determined negative beliefs. You can tell yourself this is your own business, that it doesn't really matter if you don't reach out to the full 20x people a day and write your weekly content. No one is paying attention anyway, and you have some strong prospects in the funnel. You slow down on the process and find other, more important, things to do. But then some of those deals in the funnel stall, disappear or you close them and start delivering them. Then, after a while, you don't have a pipeline of leads, and you wonder where the next deal will come from. It keeps you up at night, as the bills don't slow down, and you want to feel like a success. Eventually, you start to consider going back to work for someone else. It happens all the time.

I remember when I was just starting my business, and I had also recently been divorced, so was in all sorts of emotional and financial trouble. The kids and I were walking past my local café, and they were hungry for some pancakes, since that was our Sunday routine. I usually make them at home, blueberry was my speciality in order to get some fruit into their diet!

As we were at the shops, the kids wanted to eat out. Unfortunately, business was having a tough time, and I literally didn't have any money left over that week. I was flat broke and that realisation of being over 40 with three degrees and a strong corporate career in my not-so-distant past, made me question everything. Why am I doing this? It's far easier and more profitable to just get a job and be like everyone else. Why am I trying to create this business and dig into my soul to bring new knowledge to the world when no one really cares? "Give up!" my brain told me.

But then, after returning to our small apartment, cooking pancakes at home and feeling a bit better about life, I returned to the core reason I started the business in the first place: my kids. I have control of my time; I have control of my activities and how much I work, which relates to how much I earn, and I get to spend a lot of time with my kids.

Do the kids care that we ate at home that day? They wouldn't even remember the occasion. But they do remember all the days I went to their sports, picked them up from school, climbed trees with them at the park, cooked them pancakes. I was present for those formative years when it really counted. Unlike my dad, who decided to leave my mum and me as soon as I came home from the hospital. I chose my kids over money. It's my Values: Family over Business or Money. It's not right or wrong, just a decision I made when I had my first boy, that I would be the best dad I could with my abilities. I would NEVER leave them.

When things get tough in the business, I remind myself of why I started it in the first place. It's not to be rich or appear successful to others. It's to have control of my time so I am not jetting overseas on their footy grand final or doing a meeting when they need me to take them to a sporting event. I don't have to do these things; I choose to prioritise them over other things.

Your reasons will be different from mine. Your life story is unique to you, but you have reasons why your Values are the priorities they are. Ensure you know your story and remind yourself of it when things get tough. Your business will have plenty of ups and downs, that's the nature of these things.

With that said, hold on to your hats and let's get started!

Case Study: Carol Benton

I first met Carol Benton when I was working at IBM. She was a sales professional in one of the technology divisions and I was head of marketing for mainframe computers. We saw each other in the office but didn't have much direct communication until we both attended a conference in Sydney. My boss at the time heard that I had a side business specialising in personal branding and asked me to do a presentation for the IBM management team, which I was happy to do. Carol was in the audience, along with 100 of the top managers in the country, and she really resonated with my content and said she wanted to catch up to review her brand when I saw her after the presentation.

Months went by and we didn't get onto her brand, but one day she was asked to head up a different division by the company, and suddenly she needed her branding done. She called me and we started working on her LinkedIn with the company paying me to do so. That engagement went well and when she left IBM a year later, she called me to help her set up her brand for the future. She was unsure of what career direction to take and had never thought about working for herself. But after the Understand part of our workshops, she decided to go for it.

Carol was part of our "Launch in 12 Weeks", which is a course I created to take new corporate escapees through my e-ttraction process to set up a business in three months. She was an incredibly engaging and positive contributor to the course, who then worked hard to build her brand and business. But what really stood out to me about Carol was how she leveraged her brand to create meaningful opportunities for herself. She started out by offering just one core service, which was proposal writing for large technology companies. Very similar to what she did at IBM, so it wasn't a stretch of her skills and she had a lot of Warm connections from those companies. She loved writing and her goal was to replicate her full-time income in three years. Having a sales and commercial background helped her in this quest.

Carol started the first version of her business Words 2 Win during the "Launch in 12 Weeks" course with a revamped LinkedIn profile, new website and Facebook account. We encouraged her to connect to all of her old business connections on LinkedIn and, since she liked writing, we started blogging as her primary way of engaging them with her content. She practised her pitch, went to networking events and made appointments with old colleagues to introduce them to her new service. We created a product hierarchy and, before long, she was onboarding new clients. In the first year, she earned a respectable revenue to prove she could run her own business successfully.

In the second year, she made the equivalent of her old IBM salary, then, in the third year, more than her IBM salary – all with more time flexibility to spend with her children whilst enjoying the process more than her corporate career. She even moved back to the UK to be closer to her family and restarted her business over there seamlessly. Leveraging her brand into new areas of business was relatively easy once she established credibility with a core audience and developed her skills further. She started writing tender submissions for IT companies, as that was what she was comfortable doing because it was part of her corporate role. She then branched into other forms of writing advice as well as services for this same target market – helping businesses in the same way I help people with their personal branding. She has developed her niche ever since and kept creating value to leverage her brand into a strong business.

Carole's success was due to her following the e-ttraction process with discipline and enthusiasm. If you do all the steps to the best of your ability, you too can have your own successful business.

As Carol stated: "Andrew has a deep and detailed knowledge of social media and how to harness it for business outcomes. I first worked with Andrew when we were both at IBM, where I saw him present at a management conference and was struck by his knowledge and skill at communicating it to the uninitiated. In my current role, I have engaged Andrew and his company Social Star to work with me on incorporating this approach into my own personal and company branding, and I am delighted with the results so far."

What's Next?

Congratulations! If you have made it to the end of the book, you are in the small percentage of people who are committed to building a business for yourself.

The next step in the process is to take action. If you have digested the contents of the e-ttraction process, you will be more self-aware of what you want, the sort of business you are going to build, and the resources you have to get started.

Businesses don't build themselves, so I highly recommend getting some support to keep on track. If you feel like my process resonated with you, reach out to our team to see if we can assist you. Or do some research and ask your network for recommendations on someone who can keep you accountable and on track.

Entrepreneurship is a battle of the mind, not the market. This is one of my favourite sayings that I tell my clients. There are always clients spending money, staff looking for jobs, and investors wanting to partner with businesses. The barrier to you capturing these resources is your ability to adapt and change to meet the market. We all tend to hold on to our ideas and products too long, rather than change to suit the conditions. I highly encourage you to fix your business upon your values and vision but adapt to the conditions of the day. Small changes can make big differences in your business if you listen to others.

I wish you all the best in your endeavours and encourage you to keep connected to our community on our social media and various events. We are all in it together, so let's support each other to build our own businesses. If we do, life will be better for us and our families and, in due course, our communities and everyone around us. Entrepreneurship has the power to change the world, so play your small part in making it a better place for your team, clients and suppliers. Every little bit in the right direction helps shift the future towards something more hopeful and that's worth fighting for. Best of luck and keep going!

One Last Thing

Over the decade or so that I have run Social Star, there have been many clients who have worked with me along the entire journey. Some are referenced in this book as great examples of people who have leveraged their personal brands to start their own businesses, such as Michael Kenihan, Carol Benton, Dr Luke Crantock and Andrew Phillips. One client who I have worked with ever since I had the idea to do personal branding as my business, is someone I would like to feature as a capstone example of personal branding used well to build their own business.

Andrew "Billy" Baxter is a legend in the Australian advertising industry, having led Ogilvy Australia and Publicis Australia, before building his own portfolio business. He sits on numerous boards and advises companies all over the world through his new business: 24 Hour Business Plan.

Many of my clients have built successful businesses and when they sell them or retire from an active position in the company and start their portfolio business, they get itchy feet and want to start another business back in the industry they just left. Andrew Baxter is a classic example of this. I first met "Billy" when he was running Badjar Ogilvy and I was a client. This was in my Sensis days when we were on the cutting edge of digital projects and his team at DT Digital did some cracking creative work for us.

We would have a coffee from time to time and discuss social media and digital marketing. We were both fans of Twitter and LinkedIn back then, as it was the early days of the digital marketing industry, when Instagram and TikTok were not even invented. This was when he started talking to me about his five-year plan to leave the advertising industry and start his own portfolio business. Being the type of guy who doesn't leave anything to chance, he had already started his training to be on boards with some voluntary boards in his local community. Preparing him for larger not-for-profit boards and, eventually, commercial boards. So, I helped him fulfil his ambitions by building him a website and giving him some advice along the way.

He envisioned he would do some consulting, and more opportunities would follow. However, he ended up leading another large advertising business, Publicis Mojo, as a great opportunity came along to restructure that business, which he did. And almost as soon as he'd arrived, he left Publicis Mojo. I was always curious about what motivated him to leave so suddenly, as he was well respected in his industry and could have stayed in the CEO seat for many years to come. Luckily, I received an answer to this question when Andrew agreed to be a guest on my Build Your Own Business podcast. He said that his advertising mentor gave him the tip to get out of the game when he was on top, as it's a young person's profession and it's better to leave on your own accord whilst in control of your destiny than stay too long and be pushed out. Sage words and ones that are very difficult to live by. In theory, it's easy to consider leaving a great job in an industry where you have all the connections and respect. It's another thing entirely to actually do it, stop the monthly pay cheque and step into the unknown. I have tremendous respect for Andrew for executing his plans, even though there were still great opportunities for him in the business. But he stuck to his plan and got his board positions, started consulting, published his book and was living the full portfolio business life. But then he had an idea. That idea became a new thriving business called the 24 Hour Business Plan.

The idea, like a lot of great ideas, came from his clients. He was well respected for his strategic *nous* and had a huge network so, when he launched his portfolio business, he received many requests to do consulting work. A lot of this work revolved around strategic business planning for the businesses that he used to do advertising for. He had completed a lot of these planning sessions when leading the agencies, so he had a variety of methodologies to draw inspiration from. This led to creating the 24 Hour Business Plan format that is now a business in its own right and separate from his personal portfolio business.

Today, Andrew has kept his portfolio business vibrant and interesting with many board positions and investments whilst running his growing new business. He builds his brand consistently and authentically, which provides him endless opportunities to choose from. It really epitomises the ethos we reference in this book. That if you focus on helping people with useful knowledge alongside your branding assets, *not* trying to sell to them, you will build a powerful personal brand and always have plenty of opportunities.

Acknowledgments

O ver the years there have been many people who have supported me in business and in the writing of this book that I would like to acknowledge.

Firstly, Chris, my book coach and first cousin, who has been the push I need to submit my work every Sunday at 3 pm! Without his persistence (occasionally nagging) and attention to detail, this book would still be a half-finished manuscript. I'm good at starting things but need someone like Chris to get me finished. Nice work, mate, couldn't have done it without you.

Secondly, my kids, Hudson and Spencer who are the reason I do everything. I try to be a good example to you both, that's why I work so hard to provide whilst maintaining the alignment of my values. I'm so proud of the young men you are becoming and hope that, one day, you will find your true passion and form a business around that for yourself.

Thirdly, my team at Social Star, past and present. In the almost 15 years since I started the business part-time whilst working my corporate job, I have had the pleasure of working with dozens of young marketing professionals. I always tried my best to be a good mentor and leave you better off than when you started with the organisation. You are the foundation on which this book is written.

Fourthly, my clients are the lifeblood of Social Star. We wouldn't have been around for all this time without your continuous support

– thank you! We appreciate the referrals of new business because they have kept us growing for over a decade.

Fifthly, to my extended family. Peta and Matt you have been great supporters along the way and I know you have my back. Ros, we have raised some pretty great kids together because we work together. Thanks for being understanding and a great mum.

Finally, to all my friends and supporters, I feel so blessed to have so many wonderful people in my life. My mates, old and new, keep me grounded and laughing at life. To my work friends and colleagues, I couldn't have got through the ups and downs without those debriefs and shared learnings.

About the Author

Andrew Ford is a dynamic professional with a rich background in digital marketing and education. He is the CEO and Managing Director of Social Star and CampusLife, based in Melbourne, Victoria, Australia. With over 15 years of corporate experience and more than 12 years in industry education, Andrew has become a strategic marketer who helps services businesses leverage digital marketing to attract clients, staff, and partnerships.

Andrew's journey began with a strong educational foundation. He earned a Master of Entrepreneurship and Innovation from Swinburne University of Technology, an MBA (Executive) from the Australian Graduate School of Management, a Bachelor of Business (Marketing) from RMIT University, and an Associate Diploma of Marketing from Melbourne Polytechnic. His education equipped him with the knowledge and skills needed to navigate and excel in the marketing world.

Professionally, Andrew's career is marked by significant roles across various industries. He started his journey at RH Grierson & Co, where he learned the ropes of sales and marketing. He then moved to Hewlett-Packard, serving as the Asia Pacific Marketing Manager and, later, as the Global Marketing Manager at Vivit. His tenure at Sensis saw him as the Marketing Manager responsible for digital revolution initiatives. At IBM, he worked as the Enterprise Marketing Manager, launching impactful digital programs. His experience at Interactive Pty Ltd as the National Marketing Manager further honed his skills in digital and offline platforms.

In 2011, Andrew founded Social Star Pty Ltd, a marketing agency that aids services businesses with their digital marketing needs. He also serves as a keynote speaker, sharing his expertise on digital marketing and personal branding. His passion for education led him to RMIT University, where he has been a sessional lecturer in Digital Marketing Strategy since 2016. In 2021, he founded CampusLife, a platform connecting university students with internships and job opportunities, showcasing his dedication to mentoring the next generation of digital marketing leaders.

Andrew's unique blend of corporate consultancy and personal development coaching sets him apart. His approach combines personal development with digital strategy, leveraging his extensive experience and passion for mentoring to help clients and students achieve success in their digital marketing endeavours. His work with Social Star and CampusLife highlights his commitment to formulating effective business models that combine personal branding with passion, ensuring his clients and students achieve measurable success.

www.ingramcontent.com/pod-product-compliance
Lightning Source LLC
Chambersburg PA
CBHW040752220326
41597CB00029BA/4743